For Barbara,
May the wind ...
your back, and may the sun
shine warmly on your face.
            Bernard M. Kane
                1998

LIVE YOUR DREAMS

A FASCINATING TRUE LOVE STORY

BERNARD M. KANE
a.k.a.
CHRISTOPHER KING

BLUE NOTE BOOKS
FLORIDA

Published by Blue Note Books
a division of:
Blue Note Publications, Inc.
110 Polk Avenue, Suite 3
Cape Canaveral, FL 32920
(407) 799-2583   FAX (407) 799-1942
To order additional copies call 1-800-624-0401

ISBN: 1-878398-40-7

Library of Congress Catalog Card Number 97-075129

CREDITS
Rancho Sante Fe Historical Society
<u>Goldwater</u> by Barry M. Goldwater
Anthony's Fish Grotto, San Diego, California
Coordinator of Information - Anita Cordary
Cover Design by Don Rhodes

Printed in the United States of America

This book is dedicated to
Aileen—the blue-eyed blonde,
my true best friend,
lover, wife, mother, and editor
with a velvet hammer.

CONTENTS

CHAPTER I

We All Have a Part to Play

One Sunday recently as we left the church after Mass, Aileen stopped to compliment the young priest on his homily. After he graciously accepted the praise, he said, "My, you have beautiful blue eyes." Driving home Aileen reminded me that fifty years ago a young priest had made the same statement to her, and life since then has never been the same. I was that priest.

In my lifetime from 1916 until 1997 there have been two declared world wars, at least three undeclared wars, a devastating depression, an economic period of over twenty percent interest rates, too many mass bombings to count, and nature's revenge through earthquakes, hurricanes, and tornadoes.

According to Shakespeare, all the world's a stage and every man has his part to play. I haven't been a star, but neither have I been an extra. I haven't thrown myself on the world's stage as an aberration, nor have I been a hermit living in the woods.

Live Your Dreams

The world around me has left its mark, and so have my parents in a more intimate way. In early childhood my mother and father . . . why did I write "mother and father" instead of "father and mother"? From infancy through early childhood, the mother sets the rules of behavior, bandages the cuts, and shoos the dogs away. She's first on the scene; the first enforcer, she is the primary physician and dad is the specialist.

As an only child, I was forced by the world around me to seek and develop the pleasures I desired. There were no brothers or sisters to suggest, to share, or to give me support. In fact, with the little world around me I was compelled to be independent, self-sufficient, and a loner in the strict interpretation of the term—not the unrefined meaning of the word. As I watch my four-year-old grandson playing seriously with cars, ambulances, and even stretch limousines, I realize how much the generation in which he lives affects his life as did mine. There are two cars in his family garage; he has seen and heard ambulances racing through city streets; at O'Hare Airport before boarding a plane with his parents, he has been overwhelmed by the long line of stretch limousines.

In contrast when I was a four-year-old kid in 1920, most people did not own cars; they either walked or depended on public transportation. An ambulance with its flashing lights was a rare incident and the only time an extra long automobile went by was when it was a hearse on its way to the cemetery.

So what made the deepest impression on my young mind? It was those flicks or so called movies to which my mother occasionally took me. It was her custom to save all the picture postcards which had been sent to her over the years and in time those cards worked their way into my possession. Like our grandson with his vehicles, I would spend hours sorting out the stack of postcards in categories of local travel, far away travel, comedy, and whatever was left over. Then I would sit on the kitchen floor, use a kitchen chair as the stage, and turn the cards by hand, one at a time, with the result that there would be a complete show of a feature movie, a comedy, and whatever was left over.

Throughout the years I have never been one of the herd politically or even philosophically. My political party affiliation was never known publicly until I retired at sixty-five. There were two reasons: I did not completely agree with the two major political parties; furthermore, it would have been tactless and could have been suicidal as a news commentator to be identified as a Democrat or a Republican.

Everyone, I believe, should have some religious structure in his life. It may vary from the casualness of Thoreau to the "ex cathedra" of the Pope, or it may be a buffet of religious tenets from the time of Adam and Eve.

As an aside, recently during the Easter holidays we were vacationing in La Jolla, California. At the highest peak on city-owned land, a cross had been erected fifty years ago. Every Easter for forty years, a sunrise Christian service has been conducted on the site. In 1996, for the first time, the city fathers granted atheists permission to hold a religious sunrise service.

To me this is religious negativism since atheists do not believe in God. Truly this is a perfect example of *reductio ad absurdum* in the matter of separation between church and state. In fact, it's abysmal hypocrisy.

In my judgment, hypocrisy is not only the worst but also the most nefarious of all evils. Transgressions in every day activity are committed because of weakness, thoughtlessness, or an outburst of explosive emotions. Hypocrisy, because it is devised, plotted, and executed to deceive, is planned manipulation. In the words of Shakespeare, "Would that men are what they seem to be."

The shelves of our library at home are jammed with philosophy books. Many have been read; some have been scanned. Each author has marched to a different drummer because the times have affected each author differently. So it is with us. The filial relationships, the religious experiences, the truth and falsity of political living roll over us and beat on us, as individuals, like the ocean on the rocks of the shore.

So, you ask, what is your philosophy? Here it is. I believe in God. If the atheist is right, then at least I have enjoyed a myth with all the trappings, much as the young child enjoys Bambi.

I believe in marriage. Love is the emotional umbrella, but justice is the foundation. A youngster quietly observes his parents, their love of each other, and the importance of their mutual respect founded on justice. From these subjective sightings the offspring makes a subjective decision about his own security.

Then there is the basic principle of living either as an intrinsic member of the herd or as a self-reliant individual apart from the herd. True, we must live together, but that doesn't mean we must subjugate our personal talent for the welfare of the crowd. I strongly oppose the concept of the herd because it destroys initiative and encourages passivity and laziness. Keep all options available; use them prudently when necessary. Be ready with the tools when the pipe leaks.

It's strange, even inexplicable, how events in a certain phase of a person's life follow a logical sequence without any intellectual input by the individual. In my own family, a series of events relative to tennis confirms this idea.

As an only child, I did not participate in team sports because they were few in number, time consuming, and it was difficult to pick up a team of eleven, nine, or five. Furthermore, sports at that time were recreation, not preparation for a mega-million dollar career. I became interested in tennis by playing on public courts. Then a thought struck me. Instead of waiting hours to get a court, why not negotiate with the owners of a private court? In exchange for watering and rolling their private clay court, I would be allowed to play when it was not in use. Never was I a great player, but I have always enjoyed the sport, both as a player and spectator.

Our only child, a son named Chris, pitched for a Little League team when he was about twelve. One twilight his team was playing in the district semi-finals and they were ahead five to nothing when suddenly their catcher became wild as a bucking mustang. He was throwing the ball all over the place, even under the grandstand, with the result that Chris's team was eliminated in the semi-finals by a score of thirteen to five. Needless to say, that was a night of teary eyes and bitter disappointment.

When the trauma of losing had worn off, Chris in a casual way said to me, "Dad, I don't want to play Little League anymore."

"Why?"

"Well, you practice hard, you play your heart out, and then one kid can throw the whole thing away like that playoff game. I'm going to get into some sport where if you lose, it's your own fault, and if you win, it's your victory. Dad, you don't know how I felt standing on that pitcher's mound watching those kids cross home plate." No more was said and life went along.

At a mini graduation from the sixth grade, Chris won the Good Citizen Award. His mother thought it would be a nice idea to show our appreciation by giving him a tennis racquet. He politely accepted the racquet without enthusiasm, because obviously tennis wasn't his sport. After a few weeks of park department lessons at fifty cents a session, he entered a beginner's tournament and won it. This was the start of tennis in his life.

His determination, his competitive spirit, and his unwavering focus on a particular goal resulted in his making the varsity at University High School, the winning of thirteen state championships, and a tennis scholarship to the University of Notre Dame. Today, he is an attorney who not only plays tennis for enjoyment and exercise but also he is ranked nationally and plays sanctioned tournaments around the country.

I mention this narrative about tennis to show how casual events, unplanned and unanticipated, continually affect our lives.

Call it luck; call it being in the right place at the right time; call it taking advantage of every opportunity that comes along. To be ready, able, and willing to take a reasonable chance; to become educated to distinguish between knowledge and wisdom; to expend every effort in your being to make your dreams come true—this is the philosophy that Aileen and I have tried to instill in all the young people we have known, from our own son to thousands of men and women who have been a part of our lives in one way or another. We hope that we have, in some small way, influenced them to focus on an objective and to eventually live their dreams.

Live Your Dreams is not a documentary; however, it is an authentic commentary, a chronicle of my experiences and my observations as I remember them. It is not the purpose of *Live Your Dreams* to be censorious, but it is impossible to avoid some degree of subjectivity. That reminds me of a remark heard so often: "Why aren't the media less subjective and more objective in reporting the news?" The news itself is objective, but the messenger by nature must be subjective. Therein lies the fallacy of objective news.

CHAPTER II

The Lore of an Historical Community

As we mature, we have a natural tendency to romanticize our lives, remembering vividly the happy episodes and minimizing the less pleasant times. When the United States is called a melting pot, people usually speak from an ethnic, racial, or origin of birth viewpoint, but in my case the marriage of my parents was a perfect example of an economic melting pot.

My mother was the oldest in a patrician family of five girls whereas my father was a waif. He and his younger brother, as very small boys, were placed in the Angel Guardian Home when their mother died. Of course, I do not know why their father placed them in an orphanage, but I do know from a few slips of the lip that their father was an undertaker and a known womanizer. Anyway, when my father was eight, he sold newspapers on his staked corner in Boston's North End, and later as a teenager apprenticed under a master last maker. Lasts are the models from which all shoes are made. My father, Matthew Kane, married my mother, Bernice Bragan, when he was thirty-four and she was thirty-one.

The Lore of an Historical Community

In the early 1800's my maternal great grandfather was a simple tailor in Boston. At that time in the Bay State's history, firemen and policemen wore neither uniforms nor badges. Those citizens who could afford fire and police insurance purchased policies from small companies who hired firemen and policemen. Those who could not afford the premiums depended on volunteers. Apart from their altruism, too many volunteers were looters. The problem became so serious that the Boston City Council voted to pay firemen and policemen a salary and also to require that a standard uniform be designed for the respective public services of firemen and policemen.

My maternal great grandfather won the bid to design and to produce uniforms for the fire and police departments. A simple tailor became Thomas Bragan & Son, Clothiers.

In those days people walked or used public transportation; vacation homes were few; and expensive furnishings certainly were not common. However, my grandfather, Thomas Bragan, drove a carriage with two horses, owned a hundred acre gentleman's summer farm in Pembroke, Massachusetts, and adorned his winter home with hand made furniture and oil paintings of his five daughters.

Quincy, Massachusetts, where I lived as a teenager, was a good city in which to grow up. Only twenty miles from Boston, it was a suburb of thirty thousand people with an historical heritage of its own. Residents were proud of the roles their forefathers had played in colonial America and in the early United States of America. From that pride had sprung an intense patriotism. The Constitution of Massachusetts, a model of the Constitution of the United States, was drafted in Quincy by John Hancock, Sam Adams, and other American patriots in the law office of John Quincy Adams, who later became the sixth President of the United States. It was this man's father, the second President of the United States, who became the first chief executive to live in the White House and the first one to plant, not a Rose Garden, but a vegetable garden to trim his food bill.

The Quincy Homestead, built in 1686, was the childhood home of Dorothy Quincy before she became the wife of John Hancock. The prominence of the city of Quincy in Americana is evidenced as much by those buried there as by those born in the area. The crypt of the United First Parish Church on Hancock Street contains the remains of the second and sixth Presidents of the United States as well as the remains of their wives.

Blending with the lore of the community, the curricula of the elementary and junior high schools emphasized a love of art, an appreciation of classical music, and the subtleties of fine literature. During junior high years, we went on monthly field trips to sites of historic and cultural importance. For example, we would travel to Boston's Old North Church and there the teacher would point out the belfry where the lanterns were hung for Paul Revere's ride, "one if by land and two, if by sea." At another time we would go to the Bay State's Museum of Fine Arts where there are about two hundred galleries of classical paintings and sculptures from around the world. The real treat was twice a year when the Boston Symphony Orchestra would present a special matinee at Symphony Hall for only junior high school students of the area. The Quincy public schools offered an education that was all-inclusive; history and the fine arts were just as important as math, science, and English.

When I was an eleven-year-old kid, one of my first business ventures was selling newspapers for Howard Johnson's paper store. Howard Johnson, at that time, owned a very small smoke shop in Quincy, Massachusetts, and paper routes throughout the city. From that smoke shop Johnson went on to open his first hot dog stand on the beach of Quincy Bay where he built the first white clapboard structure with an orange roof and a cupola at the peak. There it was that he introduced the famous ice cream flavors, the tender fried clams, and the frankfurter grilled in creamy butter.

This was 1927 when bankers across the country were riding the glory train, in no way anticipating the stock market crash of 1929. The Granite Trust Company, under the chairmanship of Theophilus King, with his son Delphus occupying the president's seat, was bulging with stocks, government bonds, and depositors' cash. So they financed a six storied skyscraper in the heart of Quincy. Lawyers, doctors, and dentists occupied the upper five floors, and Granite Trust was located on half of the first floor. Theophilus King had a brilliant idea. Convince Howard Johnson, the Swedish immigrant with the hot dog stand, to move upscale by establishing an elegant restaurant in the vacant half of the ground floor in the new Granite Trust Building. The bank would put up the money. Howard Johnson accepted the idea, but as it turned out, the restaurant was too fancy for the ordinary residents of Quincy. In a short time Howard Johnson's Restaurant was on the brink of bankruptcy.

Eugene O'Neill's play, *Strange Interlude*, affected Howard Johnson in an unusual way. O'Neill's ultimate goal was an opening night on Broadway and Howard Johnson's immediate goal was to avoid bankruptcy.

Strange Interlude, a play of nine acts, took to the road in New Haven where the world-famous Baker School of Drama was located at Yale University. Yale professors would review a production and write critiques for newspapers. The critiques, whether positive or negative, were important to a producer because large sums of money could be riding on his play.

11

Live Your Dreams

In New Haven, *Strange Interlude* received excellent reviews. Then it was on to Providence, Rhode Island, where the official censor of Boston would go to preview the production. The Boston censor emphatically declared that *Strange Interlude* was indecent and immoral and would be banned from any stage in Boston. Banned in Boston meant instant success for any play.

The producer now faced a critical dilemma. The New York theater, which he had leased, would not be available for four months with the result that he had a hit on his hands, but no place to go.

A few miles from Boston, in the suburb of Quincy, was a theater with a substantial orchestra-seating section and a good sized balcony. Although banned in Boston, O'Neill's play was immediately welcomed in Quincy. The nine acts of *Strange Interlude* were divided into two separate time periods. The first five acts were presented from four-thirty in the afternoon until seven in the evening; the final four acts were performed from nine until eleven with a dinner intermission from seven until nine.

When *Strange Interlude* opened in Quincy, theatergoers flocked from Boston to see what all the fuss was about. The more that clergymen throughout New England sermonized against *Strange Interlude*, the more SRO signs became routine. In no time the two-hour dinner intermission of O'Neill's drama packed Howard Johnson's restaurant six nights a week for four months, and this was the beginning of the Howard Johnson empire as well as a Pulitzer Prize for *Strange Interlude*.

While the City of Quincy was basking in the spotlight of *Strange Interlude* and the residents were making this play a conversation item, my mother a strong minded woman, was not impressed. Instead she spent her energy impressing on

12

me the necessity of a solid, broad education. Often I heard her say that one can lose his health or his fortune, but no one can take away a good education. She, therefore, established goals and rewards—perhaps not the best pedagogy—but it worked. Each month during the school years of fifth, sixth, and seventh grades, I was assigned a long poem to learn and to recite before I could go out to play on the last Saturday of the month. My mother's pedagogy has had a lasting effect. To this day I can still remember names at a large cocktail party.

Anticipating the future, Holy Cross was the college of my choice, but I was certain that a boarding college was not financially possible. "You get A's and B's in all courses during your three years at Boston College High School," my mother said, "and I'll see that you go to Holy Cross in Worcester, Massachusetts." I kept my part of the agreement and she kept hers.

Meanwhile, during the early 1930's, life was a paradox for a young teenager. Within the family he observed the financial struggle for existence. Yet, for the individual, life was really quite simple. If parents were suffering monetary hardship, they ususally masqueraded with a bravado attitude to protect the children. Most kids, however, could read through the veneer, and so they got "help out" jobs.

From my own experience, the Howard Johnson newspaper route and then a more lucrative job selling *The Saturday Evening Post*, *The Ladies Home Journal*, and *The Country Gentleman* not only added a few pennies to the family coffer, but also taught me the basic principles of public relations and distribution. Always I would make sure the newspaper landed on the front porch, not on the grass in summer nor in a snow bank in winter. Usually the man of the house paid for magazines; therefore, my delivery hours were planned when the man of the house would be at home.

Up the pay scale ladder I moved as a helper on a Foy's grocery truck delivering food orders. My final "help out" job was second butcher to Joe Flaherty in Joe Flaherty's Meat Market which employed two people, Joe Flaherty and me. There I learned the grades of beef, lamb, and pork, but most important of all was the technique of cleaning a chicken by firmly holding the neck and then yanking from the rear. After all, chicken every Sunday was the bill of fare during the Depression.

To my mother "help out" jobs were an admirable gesture, but to her, education was so important that she insisted on perfect attendance at school. The gods, I believe, were smiling on her because every childhood sickness laid me low during vacations. Not one day from the first grade until my junior year of high school did I miss a class. Then one day in a spirit of adventure and daring, a friend and I decided to play hooky from Boston College High.

During each year of high school this had been my routine: I would walk two miles from home to the Atlantic railroad station, would ride the 7:30 a.m. steam train twenty miles to Boston's South Station, and then I would walk two miles to Boston College High. On this particular day, my classmate and I boarded the trolley car instead of the train and, to kill time, traveled all over "kingdom come" before arriving in Boston. We were just in time for the morning show at the Metropolitan Theater, which featured four vaudville acts and a first-run movie. Blissfully in a dream world I sat there in the Metropolitan Theater never thinking that a perfect attendance record was being broken.

As we walked from the dark theater into the brilliant sunlight, newsboys were hawking a headline about a train

14

wreck at the Atlantic Station. We fumbled for two pennies, bought a newspaper and there was the headline: EXPRESS TRAIN CRASHES INTO LOCAL — NUMBER OF DEAD UNKNOWN. Sure enough, it was our 7:30 local that had been wrecked at the Atlantic Station. Instinctively we beat it to Boston College High to admit our transgression to Headmaster Father Terry McGovern. Out of breath we dashed in the front doorway and there pacing up and down was Father McGovern. The moment he saw us, he fell on his knees exclaiming, "Thank God, you're safe." At graduation, I received a perfect attendance pin.

Time marched on and in 1934 I was a freshman at Holy Cross, the second oldest Jesuit college in the United States. At that time, the enrollment was 1600 and in 1996 the number was only 2700 because the College has always been proud of the low ratio of students to faculty. The undergraduate years were enjoyable and intellectually profitable, but at the start of senior year an unexpected crisis occurred. Neither for academic nor behavioral reasons, but for a dispute with the Jesuits over territorial rights, I was suspended for four days.

During my college years at Holy Cross, I had spent the summers working for Burns & Son, the largest retailer in Boston of rental clothes for proms, balls, weddings, and special occasions. The summer before senior year I went to Ralph Burns, president of the company, with this proposal. The company would provide rental caps and gowns for the entire senior class at Holy Cross and I would be the representative.

The college, unknown to me, had a contract with Russell Cap and Gown of New York whereby each senior would purchase a cap and gown to be worn at special Masses and academic occasions. The purchase price was thirty dollars; however, through Burns & Son, I could rent to each senior for an entire year cap and gown for nine dollars. This meant that each senior could save twenty-one dollars. Naturally my business flourished.

In the fall of 1937, at the Mass of the Holy Spirit, the formal beginning of the academic year, every senior wore a cap and gown, but Russell Cap & Gown of New York had sold very few. A four-day suspension of Friday, Saturday, Sunday, and Monday was my punishment for renting caps and gowns without permission. My mother wondered why I was home for four days. I just said, "Long weekend." Truly, it was a long weekend.

Foremost in a collegian's mind during junior and senior years is the choice of a career. In the late 1930's, a liberal arts degree at Holy Cross prepared one principally for medicine, law, or the priesthood. At that time, graduate school in medicine or law was financially impossible for me, but there was a special attraction about the priesthood. I did not know then what it was and to this day I still don't know. Perhaps it was the silent influence of some priest whom I had known or maybe the serenity of a priestly life appealed to me. From the sidelines throughout almost three scores of years, I have heard lay people as well as priests say, "His mother drove him into the priesthood." In my case, that statement simply is not true. It is a fact that in Irish Boston many mothers hoped that a son would become a priest. Truly, I thought that in the role of a priest, I could make a difference in people's lives. That's the reason I entered the seminary.

It was not a Hollywood-style call from God; it was a rational career decision. Were there girls in my life? Yes. Was there any relationship that had become serious? No. Why? In those days, there was no Federal safety net for those who failed in their lives. During the Depression, establishing a career came first. Then would come serious courtship, followed by marriage.

CHAPTER III

Chicken Almost Every Sunday

William Cardinal O'Connell of Boston was only a name to me, but his general reputation was that of a pompous, egotistical, power broker of the church. On the day of the entrance exam for St. John's Seminary, the trolley was running late and I was in a hurry. When the streetcar reached its destination, to make up time, I took a short cut across the seminary grounds, and suddenly there before me stood Cardinal O'Connell with his poodle and his secretary.

The Cardinal always appeared to be over seventy years of age, even when he was in his late fifties. He was about six feet tall and had a considerable paunch which went along with a tilting chin, producing an image of reverent dignity. He looked the way Sydney Greenstreet might appear in clerical clothes. Breathlessly, without kneeling or kissing the Cardinal's ring, I asked, "Your Eminence, in which building are the exams being held?" After the Cardinal asked my name, I took off.

Live Your Dreams

Two years later, the rector of the seminary recounted the Cardinal's evaluation of me. He said, "Watch out for that Kane young man. He's insolent. He didn't kneel and kiss my ring. He treated me like a traffic officer." I must say, it was not a very propitious beginning to my seminary days.

The seminary schedule with its rigorous rules, its constant vigilance by the faculty, and its long study hours accomplished the intended purpose, but was no picnic for the individual seminarian. The rector of the seminary was nicknamed "Bicky" because be was ubiquitous; hc was everywhere.

In general, the daily routine consisted of rising at 6 a.m., meditation en masse at 6:30 in the chapel, followed by Mass and breakfast; classes from nine to noon, then lunch and one more hour of class; from 2:30 to 4:30 p.m. team sports and physical exercise, followed by chapel prayers and dinner. After dinner, we walked for one hour, followed by private study in our rooms until lights out at 10 p.m.

We could neither read newspapers nor listen to the radio. We were completely oblivious to what was going on in the outside world. Our role was to do or die, but never to question why. When custodians daily cleaned the rooms of professors, who were priests, they would dump old newspapers into barrels in the common toilets on each floor. The toilets or "jakes", as we called them, were our reading rooms.

Very soon I learned that the choirs were an important part of seminary life, especially the Cathedral choir and the St. Clement's choir. My experience was not unlike a ball player making the minor league and then immediately breaking into the majors. God didn't give me a musical voice, but He gave me a deep bass one that could go boom, boom, boom. As it happened, there was at that time in the seminary population, an oversupply of tenors and altos, but very few basso profundos. Hence I went straight to the majors, the Cathedral and St. Clement's choirs, who respectively sang each Sunday morning at The Cathedral and each Sunday afternoon at a service in St. Clement's church. There were particular advantages for choir members, especially the opportunity every Sunday to visit with family and friends who came to hear the choir. The visitors also brought newspaper clippings of late breaking events in the world. In short, there was a break in the seminary routine and a chance to discover what was going on outside.

The original St. John's Seminary, built about 1890 on a two hundred acre site in suburban Boston, was the centerpiece of a serene bucolic setting. The Cardinal's residence, modeled after an Italian mansion of the Renaissance Period, anchored one end of the property while the old three-storied Theology House, which went back to the turn of the century, secured the other end. Between these two buildings, so antithetic in design, modern structures were erected over a period of time as the need arose. A separate library building eventually became necessary as well as a gymnasium and another residential hall; also, the Cardinal wanted the top echelon of priests who administered the Boston archdiocese to be at his beck and call, so he constructed a large office complex called The Chancery.

The faculty, all priests, held Doctorates in Theology earned at The Gregorian College in Rome or at Louvain University of Belgium. It is not my purpose to evaluate their respective methods of pedagogy, but I do remember well one professor, Dr. Robert H. Lord. Doc Lord, as we called him, was slim, trim, and bald. He had been chairman of the history department at Harvard University, had never married, and had become a convert to Roman Catholicism. I have always considered Cardinal John Henry Newman the prototype of Doc

Lord. Humble, scholarly, and profoundly thoughtful would be my description of Father Robert H. Lord.

At St. John's the course of studies was six years for those with only two years of secular college whereas it was five years for those who had already graduated from college. When I took the seminary entrance exam, there were over one hundred applicants, but only thirteen were accepted. We thirteen joined the fourteen, who had left college after two years, and thus became the class of 1943 with twenty-seven seminarians. Within the five years only two dropped out.

I must make a distinction between leaving the seminary and leaving the priesthood. When a young man left the seminary for whatever reason, he left with honor. He had not broken a vow because he had not taken one. He simply opted to change careers. Leaving the priesthood is an entirely different situation. According to the Catholic Church, the vow between the individual and God has been broken. With that attitude permeating the minds of millions of Catholics for centuries, a renegade priest faces a very hostile world.

Meanwhile back at the seminary, the routine was so structured and so strict, there was little opportunity for deviation from the pattern. I vividly recall, however, an incident involving my mother's friend Mrs. Rivers and a basket of chicken.

Mrs. Rivers, a widow in her forties, owned and operated a variety store near our home. A couple of times a week, when I was about four-years-old, I would walk into her store and stand there with a sad look peering into her candy case. She would fill a small bag with candy and out I would go. We moved away from that neighborhood and there was no contact with Mrs. Rivers until after I entered the seminary.

My mother met Mrs. Rivers, told her where I was, and how happy I seemed. She added with pride that I was singing in the Cathedral Choir at the eleven o'clock high Mass every Sunday. At first, Mrs. Rivers would visit me about once a month at The Cathedral and she would bring a large home-made cake or pie. These goodies were contraband, so I smuggled them into the seminary under my cape. As time went on, the confections grew into a dinner basket of roast chicken, potato salad, cold slaw, sliced tomatoes, and cucumbers, as well as pie or cake.

True, it was more difficult to screen from sight a picnic basket with a whole roast chicken in it than a cake or pie, but with uneasy skill I managed. Then there was the problem of sharing these gourmet delicacies with my colleagues. They could not partake of the feast in my room because one rule which was constantly emphasized and strictly enforced forbade visiting in students' rooms, so the old hackneyed axiom of necessity being the mother of invention took over.

The only place of refuge on the entire seminary grounds was the "jakes" because "Bicky", as the name suggests, was everywhere. So we unhitched the door on an enclosed commode, placed the door lengthwise on the barrel, which was our source of day old newspapers, and then laid out a white table cloth that Mrs. Rivers thoughtfully included in the basket. I made certain that over a period of time all twenty-seven classmates were included in these bimonthly soirées so that if anyone was tempted to squeal, he would be as guilty as I.

The sequel to the saga of the roast chicken is not a particularly happy one. For some reason the choir did not sing at The Cathedral for two consecutive Sundays and on one of those Sundays Mrs. Rivers arrived with her now famous basket. As soon as Mass was over, she boarded a trolley for St. John's, which was about ten miles distant, walked up the tree lined drive, and rang the bell at the front door. Usually the porter, a layman, opened the door, but Sunday was his day off so whatever faculty member was nearby answered the bell. As unfortunately happened, "Bicky," the rector of the seminary, attired in his purple monsignor's regalia had just returned from a special ceremony at a church in the diocese and was walking in the corridor near the front door. When the rector opened the door, Mrs. Rivers was speechless and was so confused she mumbled, "Father, will you please give this basket to Mr. Kane?"

With profound dignity Bicky responded, "Why of course, I'll be glad to."

He immediately carried out the request by summoning me to his office. Still dressed in his regal robes and with the look of a boy whose pet dog had just died, Bicky asked, "Do you know what's in this basket?"

"Yes, Father," I replied. It would do no good to fake innocence. I thought to myself, let's get this over with.

Bicky continued. "This, Mr. Kane, is a very serious breach of the rules. I suspect it isn't the first time. It will be my obligation as rector to bring the matter up at a general faculty meeting. You will have to face the consequences. Good day."

There must have been some faculty members with a sense of humor because I never heard the results of that faculty meeting nor did I ever hear what happened to the chicken.

Time at St. John's really didn't drag because we were so busy with the daily routine, yet looking ahead during those five years seemed an eternity. We were rarely away from the watchful eyes of the faculty, even in summer. For two weeks in June and for two weeks in late August, seminarians could live at home with their families. Otherwise, the period from June to August was spent at the Cardinal's camp in Meredith, New Hampshire. Some liked it, but I didn't, because to me a forced vacation is no vacation at all. True, the schedule was more relaxed; but the owlish supervision was still there. The stern regime existed as always, and complete ease was an unknown situation.

Some may wonder, and rightly so, why I endured this rigid discipline. If I didn't like it, why didn't I leave the seminary? This exacting autocratic training, I always knew, was a means to the end result, ordination to the priesthood. My career ambition was to be a priest; therefore, I, as well as the other twenty-five, was willing to undergo a five year term of maturation.

It was the start of the fifth year when the excitement as well as the anticipation of ordination grew with overwhelming force. On the outside for families and especially for parents, it was like preparing for a wedding and on the inside for us it was the pursuance of details necessary for Holy Orders. There was the ceremony of inducting us into the sub-deaconate and deaconate. Then also, it was imperative that we learn to say Mass in Latin with ease and without awkwardness.

Finally January 6, 1943, arrived, the day when Mr. Bernard Kane became Father Bernard Kane. It was a time of relief, a time of accomplishment, a time of anxiety. Truly, I was relieved because seminary days were now a memory, and there was a sense of anticipation, of fulfilling a dream.

In contrast, the world swirled with international turmoil. United States and Filipino troops on Corregidor in Manila Bay had just surrendered to the Japanese; Enrico Fermi had achieved a nuclear reaction; and less than two months previously, 491 people lost their lives in the tragic Coconut Grove nightclub fire in Boston. Indeed, I was stepping into a world full of challenges, and a white envelope with my parish assignment in it held my future. The contents of that white assignment envelope, especially during the last year at the seminary, played an apprehensive role because a general appraisal of various pastors which highlighted their positive and negative characteristics, was circulated among the seminarians sub rosa by word of mouth. Those pastors with an imbalance of negative traits we called quarterbacks and those quarterbacks with the highest negative ratings we judged as All American. In a way, it reminds one of the old Mother Goose Rhymes in which the common people satirized English royalty with names like Humpty Dumpty, little Jack Horner, and little Miss Muffett. By this craftiness the English people could communicate about the English royalty without the danger of losing their heads.

It was days before the euphoria surrounding the ordination ceremonies subsided, but then reality set in at a private reception for the twenty-five of us hosted by Archbishop Cushing, who had succeeded Cardinal O'Connell. Kane is half way through the alphabet so I just stood there and tried to appear relaxed. Loud and clear the Cardinal's secretary announced, "Father Kane." I walked to the center of the room, knelt and kissed the Cardinal's ring, accepted the envelope and returned to my place. The temptation was to rip open the letter, but the dignity of the occasion required that I await my turn until the letter opener reached me. The simple exercise of opening an envelope doesn't require much dexterity, but I acted as if it were sealed with cement. The letter began, "Dear Father, you have been..." Oh no, I had been assigned to a first string All American quarterback.

"You have been assigned as an assistant pastor at St. Bridget's Church in Maynard, Massachusetts. You will report one week from the date of this letter to Reverend G. Edward O'Bryan, pastor."—Fifty-four years later those words are still etched in my memory.

Little did I know at that time what the future had in store. I decided to go to Maynard with an open mind. After all, maybe the rumor mill would prove to be wrong.

CHAPTER IV

Across the State Line, Heading South

St. Bridget's under G. Edward O'Bryan had an unsavory reputation among priests throughout the Boston diocese as the place where a haughty, hardheaded, arbitrary martinet ruled with a heavy hand. Any variations of behavior or even new ideas were treated with austere arrogance. This may seem like a harsh portrayal, but from experience I learned that it was an accurate portrayal.

Maynard was a Massachusetts textile mill town pretty much dominated by the American Woolen Company. It was located adjacent to Concord, the scene of the battle of Concord and Lexington, where the Patriots stopped the advance of the British and drove the British back to their ships in Boston Harbor. Through the years Concord had become a community of prominent professionals, successful businessmen, and renowned scholars whereas Maynard was where the domestics, the clerks in stores, and the general laboring population lived. The greatest number of these people residing in Maynard were immigrants; therefore, with its low cost labor pool, it was an ideal location for American Woolen to establish a large mill.

Maynard was a broad conglomerate of European first generation immigrants, especially from Poland, Finland, Ireland, and Italy. They had fled their native countries to escape constant, Draconian oppression, and many of them often said to me, "Oh, even the air is so free in America."

These remarks made a deep and lasting impression on me especially since I had grown up in Quincy, a city steeped in early American history, proud of its heritage, and dedicated to the preservation of the fundamental tenets of democracy. It's true that very few of these immigrants came from Russia; however, those from Finland and Poland had felt the heavy hand of Stalin's influence, and they realized that had they remained, their future years would have been bleak and perhaps even disastrous.

On the day specified in the Cardinal's letter, I reported for duty at St. Bridget's. It took me longer to travel on public transportation from Quincy to Maynard than it does today to fly from Boston to Miami. The church was an old wooden structure built at the turn of the century and obviously in later years, it had been held together by band-aid maintenance.

The rectory was located beside a mill pond across the street from the church. It was of 1890 vintage, a large Tudor house, most likely the home of the general manager at the mill. When the barn was built, it contained six stalls which had been converted into a four car garage. Only two cars, the pastor's and the parish automobile, occupied the remodeled barn because assistants on a fifty dollar a month salary could not afford an automobile.

Across the State Line, Heading South

The interior of the three-storied house featured beautiful cherry wood accentuating the crown moldings, the chair rails, and the staircases. Originally, the first floor comprised the social rooms; the second floor was made up of the private rooms; and the servants' quarters capped the three stories. Unfortunately, through benign neglect, what was originally a masterpiece of workmanship, had disintegrated into just an ordinary edifice. On the second floor, the pastor had taken up his abode in the huge master suite; the senior assistant pastor inhabited a much smaller suite; and on the third floor, two tiny rooms were my quarters.

G. Edward O'Bryan, the pastor, was about sixty years old, a six footer tending toward obesity. He always had a cigar in his mouth. From his toe nails to his pate, he was the embodiment of austerity.

The senior assistant pastor, less formally designated as the senior curate, is comparable to the executive vice-president in a corporation. He is responsible for the day to day operations and reports directly to the pastor. In principle, that policy is currently being followed, but in the 1940's, many pastors treated a parish as their personal fiefdom and as a result they ruled arbitrarily with an iron fist.

Dave Welch, the senior curate at St. Bridget's, was a very honorable person, profoundly concerned about the welfare of people around him, and in his quiet manner he was always available to help. Dave and I performed our different regular assignments with dispatch and we enjoyed working together. About five months after I arrived in Maynard, it was a sad day for me when Father Welch received a letter which transferred him to another parish.

To complete the cast of characters of the tragic comedy at St. Bridget's, two supernumeraries or bit players should

27

be mentioned—the housekeeper Miss O'Bryan, who was the pastor's maiden sister, and Elsie O'Sullivan, the so-called cook. Miss O'Bryan, senior in age to the pastor, was a nice old lady, but she was no housekeeper. She believed that God created dust to protect beautiful woodwork, and Elsie had trouble with a soft boiled egg. I have always supported the economic precept that you get what you pay for, and it's true that Father O'Bryan got what he paid for.

When Dave Welch moved on, his replacement was an alcoholic, a tall, slim man with a bushy crop of white hair. He seemed to me to be a person who periodically in the past had tried to overcome his problem, but each time, sad to say, the ground would crumble under his feet. Actually he was only a few years younger than Father O'Bryan; yet the years of abuse had taken their toll so that he ate very little and showed the signs of dissipation.

To be quite candid, within a year, my idealism had become shattered. I was not experiencing the kindness, consideration, and understanding that one expects in a real Christian home. Rectory life at St. Bridget's was cold and insensitive. Never was there a sense of camaraderie, of good fellowship, and never a pat on the back for a job well done. From my observations, the pastor intended to maintain his rigid *status quo*.

One night I was reflecting on what could make St. Bridget's parish more attractive to the people and especially more exciting for the young folks. An idea had been developing in my mind for some time, but the presentation of it to the pastor required extreme tact as well as a certain amount of courage.

The thought kept recurring: why not start a dramatic society? At Holy Cross my roles in *Twelfth Night, Cyrano de*

Across the State Line, Heading South

Bergerac and *The First Legion* had provided some experience and a little expertise in drama. Furthermore, I had an ace up my sleeve.

With reverential awe, but determined purpose, I responded to Father O'Bryan's, "Come in." He asked me to be seated and then in his pompous voice questioned, "What can I do for you?"

"Father, I have a proposal for you to consider. I would like to start a dramatic society because it would bring parishioners together; it would be something new, and there's undiscovered talent in this town. Moreover . . ." O'Bryan broke in with absolute denunciation of my plan. "Father, you don't seem to understand that this is a Roman Catholic parish. It's not Broadway. I have no interest in your plan."

In his customary abrupt manner Father O'Bryan killed any idea he didn't like, and it was very obvious he didn't like the proposal of a dramatic society. He did not know, however, that I had already lobbied some prominent members of the parish, and the general consensus was, "Let's give it a try." Among those whom I had approached about the plan were: the head usher, who happened to be the only Catholic undertaker in town; the parish attorney, who occasionally was my golfing partner; the owner of the largest insurance agency in Maynard; and the female superintendent of the public schools, an aggressive woman with futuristic ideas.

As if deaf to the pastor's emphatic rejection of the proposal I continued, "Father, you are undoubtedly right, but why don't you get the opinions of some parishioners who are your friends and whom you trust: like Herb Martin, the undertaker; Jake Driscoll, the parish attorney; and Mary Doyle, a school superintendent with progressive ideas?"

Although Father O'Bryan's stern facial expression didn't melt, it did soften a bit as I aimed at his Achilles heel with this comment, "By the way, Father, a conservative projection of six evening performances of a play will undoubtedly net the parish over two thousand dollars."

G. Edward's knitted brow suddenly arched, his eyes popped, and his sententious attitude became milder as he reacted, "Father Kane, I'll give some thought to what you have suggested. I'll inquire around the parish and give you an answer. Is there anything else?"

"No, thank you, Father."

St. Bridget's Dramatic Society produced three plays in three years. The people, whose advice had been sought, starred in some of the plays, and to Father O'Bryan's delight each production netted over two thousand dollars. On the last night of one performance, the undertaker, who was the head usher in the parish, facetiously said to me, "This was a great idea of Father O'Bryan's. He certainly is an innovator."

"Yes, he is." was my amen to that observation.

Whenever there was a novena, a young parishioner, Doris White, a teacher in the adjacent town of Stow, Massachusetts, would frequently attend the evening services. One particular night after the service, Doris, accompanied by a colleague from Stow High School, stepped into the vestry and introduced me to her friend, Aileen Leigher. Aileen was a very attractive, sophisticated girl of about twenty-two. She had sparkling blue eyes and appeared to be about five feet four and probably weighed around a hundred pounds.

Doris informed me that Aileen had been in dramatics at Trinity College in Washington, D.C. and might be interested in the new St. Bridget's Dramatic Society. As I outlined tentative plans for St. Bridget's Dramatic Society, Aileen showed great interest so I invited her to attend the next meeting. Soon the play *The Whole Town's Talking*, a simple comedy, was selected and a cast was chosen. Except for Aileen, all the actors and actresses in this first play were raw amateurs, yet the auditorium sold out for six performances.

For the second production I decided to present one of Arthur Miller's more difficult dramas, *Death of a Salesman*. As we assembled the stage crew, chose the cast of characters, rehearsed extensively, and selected the publicity committee, Aileen and I became more involved with the minutiae, the smallest details of a sweeping production. During her college days at Trinity in Washington, she had experienced, remote as it was, a flair for drama through the influence of the renowned Father Hartke of Catholic University and his young assistant Walter Kerr, who later in life became the celebrated drama critic of the *New York Times*. This is important in revealing Aileen's modesty because never did she ever mention these facts to the cast nor to the stage crew. Even today, fifty years later, I'm the one who must relate her academic background when people ask.

Through casual conversations with Aileen, I learned that her parents had died in an auto accident and that Aileen, a Catholic, had been reared by a maiden aunt, a New York school teacher. Aileen had obtained a Master's Degree in English from Harvard University and was teaching in Stow to gain experience before applying for a position in Boston or New York City.

Meanwhile at the rectory, life was just about the same. One incident, however, upset me very much, especially by the tone and manner in which it was treated. At Holy Cross every March, a mail vote is taken by the alumni association to determine who among the graduates of the fifth, twenty-fifth, and fiftieth classes should speak at the June graduation dinner. I was chosen to speak for the class of 1938 and I was very proud to be selected. Immediately, I informed Father

O'Bryan about the honor. Because the dinner was scheduled for Saturday evening the first week of June, the time, of course, conflicted with my hearing of confessions. Father O'Bryan's response stunned me. "Father, you may be a graduate of Holy Cross, but now you are an employee of St. Bridget's parish. A dinner at Holy Cross in Worcester is of no concern to the people here in Maynard. I'll take the request under advisement, but I'm quite certain the answer will be no."

It was one thing to be denied permission, but to be called an employee of the parish was unsettling because I had always thought the priesthood was a vocation. When I informed Dave Welch about the episode with Father O'Bryan, he offered to cover for me, but unfortunately between March and June, Dave was transferred. Whenever the pastor stated that a matter would be taken under advisement, one could be very certain the matter would be conveniently and intentionally forgotten. The new senior curate offered to cover for me when he heard about my plight, and he actually did. I defied the pastor, spoke at the alumni dinner, and was in the rectory doghouse for months.

The relationship between Aileen and me had always been platonic; however, she must have realized, as well as I, that mutual respect can grow into love. After all, real love evolves from the honest esteem of one person for another. I truly felt she made the world more special just by being in it.

Play rehearsals were a pleasurable part of my life because they were the only times I could spend more than fleeting moments with Aileen. Then one day I extended the most important invitation in my life. "Aileen, have you ever been to Cape Cod?"

"Strange as it may seem, I've never been to the Cape. I hear it's a very beautiful area."

Across the State Line, Heading South

Then like a robot I blurted out, "Next Tuesday's a holiday. Why don't we spend the day on The Cape? We can visit some of those half-houses built in the early 1700's and roam through a few antique shops."

"Sounds exciting. I'd love to."

That Tuesday was Memorial Day, so the horde of summer visitors hadn't begun to arrive. It was quiet, old Cape Cod with its expansive beaches and no one on them... just soft sand and dunes, like sentinels, seeming to keep the people away. Aileen and I casually meandered through a couple of antique places as well as a few gift shops and then stopped at a half-house that had been built a couple of centuries before.

In the 1700's a new husband, a few months after the wedding, would hew the pine trees on his land, strip and finish them in a rather crude way, and then begin to build a house for his wife and himself. Today as one views a half-house— there are a few scattered around Cape Cod—the front door is situated at the extreme right, and to the left of the front door, in succession from front to back, are the parlor, the dining room, and the kitchen. Above these rooms is a dormer window indicating the bedroom. When the family grew, as children came along, the father would construct new bedrooms to the right of the front door so that the house looked like any other residence, but if the couple were childless, the house would remain in its original design. In fact, to a stranger, the half-house looked as if the owner had cut it down the middle with a chain saw and had thrown away half the house.

After luncheon in an old sea captain's mansion, which had been turned into a restaurant, we drove to a beach on the Nantucket Sound side of the Cape. At the beach, we took off our shoes and socks and, hand in hand we walked briskly along the shore, sometimes ankle deep in the cold water and, other times, we would break into a run on the wet, hard sand.

33

It was so exciting, so fulfilling, so exhilarating, that we were a couple of miles from our car before we realized it. Truly exhausted, we collapsed on the soft sand. Talking and laughing and enjoying life to the fullest—this was a day to remember. Suddenly there was an overwhelming silence, and as I looked at Aileen, I knew that life would never again be the same. I just knew it. Love understands love; it needs no talk. Reclining there propped up on our elbows, we gently looked at each other and finally I broke the silence. "Aileen, I truly love you, and I want to marry you."

With her blue eyes almost a stare and her mouth agape, she haltingly replied, "I never in the world believed you felt this way. Never did I think it was possible. True, it crossed my mind a few times, but of course I knew it could never happen."

"This is not a momentary outburst because of the romantic setting," I assured her. "These sentiments have been growing gradually since I first met you over three years ago."

"Bernie, I love you too."

The end of school was approaching, and Aileen, as she had always done, was preparing to visit a family cottage on Long Island for the summer. I was aware that she had received two high school offers, one in Connecticut and the other in Boston. In either case, it would mean separation, which I definitely wanted to avoid. Our regular exchange of letters over the summer convinced us without a doubt that two real friends had fallen deeply in love without realizing it.

The last week of August, Aileen returned to her apartment in Cambridge. All the time she had taught in Stow, she had maintained in Harvard Square her third of an apartment which she shared with two other girls. She spent every weekend there and any long holidays. This was the same apartment with the same roommates where she had lived while attending Harvard Graduate School.

One day late in August, the telephone rang and Elsie in her Irish brogue yelled up three flights, "Father Kane, it's for you."

The familiar voice on the other end informed me that she had turned down the teaching offer in Connecticut and had just arrived back in Cambridge. "Bernie, we need to talk," she said.

"Yes," I replied. "We do need to talk and I need to see you. I've missed you so much."

We made plans to meet in Harvard Square the next day, my day off. The reunion was very emotional, but I could tell there was something serious on Aileen's mind.

"Bernie, remember Jim Harris, the young man I dated when he was attending law school. Well, we were getting quite serious. I told him about you and it was a mutual decision that we should return to being just friends. As you can see, I trust implicitly every word you uttered that wonderful day on the beach at Cape Cod."

"Aileen darling, you've made a commitment and so have I. We can't continue to lead a double life. We will not be hypocrites. With brief, clandestine meetings like this, we are going to destroy ourselves. I have an idea. In seven days my three weeks summer vacation starts. Why don't we take the first three or four days driving up the east side of Vermont and down the west side playing different golf courses, relaxing at the various quaint inns, and talking out our plans?" We both realized that our love affair could lead to either a *fait accompli* or a disaster. It was up to us to control our destiny.

That Monday morning was perfect for lovers. The sun was bright, the breeze was mild, and two young people anticipated the future with confidence and hope. The world was our pearl. When I entered Aileen's apartment, there were two young ladies, not her roommates, sitting on the sofa. One of the girls I had met briefly on a previous occasion and remembered that she and Aileen had been best friends at Trinity. Later I queried Aileen about the reason for her friends dropping in at that particular time. She assured me that she was as perplexed as I about their unexpected visit.

In Vermont, the back roads, some paved and many just graded dirt, set an aura of quietude, of simplicity, and especially of romance. The green mountains provide a picturesque setting for the small towns dotted with little red school houses, white church spires, village stores, and friendly inns.

Aileen and I played a few rounds of golf, not for the exercise, but to be together alone. We sampled the Vermont sharp cheddar cheese, roamed through antique shops, and delighted in those blueberries big as Concord grapes, and we enjoyed the fluffy pancakes soaked in copper-colored maple syrup.

One incident during our few days in the Green Mountain State especially comes to mind. The poet Robert Frost had long been a favorite of ours. For many years Frost had lived on the outskirts of Arlington, Vermont, so it was natural when we stopped for lunch at Arlington Inn to ask the waitress where Robert Frost had lived.

"Robert Frost? I don't think I know him."

"Robert Frost, the poet," I added.

"Oh, I wouldn't know him. When I go back in the kitchen with your order, I'll ask the cook. She was born here."

When the waitress returned with our salads, she was beaming from ear to ear as if she had unearthed some profound truth. She informed us that about nine years before, Mr. Frost had lived down the road a piece, in the house with all the birch trees out front. I thanked her, and then we returned to our conversation of when and how to expedite our impending momentous decision.

Those three days in Vermont were a period of extremes, sometimes overflowing with merriment and exhilaration, and at other times, there were hours of deep, thoughtful concentration. Should Aileen remain in the Cambridge area while I honorably endeavored to extricate myself from a complicated situation? Should I first inform my parents or the diocese about our plans? When should Aileen tell her aunt, a very devout Catholic, about her decision? How does the public enter into this picture? Aileen and I made one immediate decision: I would call my parents to tell them I would be home the next day, Friday.

When I phoned my mother, she informed me in a kind yet firm tone, "Bishop Wright is looking for you. He's called here four or five times in the last two days. What is happening?"

"Mother, I'll tell you when I see you tomorrow. Goodbye."

How do you feel when a ton of bricks hits you? In a moment Aileen and I had fallen from the pinnacle of happiness to utter confusion. My next move was the confrontation with Bishop Wright. Bishop Wright's office was a separate building on the seminary grounds where he handled all personnel affairs for Cardinal Cushing. Up the winding tree-lined lane I drove, parked the car in a space marked VISITOR—indeed I was a visitor—and entered the foyer. Within minutes I was ushered into the bishop's office and there seated at an imposing mahogany desk was a somber, stern looking Bishop Wright.

"Father, give me the keys to your automobile." It wasn't until years later that I realized why those were the first words addressed to me. This entire session had been orchestrated by

Bishop Wright, and he was making certain that I did not bolt from the room and return to Aileen.

"Your actions, Father Kane, are reprehensible. You're disloyal to God. You've scandalized the faithful people of this diocese. You've taken advantage of a good Catholic girl."

"As a matter of fact, your Excellency . . ."

"Don't matter of fact me," interrupted Bishop Wright. "Tell me the truth. Why, why have you done such a despicable thing?"

It was obvious I was destined to take a tongue lashing until the Bishop calmed down, so the better part of prudence was to say, "Your Excellency, I don't know."

"I'll tell you one thing, Father. If you marry that girl, you'll pump gas the rest of your life, and if you can't be loyal to God, you certainly won't be faithful to her."

Just a little note: this year that girl and I celebrated our forty-eighth wedding anniversary.

Bishop Wright immediately assigned me to a room in the seminary and ordered me to remain there until I had made my peace with God. He informed me that he would call my mother in Chatham and inform her that I was spending a few says at the seminary. Next he requested Aileen's telephone number.

The old, three-storied theology building was a very lonesome place. The seminarians were at the summer camp in Meredith, New Hampshire; and the faculty, taking graduate courses or visiting friends, were scattered all over the globe. In my confinement of five days, I surreptitiously found a telephone and was able to call Aileen to tell her where I was.

When Aileen answered the phone and recognized who it was, there was an apprehensive tremor in her voice. "Are you all right?"

"As well as can be expected under the circumstances," I assured her.

"When I saw Bishop Wright yesterday, he said you were in a strait jacket at St. Elizabeth's Hospital."

"I was in a what?"

"A strait jacket. He said you were uncontrollable."

"Darling, I don't know what a strait jacket looks like and I've never put my foot in St. Elizabeth's Hospital. I've been rattling around in this seminary building for five days. When I leave here tomorrow, I shall go directly to Chatham and tell my mother and father what has been going on and announce to them our plans to be married.

At our home on Cape Cod I told my parents, incident by incident, what had been happening. Of course, they were surprised and dismayed, but like any true mother and father, they still loved me. Bishop Wright had instructed me to complete my summer vacation at Chatham, and in the fall, he would assign me to another parish.

After the initial shock wore off, my mother asked what I intended to do. "Marry Aileen," was my response. The finality of my answer was so firm and clear, she pleaded with me to wait awhile, at least until the air had cleared. I agreed on one condition and it was that she invite Aileen to visit us in Chatham. I wanted my parents to know the kind of girl I had fallen in love with.

At the Cape, my father appeared very aloof in Aileen's presence, but my mother was gracious and sympathetic. About a week had passed when one morning I was stricken with severe cramps. My mother diagnosed it as an upset stomach, too much pressure for too long a time. Aileen, on the other hand, felt that my condition was more serious than an upset stomach. She said to my mother, "Bernie needs to get to a hospital immediately."

Live Your Dreams

Aileen broke the speed limit all the way to Boston where a doctor friend of mine practiced at a metropolitan hospital. When the doctor visited me in the recovery room a few days later, he told me what had happened. My appendix had burst, peritonitis had set in, and three doctors had collaborated in the operation on my fulminating abdomen.

During my three week stay in the hospital, Aileen returned to her Cambridge apartment and visited me every day. My parents returned to the Cape, but, of course, telephoned every day to check on my recovery, which, by the way, was normal and satisfactory.

When I went back to Chatham for recuperation, Aileen joined me there. One day Bishop Wright phoned and suggested that I take a recuperative sabbatical of about three months so that any smoke of scandal could blow away. He didn't mention Aileen, and certainly I didn't. The Bishop must have thought that she had vanished into thin air. On the other hand, my parents hoped that by being kind and hospitable to Aileen, she might reconsider the situation and that I might acquiesce.

In a sense my father pretended that Aileen didn't exist, yet he was gentlemanly in his attitude toward her. My mother, I am sure, knew the inevitable was about to happen. There were many long, intimate discussions among the four of us, but the conclusion was always the same. Aileen and I decided that within four months, sometime between Christmas and New Year's, we would leave to be married. We informed my parents about leaving the New England area some time after Christmas, but before New Year's. However, we did not fill them in with the details because they had suffered enough already.

Two days after Christmas, Aileen and I drove across the Massachusetts state line and headed south.

CHAPTER V

Falling in Love—with Arizona

How true is the observation of Robert Burns, the Scottish poet, when he penned the axiom that all the best laid plans of mice and men go awry. We had decided that Phoenix, Arizona, would be our destination, principally because it was three thousand miles from New England and because Phoenix, like the mythical bird of its name, was emerging from the desert sands. Although our worldly assets totaled a little more than three hundred dollars, money could buy infinitely more in 1950 than it does today. For example, gasoline was about twenty-five cents a gallon; a comfortable, clean motel would cost about seven dollars; and a nourishing dinner would run around two dollars. These prices, I know, are mind-boggling, but a dollar in those days had much more value. Then too, we were aware that Aileen could withdraw her meager contributions from the teachers' retirement fund when our money ran out.

The first priority, however, was where to get married, and after perusing the World Almanac, we had decided on

Elkton, Maryland, a nationally famous town for elopers. The requirements to marry were the least stringent and also the waiting time was only forty-eight hours. After all, we were working on a very meager budget, so as a result there was no time for sightseeing. But alas, the best laid plans of mice and men go awry.

Two days after Christmas we drove directly from Massachusetts to Elkton, only to find out that during the holiday week from Christmas to New Year's all the town offices in Elkton were closed except for emergencies. Of course, we believed our marriage was an emergency, but we also realized the town fathers would not agree. So we kept driving southward in a southwesterly direction to Chattanooga, Tennessee, where we learned that the city clerk's office was closed, but across the state line in Rossville, Georgia, the town clerk would issue a marriage license and perform the ceremony any time.

As we entered Town Clerk Henry Bowman's office in Rossville, the heavens broke loose with a downpour. In the tradition of Aileen's Irish ancestry, there's a proclivity toward superstitions, and one is: happy the bride on whom the sun shines. Although Aileen said nothing, I presumed that the substance of that superstition was running through her mind. Just as Henry Bowman was pronouncing, "I hereby with the authority invested in me by the Constitution of the State of Georgia do proclaim . . . ," a streak of sunshine filled the Town Clerk's office.

Flushed with ecstasy, excitement, and a feeling of well being, yet with a bit of anxiety, we drove straight westward through Arkansas, Oklahoma, the panhandle of Texas into Las Cruces, New Mexico, where incidentally I enjoyed the best steak I've ever eaten. As we approached Arizona, Aileen was constantly popping her head out the window—in 1950 very few cars, if any, had air conditioning—looking for a cowboy or an Indian. Finally, we arrived in Phoenix, the capital of the Valley of the Sun, where the towering royal palms, the myriad of gorgeous pastel flowers, and the nightly clear, sparkling sky portray what many think paradise should be.

Phoenix, the hub of Arizona, is situated in a valley surrounded by mountains of various heights. That's why it's called the Valley of the Sun. The temperatures in summer soar to more than one hundred degrees, but in the other seasons the climate is pleasantly mild. Meteorologists say that the weather in Phoenix is much the same as that of Cairo, Egypt. There's low humidity in the Valley of the Sun, so residents are not affected by the heat as much as the residents in summer on the East Coast of the United States.

In the late 1940's, the city area of Phoenix was a mix of old adobe houses, a few commercial buildings, a large acreage owned by the federal government for its Indian students from the reservation, and pockets of luxury homes. There were two skyscrapers, the Adams Hotel with six floors and the Westward Ho with twelve stories. In fact, the construction of the Westward Ho began in the middle 1940's and was halted after six floors were completed because the builder went bankrupt. Then, a carpenter on the job, Del Webb, completed the structure of twelve stories. That was the beginning of Del Webb Enterprises.

When we arrived in the Valley of the Sun, the configuration of the population was unusual, especially for a native New Yorker and a native Bostonian. The population was made up of Indians, Mexicans, and Anglos who had fled the frigid winters of the North. Then too, many of the older generation had homesteaded to start a new life.

The predominant religion was Mormon. They were followed by the various other Protestant sects, and then the

Catholics and a few Jews. Over the years, Aileen and I have been associated with many Mormons and we have concluded that as a group they are honest, financially responsible, and truly dedicated to the welfare of the family.

Across the United States, the Fourth of July seems to be among the foremost of holidays, but for residents of Arizona the holiday of holidays is Rodeo Day on February fourteenth. All schools, colleges, and public offices close; stores carry on with a skeleton crew, and the climax of the celebration is the parade followed by a first class rodeo. The first rodeo parade we observed was from a third floor window of the Westward Ho Hotel. Never in my life had I seen so many horses in one place, and never had I seen so many street sweepers in their white uniforms following the horses.

When we arrived in Phoenix, our three hundred dollars had shrunk to about seventy-five. For a couple of nights we stayed at a clean, old motel on the outskirts of the city until we found an apartment in the heart of Phoenix. The make-shift apartment had originally been a large porch which the owner had divided into four very tiny rooms—a living room, a bedroom, kitchen, and bath. The rent was thirty dollars a month.

As we reflect now, forty-eight years later, we often wonder how we could have been so adventurous with so little money. It never occurred to us to worry because we always knew that tomorrow would be better. Optimism prevailed.

After we unloaded our worldly assets consisting of two suitcases, Aileen exhaled a sigh of relief with, "Just think, we're here in Phoenix, 3,000 miles away from everything we ever knew. Just you and I, here where "the deer and the antelope play."

As far as I was concerned, I could not imagine a better honeymoon—a new bride, an old car, two suitcases and less than one hundred dollars.

Falling in Love—with Arizona

I knew that Aileen was concerned about the future. How would we get started, where would it lead us, would it work? Then she suggested, "We'll begin tomorrow. I'll go to Arizona State College. The spring semester starts in about two weeks. With my Master's Degree in English from Harvard I should get something."

My situation was different. At Holy Cross I had earned a Bachelor's Degree in Arts and Sciences and at St. John's had spent five years in graduate work, but I had nothing to show for it. I did not even have a recommendation from my former employer.

At Arizona State, Aileen was interviewed by the Dean in the Teacher Training Department, and received a little encouragement when he explained, that after checking her credentials at Harvard and the Massachusetts Department of Education, he would inform her of his decision. Aileen told me that the interviewer was abrupt, yet she was certain that he was interested.

Second in the line of priorities, after finding a place to lay our tired bodies at night, was the installation of a telephone. After all, if there were an offer out there for either of us, we had to be reachable.

It seemed to me that the Arizona Department of Education was the place to inquire about a teaching job in a high school. Right up front, a clerk informed me that a course entitled *The United States Constitution* and another called *Arizona History* were mandatory before teaching credentials could be issued. Furthermore, my academic background lacked specific requirements in how to teach and how to keep records such as courses in *Tests and Measurements* as well as *Behavior in the Classroom*.

Each day our money was dwindling: furthermore, we had neither the money nor the time for me to take the state required courses at Arizona State. Early every morning I would go around the corner to a variety store to buy the newspaper, immediately turn to the "Help Wanted ads," and then scan them. To accept anything or to wait a little longer was the question when suddenly my eye caught a headline, "TV Company to Roll Cameras in Wickenburg." Perhaps they needed a script writer. Immediately Aileen and I hopped into the car and drove to Wickenburg, a real Western town, about forty-five miles west of Phoenix. Frankly, except for Phoenix and Tucson, every community in Arizona at that time was a real Western town.

Immediately after World War II, television was the new kid on the block, but radio was still the principal home entertainment medium. Radio during the war was the means of informing American citizens how our troops were doing in Europe and what the Navy along with the Marines was doing in the Pacific. Commercial television, as we know it, was on the drawing boards of research labs.

After the war, there was abysmal consternation in the television industry. Although Congress endeavored to be fair in allotting signals and wave lengths, cries of bias were heard from coast to coast. The licensee was required by federal law to air at least three hours of programming out of every twenty-four or risk losing his license. This mandate resulted in a plethora of amateur hours and old movie westerns which had criss-crossed America in small theaters so many times that a continuous black line of scratches ran through the showing of the film. Obviously this production company at Wickenburg, along with others in Arizona and California, was endeavoring to be first on the market with its entertainment package.

In Wickenburg as the car sidled up to a wooden curb, I yelled to an old timer, "Do you know where Arizona Productions is?"

"I don't know no Arizona Productions," he responded. "What do they make?"

"They don't make anything. They're shooting some movies."

"Oh, yeah. Go down this road about a quarter mile. Then turn at the first left. Continue on that dirt road about a quarter mile. Then turn at the first left. Continue on that dirt road about another quarter mile and you're there. They're new in town. It's an old abandoned stable."

We followed instructions, and there before us on the right side of the bumpy rural road was Arizona Productions, a dilapidated, weather-worn barn with two decaying smaller buildings beside it. Two 1930 trucks with cameras mounted on them were parked in the field, and deeper in the field there were carpenters building a movie set that was beginning to look like a Western street scene.

While Aileen remained in the car, I approached the old stable at an entrance, which seemed to be the office and knocked. A deep husky voice rang out, "Come in." Glenn MacWilliams, as the name plate indicated, was seated behind a huge desk, large as a drawing board, with his muddy cowboy boots resting on the edge of it. MacWilliams, a man in his mid-fifties, was about five feet eleven, and neither slim nor obese. Obviously, the rough Arizona sun had remodeled his face so that it looked like wrinkled Cordovan leather. His voice was deep with a gentle tone which made me feel at ease in his presence. "What can I do for you?" he inquired.

I introduced myself and explained that my wife and I had recently moved to Phoenix. Since I had some script writing experience in my background, meager as it was, I told him that the article in the *Republic* about Arizona Productions had sparked my interest. I went on to tell him that I had worked on *The Father Flanagan Story*, aired on the NBC Network and also *The Road Mender*, a story about a cobblestone in the street of Jerusalem when Christ was crucified. I scripted that for a Boston radio station.

"Quite unusual. Certainly a mind-catcher. But the two you mentioned are both religious themes," MacWilliams remarked, a bit of doubt in his voice.

"Yes and no," I replied. "Father Flanagan, as you know, had just been appointed by President Truman to get some control over German kids after the War. The teenagers especially, were running wild, stealing, raping, and setting fires all over Germany. They were undoing the success of military governors appointed by Truman. It really was a news documentary. The other script, *The Road Mender*, was broadcast on Good Friday, certainly a timely theme for that evening. I would like to get involved in script writing. Are you, Mr. MacWilliams, looking for a writer?"

"We're always looking for good writers. First, however, let me tell you who we are." This was a positive sign because he would not tell me about Arizona Productions if he were not interested in what I had to offer.

MacWilliams went on, "An oil tycoon out of Chicago by the name of Squire McGuire is putting the money into this endeavor. He believes that westerns on TV will be the attractions of the future in this burgeoning industry. McGuire owns an exclusive guest ranch here in Wickenburg, and that's why we're filming here instead of California. As for me, I was head camera man for most of Alfred Hitchcock's movies and now I'm taking a shot at directing."

"I'd like to see some of your work, Kane. Can you have an hour long Western script ready in two weeks. If we don't accept it, we'll pay you two hundred and fifty dollars, and that's the end of our association. If we like it, we'll pay five hundred dollars for that script and sign you to a contract to write four more at the same rate of five hundred dollars each. As you must know, five hundred dollars is about fifteen percent of what the movies pay, but this is a gamble and we're all in it together."

"I'll take the gamble, Mr. MacWilliams. Do you have a suggestion about a possible theme?" I inquired.

"It must be western, of course. Keep it inexpensive to produce. There must be a chase, about ten minutes or more. One suggestion, why don't you go to Bowman's Barn, a bar over here in Wickenburg, take a back seat and listen to the cowboy lingo and watch how the cowboys act. From listening to your accent, I wonder how much you know about cowboys. See you in two weeks."

When I returned to the car and told Aileen what had happened, she analyzed the situation at once, "You know, Bernie, he wants a script writer who won't cost him much and you want a job that pays some cash. You fit each other like a hand in a glove."

Of course I wanted to write a script that would be accepted and I certainly wanted a contract for four more. In three days Aileen and I saw five Western pot-boiler movies, took out the limit in library books about western lore, and worked into the late hours of the night on ideas and plots concerning the wild West. We saturated ourselves so deeply with western atmosphere that at times we thought we were spectators at the O.K. Corral gunfight.

We spent days and nights researching the old West, and the more we learned, the more we became enamored with life in Arizona. Soon we were calling it home and we knew that there was no more reason to roam.

We went to Bowman's Barn and observed a Saturday night in the life of a genuine cowboy. The barn was about the size of a large airplane hanger. When the cowboys entered, they went, like laser beams, directly to the bar while at the same time the coy young ladies unobtrusively ambled to the opposite corner of the massive room. Before long, the nectar of romance took effect and the tall, lean young men strode to the opposite area of the barn and each in his own way asked, "Ma'am, may I have this dance?"

We noticed that cowboys were a silent breed. The aura of their occupation, riding alone on the range, apparently tends to make them that way and thus there has developed the stereotype of the silent, tall, weather-worn cowboy. Although their language is earthy, it is by no means dirty and certainly not intended to shock the listener. Their verbal expressions rise from the atmosphere in which they work.

When I submitted my first script, *Trigger Gold*, Glenn MacWilliams liked the story line, but had very definite advice about the format. He made specific suggestions about an introduction and a closing, as well as the time allotment for commercials. He reminded me that I had forgotten to include the chase.

"Oh yes, a chase," I parroted in an attempt to hide my ignorance about Westerns.

"You decide where to put the chase," interjected MacWilliams. "Just be sure it isn't anticlimactic. A chase before its time is the death knell of any script."

When Aileen and I returned to Phoenix, we knew the script had to be reworked, but at least there was a tone of confidence in MacWilliams' voice. Then too, why would he make suggestions about time slots if he were not interested in the story?

As we were counting and maneuvering time slots as well as trying to weave a chase into the plot of *Trigger Gold*, the phone rang. After Aileen answered, there was a pause.

Falling in Love—with Arizona

"I can come tomorrow morning. About ten-thirty? Yes, I'll be there."

As she hugged me with her one hundred pound, five feet, four inch frame, Aileen cried out, "I got it. I'm signing a contract tomorrow morning. I must get my hair done."

Aileen's contract with the College was manna from heaven. Principally, it relieved the intense financial pressure and allowed us time to pause and to look at the future. Our families had rejected us. The only difference between us and the serial *The Fugitive* was the fact that no one was chasing us. The stakes indeed were high. Our future became a matter of pride, a deep personal challenge, and a dream to be fulfilled.

While Aileen was instructing in the teacher-training program at the College, I spent my time at the apartment re-working scripts, developing new plots, and about once a week I would travel to Wickenburg and stand on the sidelines to watch a shooting. In those days of early TV westerns, directors usually did not film episodes in sequence. With an eye on the budget they would shoot many variations of a similar theme and then edit those segments into one or two new stories. When a writer viewed a shooting, he generally was watching the decimation of his brain child and the creation of a new story by the director.

During one of these filming sessions, Glenn MacWilliams walked over to me and in a rather terse manner said, "See you in my office in about a half-hour." The abruptness of his remark caused me to wonder. Was he dissatisfied with my scripts? Was the company about to fold? Have they found a cheaper writer with more experience?

Many times I had entered that office, but this time the atmosphere was foreboding. As I knocked, that same brusque

51

voice called out, "Come in." MacWilliams went right on target with, "Kane, we have to change your name."

"You have to what?" I responded with gaping bewilderment.

"Yup. You see, there's too much of the name Kane in the TV series. There's Pa Kane and Ma Kane. And then there's Slim Kane and Candi Kane with a script written by Bernard Kane. That's just too much." It was a coincidence that MacWilliams had chosen the name Kane for the cast of characters long before I had arrived on the scene.

My noncommittal reply of "Well, er," together with the shocked expression on my face gave Glenn an opening.

"Tell you what we'll do. Aileen is free Saturdays and Sundays, isn't she? Why don't you both drive up Saturday about six o'clock. We'll have dinner with the cast at Bar E Ranch and choose a new name. It will be a name change by committee. Remember, this is not a legal change of name."

That evening at Bar E there was indeed a cosmopolitan gathering: a proper Bostonian, a sophisticated New Yorker, Ma and Pa Kane, whose faces showed the wear of the hot Arizona sun, Candi projecting the stereotype of a sweet, young, innocent girl and Slim, the tall, gangly, slow-talking cowboy and of course, Glenn MacWilliams rapt in the recognizable aura of a Hollywood director.

The conversational buzz at the dinner table subsided as Glenn interrupted, "I don't know whether you are aware of it or not, but the cast of characters of our series is in the process of copyright. Copyright lawyers cost money. Squire McGuire says there's too much Kane now in the series; it's just too folksy. He wants the writer's name changed or a new writer engaged." MacWilliams went on, "I find Bernard Kane quite easy to work with and by not changing personnel at every whim we can stay within the budget."

Falling in Love—with Arizona

In Glenn's remarks I read certain subtle, upbeat facts. Obviously, he was satisfied with my first script which he was shooting. Of course, I was inexpensive, a major factor in staying within the budget. Also you don't ask a person to change his name and then fire him.

So the name game began with Glenn explaining the procedure. The first or last name had to contain three syllables. As Glenn told us, rhythm makes the name, and syllables make the rhythm.

We would go around the table and have each person suggest a last name. In her earlier years Ma Kane had been a secretary. She would record each choice and then we would vote yea, nay, or none. As we went around the table calling out last names, the banter was jovial and full of humor. Some were steadfast in supporting a family moniker while others seemed to have found their recommendations in the comic strips. Finally, the majority approved the surname of King.

There was no roulette in selecting a first name. Aileen stood up and with majestic authority announced, "If I ever have a son, we both have agreed his name will be Christopher. Since we have no son at the moment, let's call Bernie, Christopher." Three years later our only child, a son, was christened Christopher. Since Biblical times, people have voluntarily changed their names for various reasons. Some have had name changes thrust upon them. I can recall a conversation with a Chicago doctor of Polish ancestry. We were discussing the contributions of Baltic immigrants to the cultural and financial preeminence of the United States. He said, "Do you realize that, except for the city of Warsaw in Poland, Chicago has more people of Polish heritage than any other city in the world."

I knew that fact, but I wondered why so many people of Polish ancestry had Anglo last names. Aileen and I would attend a party or reception in Chicago and the guests, many of Polish descent, were introduced as Jones, Wilson, Cummings, Bartlett and many other typically American names. The good doctor explained the apparent contradiction. In his slow, precise manner he explained that when Polish immigrants arrived on Ellis Island, of course they couldn't speak English. On the other hand, the immigration officials couldn't spell Baltic names. As a result, if a newcomer said his name was Walenoski, the officer would jot down Walen and push him along. In the same way Janulevicus became Jensen, and Washelewski had the good Irish name of Walsh forced on him. The immigrants were so busy trying to make a living, they didn't have time to rectify the mistake even if they could find the courthouse. And so generations of Poles became Anglos in name because immigration officers couldn't spell.

The name change in my case has been expedient throughout the years for one particular reason. The name Bernard Kane is harsh like so many Northern European names whereas the "also known as" Christopher King is fluid as well as soft like so many Spanish and Italian expressions. As a result, I have lived very comfortably with the two identifications, Christopher King on radio and television and Bernard Kane in academia and in my personal life.

As they say in Westerns, "meanwhile back at the ranch," the situation at Arizona Productions gradually became uncertain, financially insecure, and as Glenn MacWilliams said, "This is a gamble, and we're all in it together." At this point, Aileen reminded me in a subtle way that we were in no position to gamble.

Furthermore, small production companies of TV westerns were popping up all over Arizona hoping to fill the vacuum of programs caused by the Federal law requiring so many hours of broadcasting or the loss of a television station's license. As a result, many companies failed, others merged, and scripts were being sold and resold for substantial profits. From this mishmash of turmoil, there emerged a few westerns like *Gunsmoke* and *Stagecoach* which went on to extraordinary success.

After finishing five scripts, I informed Glenn MacWilliams that I was deeply appreciative for the opportunity of working with him, but that I had to have a more certain and more secure future. So then I spent most of my time taking required classes, preparing for exams, and sending out inquiries to various high school districts. Finally with an Arizona teaching credential in my hand, I made an appointment for an interview with the Scottsdale School Board, which had previously indicated an interest.

The interview was a session I'll never forget because it was the onset of an exciting, fruitful, and happy life. The five-member Board consisted of a rancher, an undertaker, an attorney, and two housewives. They met in a large room adjacent to the superintendent's office. The enrollment in Scottsdale High School was about one hundred thirty-five students, and the old one story building, constructed perhaps about the early 1920's, was in need of repair. In the dirt parking lot were lines of rustic hitching posts where many students tied their horses when they came to school. Faculty automobiles were mixed among the tethered horses. Frankly, the night of the interview I had to watch my step, walking from the parking lot to the front entrance, because of the state of the soil in the lot.

The Board of Trustees, who were seeking an additional English teacher, seemed especially interested in my scriptwriting experience because, as a couple of members mentioned, it would add an extra dimension to the English curriculum. That evening at the meeting, the Board offered me a teaching position in the English department which comprised three instructors. Later I learned that while my subject was English, I would also teach Latin, head the Speech department, and produce two plays a year.

Scottsdale of today has its Neiman-Marcus Department Store, its five star Phoenician Resort, and its McCormick Ranch. It bears no resemblance to the Scottsdale we knew in 1951. Back then, there were only about four paved streets. The center of town consisted of fewer than ten small stores. The town was bordered on the north by a dangerous, wide canal; on the east by an Indian Reservation; and on the south by a river bottom. Phoenix adjoined Scottsdale on the west; in fact, Scottsdale seemed the last outpost of civilization.

For such an insignificant town, Scottsdale was remarkably cosmopolitan. There were descendants of the early pioneers, Indians from the nearby reservation, and transplanted successful Easterners who had built mansions in Paradise Valley, just north of Scottsdale. I observed this heterogeneous combination one time when Connecticut's Senator Benton's daughter sat in my English class next to an Indian from the reservation, and the grandson of Fowler McCormick, of the famous McCormick family of Chicago, worked on stage scenery with the son of a local rancher. The artist and originator of the internationally popular pin-up Petty Girls used to draw his curvaceous models at the bar of the Pink Pony, located at the intersection of the two main streets in the center of Scottsdale. An interesting incident concerning Frank Lloyd Wright was related to me by a young lady, a senior in my advanced English class.

She worked after school in Lute's Drug Store which sold everything from pharmaceuticals to small appliances. One afternoon Mr. Wright walked into the store and ordered a toaster. She went to the back room, and returned with a toaster.

She told him, "That will be fourteen dollars and ninety-five cents."

"Charge it," rang out the sententious voice.

"I'm sorry, but we can't do that."

"Young lady, do you know who I am?"

"Yes. And that's why we can't charge it."

Life for Aileen and me became more settled and less worrisome. She was happy with her classes at the College, and I felt more relaxed at Scottsdale High. We moved from the made-over porch apartment as soon as we could and rented a two-bedroom home in Tempe.

The first drama production at Scottsdale High was so nondescript I don't even recall the name of it. Doting parents, relatives, and close friends of the cast as well as those related to the stage crew made up the audience. They were not the ingredients of a sell-out show.

The eagerness and the talent of the drama students at the high school, together with the worldly experience of the Scottsdale population, germinated an idea. Why not blend the two segments into one and make it a community enterprise? This endeavor would require diplomacy because any play heavy with adults, or in reverse, any script heavy with students would splinter the experiment. Also it was prudent for me to remember that my salary came from the school district and not from the town.

After scanning Baker's catalogue of plays, time and time again, for the drama most appropriate for our situation, I chose Clarence Day's *Life with Father* because it was a family story with an excellent balance between adult and youthful actors. Before I selected a cast, I personally contacted some nationally known personalities who were residents of Scottsdale and Paradise Valley. I asked two questions: Do you approve of joint theatrical productions involving both the community and the high school? If you were asked, would you accept a role?

Bettina Rubicam, wife of the founder of Young and Rubicam, endorsed the idea enthusiastically, but she did not wish to take a role because, as she said, her days of acting on Broadway were pleasant memories for her and she did not want to disturb them.

Martha Lee McDaniel, mother-in-law of Dick Searles who at that time was Under-Secretary of the Interior in Eisenhower's Cabinet, not only supported the concept but also played the part of Mrs. Clarence Day. It was a coincidence that Mrs. McDaniel actually had four sons and a husband named Clarence, used to live at 48th and Park Avenue in New York, and even patronized Sherry's Ice Cream Parlor which was depicted in *Life with Father.*

Scottsdale residents became most enthusiastic about the project. W.W. Dick, the superintendent of schools, not only acclaimed the venture but also agreed to play the role of Dr. Somers; Elizabeth Haas, the wife of the general manager of Phoenix's Chamber of Commerce, had never before appeared on any stage. As it turned out, she was outstanding as Aunt Cora, a principal character in *Life with Father.* Jovial Cecil Raleigh, the founder and owner of the largest insurance agency outside the city of Phoenix, reveled in his enactment of the staid, somber Reverend Doctor Lloyd.

The four Day boys, ages six, ten, fourteen, and eighteen, were all redheads like their father and mother, Clarence and Vinnie Day. None of these principals in the cast was a natural redhead, so it was necessary to have their hair dyed before the curtain went up. About a week before opening night Lute Wasbotten of Lute's Pharmacy, his wife Marian and the three employees in the store wanted to create interest in the show, so they dyed their hair red.

Falling in Love—with Arizona

On the evenings of April 21, 22, and 23, of 1952, in the Scottsdale High School auditorium, *Life with Father* played to sell-out audiences, and on that opening night The Scottsdale Community Theater was born. The theater continues to this day, a magnificent structure, a dream come true.

It's time to put together the bits and pieces of *Life with Father* and wrap them with a blue ribbon. It is true, that whenever any event is a sell-out, everybody wants a ticket. The newspapers in the area had played up the fact that *Life with Father* was sold out well before opening night. On the day of the last performance, business manager Lucille Raleigh answered the telephone and heard: "I am calling on behalf of Crown Prince Franz Joseph of Liechtenstein. The Prince has read about all the excitement in downtown Scottsdale. Would there possibly be two cancellations for the Prince and Princess?"

Mrs. Raleigh, the astute wife of jovial Cecil Raleigh, calmly answered, "Although we are sold out, I'll check and return the call within ten minutes."

There had been no cancellations, but if a cat can look at a queen, we certainly could make arrangements for His Royal Highness and his wife. At the end of the center aisle in the rear of the auditorium, we placed two comfortable but not ostentatious chairs, and there royalty viewed *Life with Father*. Later we learned that the Prince and Princess were leasing a mansion in Paradise Valley.

Another item of interest concerns the Raleigh family. The husband Cecil played the Reverend Doctor Lloyd, while Lucille was business manager. Their son Barry Raleigh, who portrayed Clarence Day, Jr., later became a renowned scientist and is internationally famous as an authority on earthquakes.

Then, there was the reformation of Elizabeth Haas, who took the part of Aunt Cora. Before her marriage, Elizabeth had been a journalist in San Francisco. When I first approached Elizabeth for her opinion about a community theater, she heartily endorsed the proposal but remarked with definite firmness, "Acting's not for me. I've always hidden behind the written word. I'd rather die than go on the stage. Furthermore, with Lew's position as general manager of the Phoenix Chamber of Commerce, I don't especially want to make a fool of myself in front of his friends and business associates."

Elizabeth Haas was a clone of Aunt Cora so every time we met, I would cajole her with honeyed words until at last she laid down the gauntlet.

"All right. I'll struggle through the part of Aunt Cora if you'll play Father." She never thought that I would accept the challenge. Throughout my sampling of re-actions about a community theater, I learned that most adults who had never been on a stage, feared that *Life with Father* would fall apart unless there was someone on stage to hold it together. The cast voted unanimously for me to play Father and they were ready to rehearse with enthusiasm and confidence. Everyone in the cast performed superbly, especially Elizabeth Haas, who in future years studied oil painting, and under the name Chabela won national recognition.

The expectations and disappointments, the illusions and delusions, the successes and failures of life occur in the strangest places at the oddest times. Who would ever surmise that a drama about an autocratic Manhattan family would play to sellout audiences on the arid sands of Scottsdale, Arizona? Who would imagine that the Crown Prince and Princess of Liechtenstein would be sitting in portable seats at the final performance? Who would ever believe that the tiny town of Scottsdale in 1953 would become the famous city of Scottsdale we know today?

CHAPTER VI

1953, A Banner Year

Our private lives settled down for a short period of time. We bought an attractive double-brick house just outside the Phoenix city limits. An incident at that house, truly an insignificant episode in itself, illustrates the hackneyed adage, what goes around comes around. In a previous segment referring to my great grandfather, I wrote about small insurance companies with their own private fire brigades in Boston, and in a sense, the circumstances over one hundred years ago in Boston, recurred when our home in Phoenix caught fire because of a cracked flue in the chimney.

The Phoenix Fire Department in 1952 would not go outside the city boundaries with the result that private fire districts, another name for an insurance company, would send their volunteers if the owner was a policy holder. If he were not, he'd watch his home burn to the ground. Fortunately, we were members of the fire district, so there was very little damage. Just a word of caution to many Easterners who go West, particularly near large cities, don't assume that fire protection is automatic. That is not necessarily true. Check the boundaries of the area where your home is located.

Teenagers and adults working together in the production of *Life with Father* planted in my mind the seed of *Arizona Youth Forum*, a radio program in which young people would interact with experts on subjects such as education, politics, sports, family relations, and philosophy. KRUX was a small radio station with studios in the Westward Ho, the tallest, the newest, and the best hotel in Phoenix. When I approached the general manager of the radio station with my plan, he responded enthusiastically, provided that I could gain approval of the twelve high school districts in the Phoenix area and the suburbs.

The greatest obstacle I faced was the fear of board members that the students would be commercially exploited. It took a lot of rhetoric to convince the members of the first three districts to whom I made the proposal, but thereafter the other districts fell in line. This was the agreement with KRUX: the station would provide one hour of prime time each week for twelve weeks; I would produce, moderate, and provide the talent at no expense to KRUX; if the show was not sold at the expiration of three months, the station had the option to cancel.

Arizona Youth Forum was exciting for the students, but unfortunately the audience ratings were low because, I presume, listeners accustomed to cowboy music were shocked by a panel program of teenagers. In 1952 the general attitude of audiences, so different from today, was that children didn't belong on radio or TV. The program continued, but the ratings remained low with the result that the station manager informed me that the show had not been sold, and therefore, would be canceled in two weeks. Gradually I was learning that the entertainment business is an uncertain business.

The salesman who had been assigned *Arizona Youth Forum* went to the KRUX business office to pick up his weekly paycheck, and with the paycheck was a pink slip. To drown his sorrow, the salesman went to the bar on the lobby level of the hotel, and next to him at the bar was a man obviously also bemoaning some misfortune. It turned out that the man was a builder, and his cash assets were dwindling because his one house, built on speculation, was being foreclosed by the bank.

Sometimes the strangest happenings take place at bars. After a few drinks, the builder who was going broke, bought the sponsorship of the *Arizona Youth Forum* from the salesman who had just been fired. I assume the builder sold his house because in later years he became the developer of huge subdivision communities in Arizona, California, and Florida. To complete the episode, the salesman was rehired.

There were three schools in the Phoenix High School District participating on *Arizona Youth Forum*; they were Tech High, Phoenix High, and Carver High whose enrollment was entirely Afro-American. Since Carver High had all Black students, the Westward Ho informed me that the students from Carver would have to use the freight elevator to reach the KRUX studios on the third floor. This order was reprehensible to me, but then I began to recall how European immigrants had been treated on the East Coast during the early 1900's. I remember that in 1931 when I would walk from Boston's South Station to B.C. High, I would see in store windows many signs stating, HELP WANTED—NO IRISH NEED APPLY. It seemed that the Bean Town streets were being repaved only by Italians, all laundries were operated by Chinese, and all the tailors were Russian Jews.

Live Your Dreams

As I look back, Afro-Americans during the past forty-five years have become an integral part of America as the European immigrants did. In this evolution of Blacks, I have observed first hand the embarrassment and rejection they have suffered as they have struggled to become an integral part of America. On the other hand, Tiger Woods' spectacular success in the Masters Tournament at Augusta, Georgia, proves that ability is the basis of success. Color has nothing to do with it.

For years the professional summer theaters in Maine had been begging *Life Magazine* to do a feature story about their successes. At last *Life* agreed to send a writer and one of their top photographers. The owner of Boothbay Harbor's Sprucewold Lodge, where that summer my Mutual Network show originated each week, had offered accommodations for the reporter and photographer. When the two from *Life* drove up to the office, the owner actually panicked; the writer was white and the photographer was black. In 1956, the time of this incident, the Supreme Court had not yet handed down the revolutionary decision about Afro-Americans riding in Alabama buses.

It is necessary to capsulize the background of Sprucewold's owner to really understand his dramatic reaction. He started as an employee with the Post Office; after that he opened a hot dog stand at Maine's Old Orchard Beach, and then with his savings, bought an old run-down summer hotel at picturesque Boothbay Harbor in Maine. In a period of twenty years, he had restored the weather-beaten property to a magnificent resort hotel which every year was booked to capacity from early spring to late fall. He was training his two sons, both Stanford graduates, in the operation of the business. The unusual attraction at Sprucewold was that fresh lobster, any way the diner wished, was served as one of the entrees at all three meals each day.

Swift action was necessary because the owner found himself on the horns of a dilemma. Never had he registered a Black, not by design or policy, but it just never happened. Since the dining room was a separate building overlooking the Atlantic Ocean, the Afro-American would be highly visible. The owner, I know from many years of friendship with him and his family, harbored no animosity toward any group of people, but he was thinking about the repercussion of his guests, the negative effect on his resort, the future of his sons, and especially how untrue statements would spread on the gossip network.

On occasion when dignitaries would vacation at Sprucewold, the owner would turn over his private home for their enjoyment. His secluded home was located adjacent to the hotel grounds on a narrow peninsula jutting out into the Atlantic Ocean. There was a housekeeper at the family home, but all meals were prepared in the hotel's kitchen and were delivered by a bellboy.

While employees were scurrying to put the house in immaculate order, the owner invited the writer and photographer to have an arrival drink with him in the cocktail lounge. He informed them about the custom at Sprucewold. "When celebrities come to Sprucewold, they come to completely relax. For that reason, I turn my home on the peninsula over to them for privacy and seclusion. My home is your home for the time you'll be here. All your meals will be delivered by a bellboy. Phone the desk for anything you need." The reporter and photographer during the day were usually away on their assignments at summer theaters, and in the evening they would relax at their private retreat on the peninsula.

Live Your Dreams

Everything went smoothly at Sprucewold. The reporter and photographer from *Life Magazine* seemed to enjoy themselves; the guests were not aware of any extraordinary situation; and an eight page pictorial spread appeared in *Life Magazine*. The Black photographer—who holds 28 honorary degrees and received the National Medal of Arts from President Reagan in 1988—was the internationally renowned Gordon Parks.

I was a spectator at another racial event; this time, in Montgomery, Alabama. My radio program, *Christopher King's Sounding Board*, was originating from Montgomery where there was a city ordinance requiring Blacks to sit in the back of a bus. Blacks protested the ordinance by forming car pools with the result that the bus company, owned by the city, was losing money. The City of Montgomery retaliated by accusing Blacks of operating taxis without a business license, and this confrontation led to the significant Supreme Court decision which was a lethal blow to racial segregation.

The Supreme Court handed down the decision on desegregation at four in the afternoon with instructions that on the next morning, buses would roll with Blacks sitting anywhere they wished. Rosa Parks was on the first bus to leave the garage the next morning, and I was there among the crowd to record the reactions for a later *Sounding Board*.

Another involvement in the process of desegregation was more personal to me. It happened in San Diego where I lived. There were two gentlemen by the name of George Smith, both Afro-Americans. One George Smith was a constant gadfly at meetings of the San Diego City Council, while the other George Smith was a Methodist minister. The gadfly was getting weekly coverage in the *San Diego Union* because his weird antics were good copy. The Reverend George Walker Smith decided to run for the San Diego School Board, but the campaign couldn't seem to get off the ground. The voters were confusing the identity of the two George Smiths.

The phone rang and the voice on the other end said, "This is Reverend George Walker Smith. Is Christopher King there?"

"You're talking to him."

"Chris," continued the Reverend, "I need your help. It's a case of mistaken identity. The public is mixing me up with the George Smith who's always disrupting Council meetings. For that reason, I can't get my campaign moving."

"What can I do for you?" I inquired.

"Your talk show *Vox Pop* has a terrific audience. People mention it to me often. May I be a local guest to clear up this confusion about the other George Smith?"

I told George Walker Smith that he could be a guest for about ten minutes to rectify the problem; however, he could not say a word about running for the School Board because that would be a violation of the equal time law. In a clear, professional manner, the Reverend cleared up the mistaken identity, won the election, and served admirably on the Board.

During the eight years George Walker Smith was an incumbent on the School Board, he and I developed a friendship with the result that when Smith announced his candidacy for the nonpartisan San Diego Board of County Supervisors, he asked me to ring doorbells in his behalf. Since local elections of San Diego didn't involve party politics, I readily agreed.

In an area where most of the residents were employees of General Dynamics, one of the nation's largest suppliers of aeronautical parts, I rang over fifty doorbells. Usually the lady of the house answered, and I began my spiel about George Smith's service to the community, about his integrity, and his plans for the future of San Diego.

Live Your Dreams

At many houses, as I was about to leave, and was handing the lady a brochure with George Smith's picture on the front, I would hear, "Oh!" or "Is this Mr. Smith's picture?" The remarks didn't make any impression on me until I realized that those remarks were common at almost every home I visited. Then I put two and two together. Every one of the houses had under the doorbell a bronze medallion stating: "This is a General Dynamics home." Obviously, the residents of each home, when they saw Smith's picture, were fearful about their economic security. I believe that to the residents in those General Dynamics homes, George Smith was a symbol of a horde of people who might take away their jobs. How often an incident involving one person can be the source of a stereotype of all people in that class. George Walker Smith lost the election.

From these experiences relating to Afro-Americans, I've reached three general conclusions. Blacks in the past were treated badly; they have been entering the mainstream of American life at a reasonable rate; but underlying that progress is a resentment based on a fear that one's economic stability is being threatened by the emergence of Blacks.

Arizona Youth Forum was well received by the high school boards of the Phoenix area as well as by the listeners. The ratings rose, resulting in an offer from the Phoenix NBC television station to join their weekly lineup of programs.

The general manager of the radio station where *Arizona Youth Forum* had begun asked me to create a show to fill the void left by the youth program when it moved to television. Aileen and I tossed around many ideas before we eventually came up with *Arizona Cavalcade*. This was the format: each week on Saturday we would travel with an engineer and his portable recording equipment to an Arizona community. A few communities were relatively large in population like

1953, A Banner Year

Flagstaff and Tucson, but most were small towns off the main roads. A welcoming greeting from the mayor, two renditions by the high school band, an essay about the community by a sixth grader, interviews with the town's oldest resident, the merchant with the largest business and the citizen who had the strangest tale to tell comprised the show. It was entirely unrehearsed, and the spontaneity is what made the program different. For Aileen and me this was an exciting show because it enabled us to see every nook and corner of Arizona, our adopted state.

Radio station KOY loved *Arizona Cavalcade*. The various communities were happy to boast about their local attractions, and we were enjoying every moment traveling around the state. *Live Your Dreams* is not a travelogue, so I'll recount only two of the many unusual incidents which occurred.

In 1952 Eisenhower and Stevenson were campaigning for the Presidency of the United States. Since Aileen and I were traveling across Arizona each weekend, KOY suggested that we do a five-minute segment at the same time, a poll of the voter's preference for Eisenhower or Stevenson. The most humorous interview took place in Show Low, Arizona, a town of about six hundred residents. Show Low was named for a card game that settled the ownership of land in the pioneer days. After my radio dialogue with the owner of the general store, who narrated some extraordinary stories, I spied a bearded, crusty-looking old timer sitting on a cracker barrel at the opposite end of the store.

My first question, "What is your name, sir?"

"None of your business," was the terse answer.

"Do you prefer Eisenhower or Stevenson to be the next President of the United States?" I inquired.

"None of your business."

Live Your Dreams

The old man was obviously stonewalling, so I tried a different tack. "May I ask you, sir, what is your occupation?"

"Just a settin'."

That colloquy, I suppose, was one of the briefest on radio, but listeners commented about it for weeks afterwards.

The most poignant experience on *Arizona Cavalcade* happened at Vicksburg, Arizona. When the letter agreeing to host a program arrived, there was no letterhead to indicate the sender. The letter agreeing to host a program was handwritten on ordinary note paper and under the signature was the man's title as president of the Chamber of Commerce. I had never heard of Vicksburg, Arizona, and neither had anyone whom I asked. In fact, it wasn't even on the map.

Aileen and I followed the directions to Vicksburg as stated in the letter and finally arrived at the isolated community which was about fifteen miles off the main road between Phoenix and Yuma. Vicksburg was a commune of Afro-Americans whose ancestors had homesteaded the land after the Civil War. The original settlers had left Vicksburg, Mississippi, to be really free, much as the earlier Pilgrims had sailed from England to live in an aura of freedom. The complex was mostly rehabilitated boxcars decorated with attractive pastel colors; the people were gracious and eminently hospitable. The homesteaders and those who came after them converted an arid desert plot into a fertile, productive piece of land. The residents lived off the land; the women did needlework which they sold at little stands on the main highway; and the men worked in the nearby pima cotton fields.

At Vicksburg there was no high school band, no mayoral greeting, not even an old codger sitting on a cracker barrel; however, the stories they told during interviews on the air were fascinating. They related that their forefathers had left Mississippi during the turmoil after the Civil War, and that

70

they had cultivated the desert sand by very primitive irrigation to make it a source of their food supply. They told how wild camels, originally brought to the Arizona desert during the 1870's and 1880's as pack animals by Ex-Confederate soldiers, roamed at will among the saguaro cacti. The camels over the years became extinct because mules and camels cannot live together, and mules were the entrenched beast of burden at that time. For fifty weekends we viewed the majestic beauty of Arizona; we met people of different backgrounds with divergent interests, and we had fun doing it. Then something unexpected happened.

I was standing on the front patio of our Phoenix home when Aileen drove in to the driveway. Usually she put the car in the garage and locked the garage door, but this time she left the car in the driveway with the motor running, dashed out the driver's door, and exclaimed for all the world to hear, "Bernie, we're going to have a baby!" Unknown to me she had stopped at the doctor's office on the way home. Aileen had always been attractive to me, but after her announcement she seemed to blossom even more. I have heard that all expectant mothers react in much the same way, yet in Aileen's case she seemed to radiate confidence and a positive attitude of peaceful happiness that was unusually beautiful.

This was 1953, a year of bountiful opportunities which radically changed our lives. Aileen and I still held our respective teaching positions at Arizona State and Scottsdale High. *Arizona Youth Forum*, sponsored by a local chain of office supply stores, was firmly established on TV, and *Arizona Cavalcade* had a projected life span of five more months.

KOY, the flagship station of an Arizona radio network and the station from which *Arizona Cavalcade* originated, desired to continue the general theme of Arizona, so the management asked me to design a show for that purpose. It was called *Arizona Town Hall*, and the format was very simple. Each week a controversial subject especially identified with Arizona would be selected; two experts, one supporting and one opposing a proposition, would be allowed two minutes each to state their positions; then, with a microphone, I would walk among the audience for their reactions.

Panel shows in the early 1950's were much different from those of today. In those years they were entirely unrehearsed, and controversial subjects of general community interest were discussed. Today the warm-ups for a talk show are dress rehearsals; furthermore, most of the topics belong in the privacy of a bedroom, and not on a public forum like TV or radio. Too many of the hosts are aberrations; in fact, they're not even entertainers. These days the amount of expensive publicity spent on a new show will determine the program's success or failure. Substance is subservient to spectacle.

In the beginning, *Arizona Town Hall* experienced difficulty because we could not attract a diversified studio audience each week, and a studio audience was in fact the backbone of the show. We tried everything from originating at a civic club meeting to inviting tour groups who were staying at the Westward Ho to be part of the studio audience. Finally, as an act of desperation, we asked employees who were free to be the studio audience. The knell of *Arizona Town Hall* was about to peal loud and clear.

What I needed—and immediately—was a captive audience. Jack Stewart, the manager of Scottsdale's famous Camelback Inn, came to mind. I did not know Jack Stewart personally, but his reputation was well-known. He was generally recognized as one of the best innkeepers in the country, and furthermore he was praised by his colleagues in the hotel industry as an astute businessman. In my mind, *Arizona Town*

Hall and Camelback Inn were made for each other, but I was aware that Jack Stewart was known for his bargaining prowess.

We set the time for an appointment at Camelback Inn, and at the designated hour I was there, armed with every possible persuasive reason. From the telephone conversation, Jack Stewart knew in general the purpose of my visit, but he wanted to know more particulars.

"Your program sounds good, but I wonder if it fits into our schedule at Camelback. Guests come here to play and to relax. They don't want to do any heavy thinking. We do that for them."

I was ready for this objection. "Mr. Stewart, a guest can choose whether he wishes or not to participate. At least, he can learn what his fellow guests are thinking."

"What you say is true, Mr. King; however, from time to time there are lecturers who come here during the winter season. Since the speakers come occasionally, we're not tied down to any regularity. Inasmuch as your broadcast is set for every Thursday evening, an element of routine would be settling in, and as I said, guests come here to relax and to play."

I knew it was time to change the conversation, so I said to Mr. Stewart, "I noticed in your weekly program that Thursday seems to be a free night. On Tuesdays and Fridays, there's Bingo. Some form of a musical is scheduled for Mondays and Wednesdays, and so Thursday is the only free weekday night."

"Yes, it's planned that way. It gives us flexibility. Tell you what I'll do. We will list *Arizona Town Hall* at nine in the evening for the four Thursdays in January. If the guests like it, we'll continue every Thursday until June first when the winter season ends. If they don't like it, you know what the answer is."

"Indeed I do, Mr. Stewart. Thank you for the opportunity."

"By the way, you and your wife will be my guests for dinner at Camelback Inn on those Thursday evenings."

From experience I knew that most radio or TV programs needed at least two months of what is called seeding time. That's the period of time when listeners or viewers hear about a show or when they perchance happen to tune in for the first time. In 1953 there was little publicity about regional or local programs. Even though there was little promotion of the show, I was aware that the origination from Camelback Inn cloaked *Arizona Town Hall* with respectability and a certain degree of prestige. Jack Stewart's proposal of four initial programs was at least a beginning.

In two weeks *Arizona Town Hall* would be presented for the first time at Camelback Inn. Aileen had just announced that our baby would be born during the latter part of September or in early October. With a new baby on the way, I was walking on clouds. Then a surprising event occurred which completely changed our lives. I met W.S. Woodfill, the owner of Grand Hotel on Michigan's Mackinac Island. He loved his hotel and always referred to it as the world's largest summer hotel. As I got to know Mr. Woodfill, I labeled him the "reasonable eccentric" and I did so with profound admiration and respect. All this happened in January of 1953.

A series of circumstances against a backdrop of widespread corruption led to my first meeting with Mr. Woodfill. Before 1950, Phoenix and the area around it was a Sodom and Gomorrah where more than forty whorehouses openly plied their businesses in the downtown section, and where there were more than twenty betting parlors. In those years, the law enforcement agencies either were totally blind or were taking graft. Gambling, even bingo for charity, was illegal in Arizona.

On November 8, 1949, a reform, nonpartisan slate of city council candidates led by Barry Goldwater swept every precinct, and that's when the cleanup of Phoenix City Hall began. After one year in office, the new council drove crime underground, had a balanced city budget, and produced a reserve of $275,000.

By January of 1953, the Phoenix area including Scottsdale was a decent, respectable place. First class resorts were scattered throughout Scottsdale and adjacent Paradise Valley, and the jewel among them was Camelback Inn. Jack Stewart possessed the unique ability of managing a rigid operation with the appearance of complete casualness. Even in those days Camelback Inn was very expensive, but its clientele from New York, Chicago, Boston, and the entire East was willing to pay for quality.

Even though bingo was unlawful in Arizona, every resort, big and small, had bingo at least one night a week. Law enforcement officers looked the other way because tourism was producing significant public revenue. Money talks. Easterners, who were accustomed to playing bingo for charitable causes in their home towns, demanded bingo at their vacation spots. Camelback, of course, complied.

On the Tuesday evening before the second Thursday night broadcast of *Arizona Town Hall* from Camelback Inn, the resort was raided by a deputy sheriff for violation of the Arizona gambling laws. Jack Stewart and his wife were arrested for running a gaming establishment, and the mother and father of a ten-year-old girl who had just won a bingo jackpot of ten dollars were also arrested for contributing to the delinquency of a minor.

Live Your Dreams

The next day newspapers carried the headline: Camelback Inn Raided. The caption could have read: The Devil Storms Heaven. Although I had chosen the topic for that Thursday's broadcast, I quickly canceled it, and instead substituted the question: Should Bingo be legalized at Arizona resorts?

When word circulated about the raid, as well as the change to a new topic for *Arizona Town Hall*, SRO became the sign at Thursday night's broadcast. The sheriff's department reluctantly sent a spokesman to defend its actions, but the audience wasn't swayed by his halting, dull explanations. The guests were out for blood and they made it known. It was an unusual sight to observe in the audience a tycoon of a megamillion dollar New York Corporation verbally defending bingo against the lonely speaker from the Sheriff's department. Then toward the end of the program, the ladies in the audience released their fury, and verbally demolished the law and order spokesman.

After the show, the spokesman for the Sheriff's office departed quietly and very quickly while members of the audience milled around conversing with one another. Jack Stewart, who after the raid had been released on his own recognizance, tapped me on the shoulder and as I turned around he said, "I guess it will be every Thursday until the first of June."

Aileen had an important faculty meeting that Thursday night, so she was not at Camelback Inn. I was anxious to get home because honestly I was exhausted by the give and take during the evening. As I was leaving, a distinguished looking gentleman wearing a camel hair coat, Italian cut trousers, alligator shoes, an ascot, and carrying a walking stick, stepped up to me and said, "I am W.S. Woodfill, the owner of Grand Hotel on Mackinac Island, Michigan, the largest summer hotel in the world. I liked what I saw tonight. Get me a coast to coast national network and the biggest names in Washington. I'll pay all expenses; I'll give an honorarium to the two principal speakers, and I'll reward you handsomely. In a special delivery letter, I'll write the details. Good night."

When I arrived home and repeated the gist of W.S. Woodfill's remarks, Aileen's facial expression showed not only unbelievable amazement, but also extreme doubt. "Are you kidding me?" she asked.

"No, it's the absolute truth."

"Well let's wait to see if the special delivery letter ever comes," Aileen advised.

Waiting for Mr. Woodfill's letter was like waiting for the next episode of a soap opera. Will the letter come? What's in it? Is it good news or bad news?

After a week and no special delivery letter, our interest began to wane. Then one afternoon when we returned home together, there on our door knob was a notice instructing Aileen to pick up a special delivery letter at the post office. Why would it be addressed to Aileen?

We signed for the letter, and then saw it was Registered/Special Delivery postmarked from Boston. About two months previously Aileen had requested that her shares in the teachers' retirement fund be sent to her, and sure enough, a check for the amount was in the letter.

Hope for the important special delivery from Mr. Woodfill had almost faded when at last the postman rang our doorbell and asked us to sign for a special delivery postmarked Scottsdale. Aileen and I looked at the front of the envelope, then we looked at the back. She put it down on the dining room table, and went into the kitchen for a letter opener. Finally, we carefully slit the envelope.

Live Your Dreams

There were two sheets of letter paper in the envelope. One was the letter requesting a visit with Mr. Woodfill at his home on a particular afternoon at four o'clock to discuss his proposal. The other sheet of paper was a work of art, all in English script. At the heading was the name of his home called Armageddon, and beneath the name was the Biblical explanation. At Armageddon on Invergordon Road in Scottsdale, good and evil fight to the finish within Mr. Woodfill and, of course, good wins.

The rest of the page was a colored map of the United States. The principal landmark was an artist's rendition of Armageddon, and scattered across the map were replicas of well known sites with the exact mileage noted between Armageddon and the particular location. For example, the map I received showed the precise mileage between Armageddon and Zsa Zsa Gabor's home in Los Angeles; between Armageddon and President Truman's winter White House in Key West; and between Armageddon and the United Nations Building in New York. At the bottom of the sheet was this instruction: Kindly turn the page.

On the other side was a caption denoting the proper manners for a person visiting Mr. Woodfill's home. Some were these: a guest is always on time; conversation is always informative, never argumentative; a guest should depart with a sense of enrichment. Aileen and I just looked at each other and stared, not saying a word.

CHAPTER VII

Armageddon on the Desert

It was about ten minutes before four o'clock when I drove up to Armageddon. There it was—a sprawling one-story house, completely walled with a wrought iron gate at the entrance. The gate was open, so I drove in. A turnaround inside the wall was edged by magnificent, pastel flowers, and in the center of this floral array was a sign in English script: "If you do not have an appointment, keep driving." The driveway led right out to the street.

Since I had an appointment, I parked the car and walked over to another wall which was attached to the house and was adjacent to a lovely garden. Over the lighted buzzer was another sign in English script: "If you do not have an appointment, don't ring. If you have an appointment, there's no reason to ring." So I stood there. At four o'clock the door in the wall opened, and before me appeared Mr. Woodfill dressed impeccably in a black camel hair sport coat, an ascot, white linen trousers, and burgundy loafers. He stood about six feet, one hundred eighty pounds, and he appeared erect as a steel rod. His manner was hospitable and especially gracious. He was a perfect gentleman.

The flower garden inside the entrance was so manicured one would think an artist had painted it. As we strolled onto the patio, I noticed that the slats overhead were arranged in an unusual pattern. Mr. Woodfill observed my bewilderment because he immediately said, "I can see by your expression that you are wondering about the position of those slats. Well, these are the reasons why they are slanted in such a strange way. Each year I come to Scottsdale from November until May. My custom is to retire at four in the morning and to arise at one in the afternoon. Therefore, I have calculated for sun bathing the position of the sun during the months when I am here, and also when I'm awake. Reasonable isn't it?"

"It certainly is," was my prosaic remark.

I should make it clear that my host was always addressed as Mr. Woodfill, and always referred to as W.S. Woodfill. No one ever considered calling him Bill or Stewart. For thirty years I called him Mr. Woodfill.

The living room was lined on three sides with built-in bookcases, and there wasn't room for one more book. The room was tastefully furnished, but not lavishly. I could see into the dining room, and the set of furniture caught my eye because I had never seen anything like it. It was not the standard height of a dining room table nor were the chairs typical of what one sees in most homes.

Mr. Woodfill sensed my curiosity. "Frank Lloyd Wright designed that suite for me. English Victorian furniture is self-torture when a man is eating, and the Romans were a bunch of hedonists when they would recline for a meal. So I said to Wright, "Design me a dining set that's half way between the rigidity of the English and the laxity of the Romans.""

Seeking some remark that wasn't too inane, I said, "You certainly are a man of originality."

"Sit down in one of these chairs. Feel how comfortable and relaxing they are. Ten people can sit around this table in these reclining, low chairs, and no one's knees, ankles, or feet will touch the person seated next to him. So much for furniture. Now let's get on with the business of the afternoon."

Before Mr. Woodfill began to outline his plan, two questions were running through my mind. Was there a Mrs. Woodfill? What does he do to occupy his time here?

Mr. Woodfill realized that I had questions, but he knew that it would be impudent of me to even suggest them. So he interspersed some details of his personal life with his plan for a national network program from Grand Hotel.

There was a Mrs. Woodfill who preferred the Chicago society life to one of living on the quiet, lonesome Arizona desert. The Woodfills reached a compromise whereby she would remain in Chicago at their apartment in the Whitehall Hotel from November until May while he would stay at their home in Scottsdale during the same period. Otherwise, they lived together at the Whitehall and at their home on Mackinac Island overlooking the Straits of Mackinac.

Mr. Woodfill gradually delineated the overall proposal for his version of *Arizona Town Hall*. He, of course, recommended a name change since he expected that the show would be aired nationally. In general, Mr. Woodfill approved of the same format he had observed at Camelback Inn. He wanted the two principal debaters, one for the proposition and the other against, to be nationally distinguished personages. He assumed that the network would offer the half-hour free, and that he would be responsible for all the other expenses. All he requested was that Grand Hotel be mentioned as the site of the broadcasts. He would pay the transportation costs for the two celebrities and their spouses wherever they happened to be in the United States; moreover, he would furnish complete accommodations, and at the end of their stay at Grand Hotel, he would give each participant an honorarium.

Mr. Woodfill informed me that he had made a background check on me; furthermore, he assured me that he would exert every effort to make the summer broadcasts a reality and that he would financially reward me at the end of the summer. This was a chance in a lifetime so I instinctively responded, "I'll do my best, Mr. Woodfill." Those words were the beginning of a formal friendship which endured until Mr. Woodfill's death many years later.

At the conclusion of our first meeting at Armageddon, Mr. Woodfill handed me a box of Grand Hotel stationery and a roll of stamps, shook hands, and said, "Good luck." From that time on I would confer at least twice a week with Mr. Woodfill at his home. After three weeks of these bi-weekly conferences, Mr. Woodfill gave me his new unlisted telephone number with the comment, "I give my unlisted telephone number to so many people, I have arranged with the telephone company to change it every month. So, if I forget to tell you the new number, remind me."

Meanwhile back at 44 West Oregon, where the Kanes lived, Aileen and I spent every free moment writing letters of invitation to Members of Congress. It was slow going. Since we were meeting regularly, Mr. Woodfill would inquire, "How are we doing?" and my answer would remain the same. "We have one Senator, Joe McCarthy, and no network." Woodfill's response was always the same—"Don't worry; we'll make it." Despite Mr. Woodfill's optimism, I did worry because a real debacle was in the making. What would happen if I had an acceptance list of celebrities, and no network on which to present them? Politicians, especially those who make the news, have their appearances booked six months in advance. Did I worry? I certainly did, but I never indicated in Mr. Woodfill's presence how I felt. Then an ingenious idea crossed my mind.

Jim Overpeck, a friend whom Aileen and I had met while traveling the state with *Arizona Cavalcade*, was a super salesman and a real entrepreneur. Jim could sell anything as long as it was big, expensive, and unusual. His attitude was why spend time selling automobiles and ordinary houses, when the sale of large acreage, mansions, and pricey collectibles paid far more for the same amount of energy. Apart from the money, he loved the challenge.

I introduced Jim to Mr. Woodfill. As a result, Jim Overpeck flew to New York City in search of a network. The CBS radio network turned down his proposition and so did NBC. Then Jim contacted the Mutual Network, which at that time had a string of over four hundred stations across the country. The network's national program director, Hal Wagner, did not immediately reject Jim's proposal nor did he accept it. He needed more time to dwell on the proposition and advised Jim to phone him before returning to Phoenix.

Mr. Wagner told Jim that the Mutual Broadcasting System would air the show for ten weeks on a trial basis beginning the first week of July. The details of a contract were to be negotiated between Mr. Woodfill's lawyer and the legal department of the Mutual Network. I never did learn what the arrangements were between Jim Overpeck and Mr. Woodfill.

Every time I visited Armageddon, the first question always was, "How are we doing?", and the answer was always, "We have the Mutual Network now, and Senator McCarthy." From Mr. Woodfill it was always the same positive encouragement, "Don't worry. We'll make it."

Live Your Dreams

In the bi-weekly conversations, Mr. Woodfill would interlace some of his personal life story with talk about the impending broadcasts. He was a skilled raconteur, and during one of the story telling sessions he told about his four years at Bowdoin College and the years following his graduation. The campus of Bowdoin in Brunswick, Maine, is where Henry Wadsworth Longfellow began his teaching career in the modern language department before he went on to Harvard. Harriet Beecher Stowe's husband was the minister of the Congregational Church in Brunswick, and in the manse at Brunswick, Harriet Beecher Stowe wrote *Uncle Tom's Cabin*. W.S. Woodfill attended Bowdoin College when the United States was fighting Germany in World War I. His scholarship was under the aegis of the Federal Government in exchange for military service after graduation. The war ended during Woodfill's senior year so the government did not need his service. W.S. admitted that he did not study, and as a result he learned very little.

After graduation he obtained a job as second cook in a Michigan lumber camp. He chose the job because he frequently suffered severe asthma attacks. The clear, clean northern Michigan air lessened the congestion of his lungs. Since Mr. Woodfill was the second cook in the logging camp, he was required to get up at four in the morning to make the fires for the first cook. Then and there he decided that if he ever became rich enough, he would never arise until one in the afternoon.

It was also in northern Michigan that W.S. made another decision. Since he didn't spend a lot of time studying at Bowdoin, he determined that if he became rich enough, he would set aside so many months each year for learning. Those two decisions I observed in practice at Armageddon in Scottsdale. Mr. Woodfill was never available until after two o'clock in the afternoon. Furthermore, he spent most of his time each year from November to May studying and writing and rewriting theses on various subjects such as astronomy, mathematics, and physics. During the winter I met him, he was deep into astronomy. Not only did he study a particular subject from books and tapes, but he also invited experts to be guests at his home so that he could get to the root and the source of the subject matter. I remember that for a couple of weeks that winter, I didn't see Mr. Woodfill because he was hosting an astronomy professor from the University of Pennsylvania and another professor from Sydney, Australia. He would never permit any intrusion on his study time. These professors, like most of us, were unaccustomed to Woodfill's waking hours. They found it exhausting to work from late afternoon until two in the morning. Mr. Woodfill, however, rewarded them handsomely for their time and expertise.

Upon completion of the thesis, he would send the manuscript to Donnelly Brothers in Chicago, printers for the Grand Hotel. At his request, they would print and bind the manuscript, make several copies, and return them to Mr. Woodfill. Since he did not have any children of his own, he would send a copy to each of his nieces and nephews. After reading his copy, he would toss it in the fireplace and watch it go up in flames. This whole procedure made a dynamic impression on me which has lasted to this day. It made me realize that true learning becomes a part of a person; it is not merely a page in a book.

Spring had arrived. Mr. Woodfill was preparing to leave Scottsdale. The two radio programs, *Arizona Cavalcade* and *Arizona Town Hall*, were coming to an end. Aileen and I had covered much of the state with *Arizona Cavalcade*, and *Arizona Town Hall* was scheduled to conclude at Camelback Inn the first week of May. Schools were closing for the summer so *Arizona Youth Forum* on TV took a four month hiatus.

Before Mr. Woodfill flew to Mackinac Island, he invited Aileen and me to dinner at Armageddon. He informed us it would be just the three of us as he wanted to give instructions regarding Grand Hotel.

At every meeting during the winter at Woodfill's home, the conversation opened with the same question, "How's it going?" and the answer was always the same, "We have the Mutual Network and Senator Joe McCarthy." This dinner conversation was no exception.

Beneath Mr. Woodfill's apparent austerity, there was a great deal of tenderness and thoughtfulness. He showed it that evening. Before any discussion concerning the Grand Hotel, the network program, or possible participants, he turned to Aileen and said, "I have sensed your apprehensions about being pregnant on an island where there is no hospital and the only transportation is by horse and carriage. To alleviate your anxiety, I assure you that on the island we have an excellent doctor who was delivering babies before you were born. When I arrive on the Island, I shall alert the Coast Guard, so that in case of an emergency, they will escort you to the mainland." Aileen said nothing, but I judged from her facial expression that she would have preferred to be anywhere else than on an island.

Then we got down to details. It was arranged that Mr. Woodfill would send us air tickets to Detroit and also sleeper train tickets for the overnight trip to Mackinac City. We would arrive at Mackinac City about nine in the morning and then take the one hour ferry sail across the Straits of Mackinac to the Island. He would not be at the pier to greet us because, as I well knew, Mr Woodfill never arose until one in the afternoon. In his place, the social host of the Grand Hotel would be at the wharf to expedite our needs.

Mr. Woodfill told us most emphatically that we were going to the Grand Hotel as his guests and not as employees of the resort. For the three months of June, July, and August, we would live in a suite and be treated the same as any paying guest. He would supply an office and a secretary for the duration.

Before leaving for Mackinac Island, it was necessary that I inform Scottsdale High School about my future plans. Since the baby was expected in early October, Aileen would not be returning for the fall semester at Arizona State.

In my case, however, uncertainty abounded on all sides. After the ten week series at Grand Hotel, what would happen? Would the show, *Christopher King's Sounding Board,*—that was the title Mr. Woodfill had selected—be continued or would it be canceled? Would the weekly program originate from the East Coast or from the West Coast? Would the Mutual Network offer an extended contract or would the ten weeks at Grand Hotel be just an exciting summer vacation?

The teacher training department at Arizona State was very kind. They agreed to rehire Aileen when or if she wished to return. Scottsdale High also was very considerate. The board would assume that I was returning in the fall unless they were notified to the contrary by August fifteenth. All the loose ends of our life, at least for the time being, had been gathered and tied together. Indeed, great expectations awaited the Kanes at Grand Hotel.

The tubby ferry tooted its steam whistle three times, weighed anchor and slowly turned the bow toward Mackinac Island. The trip across the straits from Mackinac City required one hour. Suddenly the majestic Grand Hotel appeared on the horizon. From a distance the Hotel seemed as large as the island itself. Then as we approached, the magnificent features became more distinguishable. It was four stories high, a glistening white clapboard building with a crimson roof. Turrets were scattered in an irregular design across the massive red roof. As we neared the pier, the expansive veranda supported by gleaming white pillars displayed a large American flag from each column. Mr. Woodfill once told me that the front porch of The Grand was a quarter of a mile long.

As we were disembarking, Aileen tugged at my sleeve and pointed to a sign written in English script. It read: Welcome to Grand Hotel, Mr. and Mrs. Christopher King. The man holding the sign aloft was Driscoll Wolf, the social director at the hotel. He greeted us hospitably, directed our luggage to a waiting dray, and then led us to Mr. Woodfill's personal carriage. The carriage drawn by two sleek, crimson-plumed horses was reined by a uniformed driver named Teddy, who in his younger days had been Speaker of the House of Representatives of Michigan.

The red carpeted steps at the entrance blended into a spacious veranda spotted everywhere with potted red geraniums. The lobby was huge, and the deep pile in the crimson carpeting almost reached one's ankles. Later I learned why there was so much red at Grand Hotel; Mr. Woodfill was color blind.

We were almost completely settled in our suite when at two o'clock a bellboy knocked on the door. "Mr. Woodfill wishes to see Mr. King at his home within one hour. I'll dispatch Teddy with the carriage if you desire."

"No, thank you. I'll walk."

It was about a ten minute walk down the hill to Mr. Woodfill's house, which was an imposing, magnificent structure of early 1900 architecture. The residence, walled on all sides, overlooked the Straits of Mackinac. It was two storied, painted white with bright green shutters. Mr. Woodfill answered the bell at the gate and then directed me to the barn at the rear of the house.

The barn was a home within a barn. What in the past had been a stable, was attractively remodeled into a complex of oak paneled rooms. There was a library, a bedroom, and a convivial room where Mr. Woodfill entertained his close associates. There was another section of the stable I must mention because it indicates how Mr. Woodfill organized the results of his learning sessions each winter in Scottsdale. One winter before I had met him, he had flown in historians from various sections of the country since the topic that particular year was American history.

The recipients of his generous hospitality would often ask Mr. Woodfill what in the world they might give him as a token of their appreciation. He would respond that a most treasured gift would be a walking stick carved from wood directly associated with an event in American history. In the stable there were over one hundred walking sticks. I recall that one had been made from the remnants of a sunken slave ship whereas another had been carved from the limb of a mighty chestnut tree, which as a sapling had stood on Lexington Green during the Revolutionary Battle of Concord and Lexington.

This first visit with Mr. Woodfill, in Woodfill's barn, was a surprising as well as a pivotal episode in my life. Mr. Woodfill began by handing me a round trip air ticket to Washington as well as confirmation of reservations at the Statler Hotel. Then he handed me two checks and explained, "These two signed checks are for you to host two cocktail parties at The Statler. Invite enough VIP's so that you have at least twenty, and perhaps a couple of back-ups to complete the roster for *Sounding Board.* You will leave for Washington tomorrow morning."

I sat there aghast, but said nothing. During the biweekly visits to Armageddon, I had learned to expect the unexpected, but this immediate trip to Washington completely overwhelmed me. What was I to do? Walk around Washington with two blank checks and say to strangers, "Come to my party."

I knew Mr. Woodfill recognized my consternation when he reassured me, "I am aware that this is a challenge, but I am certain you can meet it. There are only two requests I have to make. One, I want you to phone every night to fill me in on the progress. Two, as you have learned from some of my comments, I am a great admirer of Doctor Albert Einstein. Einstein is now a professor in residence at Princeton, so I want you to stop at Princeton and get him as a guest for *Sounding Board.* This means a lot to me."

On the walk up the hill to The Grand, I pondered how best to break the latest news. When I opened the door to our suite, it was obvious that Aileen was preparing for a lengthy stay at Grand Hotel. She had made it as home-like as any five star resort can be.

She was the first to speak, "Well?"

I gave her tummy a little love pat, and then began to explain that I would be flying to Washington the next day. I showed her the airline tickets and the two blank checks.
She remarked, "The checks are signed, but they're not filled in. Mr. Woodfill surely does trust you." I explained that the two checks were to pay for two cocktail parties at the Statler Hotel. I was to invite enough guests who were national personalities to fill the roster for the *Sounding Board* programs that summer at Grand Hotel.

Armageddon on the Desert

The next day I flew to Washington, checked into the Statler, and laid out my plan of attack. The two cocktail parties, I decided, would be the *coup d'etat* of my siege on Washington. In the Capitol there were three acquaintances who could direct, make suggestions, and even open doors for me. Pat Balen had been a student at Arizona State, and when I went to Washington, he was a page in the Senate. John Rhodes was a new Congressman from the Phoenix district whom we had met during his campaign. His wife and Aileen had become good friends through meetings of University Women. Orme Lewis had been appointed Under Secretary of the Interior by President Eisenhower, and it was Orme Lewis's son who had just finished his junior year in my class at Scottsdale High School.

As a page, Pat Balen knew many senators on a friendly basis, and as a result, introduced me so that I could extend them an invitation to be guests on *Sounding Board*. The Senate cloak room was a happy hunting ground.

My strategy in lining up personalities for the ten broadcasts was to inaugurate the series with a highly charged, controversial topic. The two most debatable topics were the Cold War and the diplomatic way the United States could get out of Korea without losing face. The Chinese Nationalist regime of Chiang Kai-shek had crumbled fast before the onrush of the Communists, and it was obvious to the world at large that Soviet Russia was agitating these upheavals.

The Russian ambassador to the United States had never been on radio or television in the USA. To snare the ambassador for the initial show would be a coup. If I had phoned the embassy for an appointment, I was quite certain that the request would be denied, so I strode down the street from the Statler and rang the doorbell of the embassy.

Live Your Dreams

A tall, thin, sallow young man answered the door. I told him what my mission was, and to my surprise he ushered me into a foyer with a marble floor, marble walls, and marble columns. In the foyer, there was not a single piece of furniture. The young man then directed me to a sun room off the foyer, motioned to a wicker chair, and when he closed the door, he locked it.

It was the first time I had ever entered a home and had been locked in a room. Frankly, I was eager to get out of that room and out of the embassy. After a few minutes, the lock clicked, and in walked another young man, sallow, thin, and tall like the first. In his hand was a questionnaire he asked me to fill out, and then left the room, closed the door, and locked it.

The questions mostly concerned my relationship with the Communist government of Russia and what I had done to enhance the Soviet image in the United States. I filled out the inquiry with so many anti Russian answers that I knew the overture to Ambassador Georgi Zirubin was a dead issue. When the young male secretary returned, I handed him the questionnaire, whereupon he informed me that the ambassador would phone me within two or three days.

From the embassy I went directly to the Capitol. Between the House and the Senate buildings, there is an underground tunnel. On my way to the Senate cloak room, I met Senator Barry Goldwater coming in the opposite direction. We did not really know each other, but I had seen him at political rallies in Phoenix, and I presume he had seen me on television. Quite firmly he said, "I'd like to see you in my office. Follow me."

Since every voter is a possible constituent, Congressmen and Senators usually introduce visitors from their home district or state to the aides and secretaries in their congressional suite. Senator Goldwater, however, walked straight through his reception room, right on through the private office where his employees worked, to his personal office. Opening the door he ushered me in, designated a chair, and then asked rather sharply, "What were you doing this morning at the Russian Embassy?"

Stunned by the Senator's question, I promptly gathered my wits and explained in detail why I was at the Soviet Embassy. Goldwater's face began to relax and to lighten up, and then he accounted for the question. "You see, the FBI have a twenty-four hour camera on the main entrance of the Russian Embassy and another on the rear. Your picture popped up. That's all I can tell you except to say that I'm satisfied."

Then it was my turn to ask a question. "Senator, would you be willing to appear as a guest on my new network show which I have just referred to?"

"Send a letter to my office with the details. Please specify three possible dates. I'd enjoy very much being with you."

As I left Senator Goldwater's office, I felt like a spy who came in from the cold.

On my prospective guest list for *Sounding Board* was Owen Lattimore, a top expert for Chinese affairs in the State Department. At the time Lattimore was under Federal indictment for the role he played as a State Department adviser in the cataclysm which resulted in Chiang Kai-shek's army being driven off the Chinese mainland. Even though Owen Lattimore had been indicted, he was innocent until proven guilty. I drove to Johns Hopkins University in Baltimore where Owen Lattimore was teaching, and enjoyed a delightful hour with him and his wife. He accepted my invitation to appear on *Sounding Board* at Grand Hotel.

Live Your Dreams

As I previously mentioned, Orme Lewis was Under Secretary of the Interior in Eisenhower's cabinet. The Secretary and his wife Barbara were very cooperative in arranging the two cocktail parties. During the two social gatherings at The Statler, the Lewises and I completed the roster for the ten Mutual broadcasts at Grand Hotel. The list contained names of national personalities prominent in 1953. Among them were Senators Homer Ferguson of Michigan and Guy Gillette of Iowa; Polish Frank Jurecki, who made news by flying the first Russian Mig from behind the Iron Curtain to freedom in Denmark; former Vice President Henry Wallace; Congressman Fred Hartley, co-author of the Taft-Hartley Labor Law; and Theodore Sachs, chief counsel for the AFL-CIO.

Some of the other luminaries were Michigan's Governor G. Mennen "Soapy" Williams; Congressman Harold Velde, Chairman of the House Un-American Activities Committee; United States Senator Tobey from New Hampshire, the irascible Chairman of the famous Tobey committee; and Dr. You Chan Yang, Korean Ambassador to the United States.

The mission to Washington was accomplished except for one piece of business, the trip to Princeton to contact Albert Einstein. Intentionally, I had delayed the visit to Einstein because Princeton, New Jersey, was on the mainline between Washington and New York, and Hal Wagner, Vice President of the Mutual Network, had insisted that he approve the guest list and he also wanted to inform me in person about the guidelines for each show.

At Princeton, I alighted form the train, took a cab to the residence where Einstein was living, and rang the bell. A rather elderly man greeted me at the door and guided me into a parlor. When I told him the reason for my visit, he quickly

Christopher King, Bob Phail, Senator Barry Goldwater, Baron Silvercruys
(left to right)

Pulitzer Prize Winner Arthur Schlesinger, Jr., Christopher King,
Judge William Treat (left to right)

and knowingly informed me that Dr. Einstein had turned down all radio and television requests and although his English was satisfactory for seminars, it wasn't the quality for radio or television.

The gentleman, who seemed to be a protector, went on to explain that Dr. Einstein charges very high fees for public appearances and donates those fees to private Jewish schools.

I thanked him for his time and quickly departed for New York City to confer with Mr. Hal Wagner at Mutual.

On many occasions I had conversed with Mr. Wagner on the telephone, but this was the first time for a face to face meeting. If it's possible to describe a typical radio network executive, I would picture Mr. Wagner as a stereotype— gracious, hospitable, and impeccably attired was this six foot athletic-looking executive.

After exchanging pleasantries, Mr. Wagner perused the *Sounding Board* guest roster, and then commented, "This is an impressive list. How you pair up these personalities will determine the success of the program." I assured him that I would stay on top of the news each day to determine what controversial subject would be highlighted on the *Sounding Board* show that particular week."

"Good idea," interjected Mr. Wagner. "Too many moderators put on a couple of well-known names and often you end up with just a half hour of wind. Your range of guests is broad. They encompass a wide spectrum of topics."

"That is my plan. That's why the list of participants is heavy with Senators and Congressmen," I added.

"I see here one person that you will have to delete," advised Wagner. "Owen Lattimore. He has been indicted by a Federal Grand Jury, and I'm certain the legal department will never approve him. Furthermore, it is not our role as a nationwide network to offer our facilities as a sounding board to those under the cloud of indictment."

After checking in at the Hotel Pennsylvania in New York City, I phoned Mr. Woodfill at the Grand Hotel to fill him in on the day's progress. The manager informed me that Mr. Woodfill was off the Island, but he would be willing to convey any message. I gave him the following message: Kindly tell Mr. Woodfill that I have cleared the guest list with Mutual. Also tell him that they won't accept Owen Lattimore because he is under indictment for something he has done concerning the Communist take-over in China. And by the way, advise Mr. Woodfill that Dr. Einstein can't go on because he doesn't speak English well enough."

Unknown to me pandemonium broke loose while I was returning on the train to Grand Hotel. It so happened that when Mr. Woodfill arrived back on Mackinac Island, the manager told him, "A Mr. Lattimore doesn't speak English well enough, and Dr. Einstein had been indicted as a Communist."

Mr. Woodfill exploded, but he had to be circumspect. So he sent a telegram to Dr. Albert Einstein telling him that maybe the Mutual Network considered him a Communist, but to him Einstein was no Communist. That was the first time Dr. Einstein had ever heard himself referred to as a Communist.

Fortunately, the media did not dig their talons into these two misstatements. If they had, there would have been an uncontrollable brouhaha in the press. As soon as Mr. Woodfill learned the facts, he immediately sent a telegram of apology to Einstein, and Einstein in return sent a handwritten letter accepting the apology. Mr. Woodfill was ecstatic because now he owned a personal letter hand written by Dr. Albert Einstein. He promptly had it framed and displayed it over his desk.

Live Your Dreams

Chatham on Cape Cod was less than an hour's flight from New York City. I had decided to fly there to spend a couple of days with my parents before returning on the train to Mackinac Island. This would be my first meeting with my parents since I had left Massachusetts nearly four years before. As I walked through the doorway, my mother, her eyes welling with tears, threw her arms around me and hugged me affectionately. I had been taught since early childhood that men don't cry, but I couldn't hold back the tears. My father, the staunch, stoic New Englander that he was, extended his hand and said warmly, "Welcome home, Son." My father and I walked through the house while he proudly pointed out the improvements he had made. Frankly, it looked the same as I remembered it. I must say, it was good to be home again.

The next few days my mother quietly pampered me by making some of my favorites, especially New England clam chowder and blueberry pie. We took a drive around Chatham viewing the old landmarks like Chatham Lighthouse, Chatham Bars Inn, and the Old Fish Pier so frequently visited by tourists.

I had been trying ever since my arrival to find the right time to announce that in just a few months my mother and father were going to be grandparents. When I told them, my mother's eyes again welled up in tears—tears of joy and happiness—as she exclaimed, "Isn't it wonderful, Matt? I never thought I would be a grandmother."

Before I left, I invited my mother and father to spend the winter with us in the warm, sunny climate of Phoenix, so different from the cold, slashing Nor'easters on Cape Cod. Without a moment's hesitation my mother accepted. Obviously she wanted to be on the scene when the baby arrived.

The emotional visit at Chatham, especially since there had been an interval of almost four years, was the beginning of a healing process. The birth of our son Chris became the cornerstone in the reunion of both families.

An episode, which happened when Chris was eight years old, even today flashes before my eyes. My father was an avid Red Sox fan. He bought Chris a size eight Red Sox uniform and very often the grandfather and grandson would play catch for one or two hours. Then one day Matt suffered a heart attack and died. During the mourning period Chris would quietly weep as might be expected. On the way home from the cemetery Chris burst into a flood of tears. "I made Matt die," he uncontrollably cried out. "I made him play catch with me too long."

CHAPTER VIII

Getting to Know the Real W.S.

Meanwhile back at the Grand Hotel, Mr. Woodfill was making grandiose plans for the first broadcast of *Christopher King's Sounding Board*. He had already arranged for a bell-boy, dressed as the town crier, to walk through the downtown of Mackinac Island ringing his bell and announcing, "*Sounding Board* from the ballroom of the Grand Hotel—Tonight—Nine O'clock—Everyone Welcome."

The night of the first broadcast the ballroom was packed, not only with Grand Hotel guests, but also with guests from neighboring hotels on the Island. Governor "Soapy" Williams, a summer resident on the Island, was in the audience as was United States Senator Phil Hart. The participants on the show were Dr. You Chan Yang, Korean Ambassador to the United States, and Wisconsin Congressman Alvin O'Konski, who was diametrically opposed to Yang's plan for an armistice. Actually the cease-fire talks of the Korean War began one week after the appearance of Ambassador Yang and Congressman O'Konski on *Sounding Board*.

Getting to Know the Real W.S.

I must return to the remembrance of that train trip from Chatham to Mackinac Island. The train was traveling at the legal speed, but for me so anxious to see Aileen again, I thought it was lumbering along with its brakes on. I reflected how my mother and father had always manifested their deep love for me in big and small ways. I recalled how hard my father had worked to get us through the Depression. I remembered so vividly that day when my mother said to me, "You get all A's and B's at Boston College High, and I'll see that you go to Holy Cross." But that day on Cape Cod when I was reunited with my good parents, when my mother burst into tears and my father extended his warm hand of welcome, I knew two courageous people still loved their son very much.

When you sit on the upper deck of a ferry as it plies across the Straits of Mackinac, you feel you are in the best seat of a theater watching a three dimensional movie unfold. First, the majestic, glistening white Grand Hotel with Old Glory fluttering from each pillar appears in the distance. Then gradually the large Victorian houses on the shore, which first looked like matchbox cottages, take on their grand style.

That day in June the ferry was maneuvering to the wharf, and where the street meets the pier, I beheld a sight I'll always remember. There was Mr. Woodfill's carriage with the two sleek, black horses. Teddy, attired as always, in a black top hat, a crimson riding coat and white breeches was perched in the elevated driver's seat. And there in the rider's section was my beloved Aileen looking like a queen overseeing her realm.

The chains were clanging against the piles, and it was then that I caught sight of Aileen alighting from the carriage. Quickly I dashed to be first off, and when the gangplank went down, I sprinted through the crowd with a zig and a zag to hold Aileen in my arms. I had been on the Island only one night, but now going home meant wherever Aileen was.

On the ride up the hill to The Grand, Aileen told me how wonderful she felt, how the weather had been superb, especially for an expectant mother, and then she said something I can recall to this day, forty-three years later.

She said, "To some, Mr. Woodfill may appear pompous, but I know from fourteen days of experience he has a compassionate streak that extends from the top of his head to his big toe."

Quizzically, I stared at her, but said nothing. Aileen continued, "Do you know, Mr. Woodfill assigned to me one special bellhop who would fly over those stairs any time I rang the desk. Mr. Woodfill called me every evening to learn how that particular day had gone. And one afternoon as Mr. Woodfill and I were strolling along that quarter mile veranda, he turned to me and remarked, "I never had a daughter of my own. As long as you are my guest at Grand Hotel, you shall be treated as my daughter."

That evening I walked down to Mr. Woodfill's home and explained in detail about the Washington trip. He was really elated and boastfully exclaimed, "I told you we could do it."

Generally, the *Christopher King Sounding Board* programs went smoothly. There were a few exceptions, as when Senator Tobey of New Hampshire died two days before the show, and when Ambassador Yang arrived in a small vegetable scow because the water was too choppy for the passenger ferry. Each week the Mutual Network would inform me about the ratings across the country. The ratings were substantial, and the Network was satisfied.

After the fifth show, Mr. Woodfill proposed an idea. He suggested, "The Network seems pleased. You have a tiger by the tail, and you don't want to let it go. And I don't intend to subsidize *Sounding Board* forever. So I put all these thoughts into a boiling pot, and like the witches in *Macbeth*, I came up with an idea."

"From knowing you these past six months, I can be certain the idea will be successful."

Mr. Woodfill told me his plan, "I shall send a personal invitation to the president of the Mutual Broadcasting System inviting him and the vice president, with their wives, to be my personal guests at Grand Hotel for a long weekend. I'll entertain them with a red carpet hospitality they've never experienced. We have to get a long term contract from them. We can't let this bird in the hand perish."

The VIP's from Mutual came; they left after offering me a five-year contract. I was to produce a weekly program of the quality they had just seen at the Grand Hotel. I was also to arrange for the programs to emanate from prestigious resort hotels.

Mr. Woodfill enjoyed an excellent reputation among his peers in the resort hotel business. With his endorsement it was easy to line up long term engagements at hotels such as *The Broadmoor* at Colorado Springs; the *Cloister at Sea Island*, Georgia; *San Marcos Golf and Country Club* in Arizona; *Wentworth by the Sea* at Portsmouth, New Hampshire; and *Del Coronado* in California. Woodfill always said, "If one has to work, he should choose the most enjoyable surroundings."

Even though I had learned a great deal about Mr. Woodfill from my personal association with him, I gleaned even more from conversations with employees at The Grand. Most agreed that he was fair and honest, but a very demanding employer. They all concurred that he was a very caring man. This is one memorable story about him.

Republican Congressman Chenowith, Christopher King,
Wyoming U.S. Senator Joseph O'Mahoney (left to right)

Judge Louis Perez of New Orleans, Christopher King,
Governor Marvin Griffin of Georgia (left to right)

Getting to Know the Real W.S.

All the waiters at Grand Hotel were Afro-Americans. As with everything Mr. Woodfill did, he had substantial reasons. To him college students were unreliable because after a few weeks, they would fall in love and then be too tired to serve breakfast with a smiling face. So, in the off season the manager would go down to Detroit and recruit Black waiters at various hiring halls.

This particular incident happened before I knew Mr. Woodfill, but it was told to me by one of the employees. An Afro-American waiter, who had just finished his junior year at the University of Michigan, had been chosen as the spokesman for all the waiters. At the beginning of that summer season, the student presented to Mr. Woodfill a list of grievances, among them requests for better housing and higher wages. Like the true businessman he was, Mr. Woodfill stonewalled. The young man kept pressuring Mr. Woodfill until the first week of August when, as leader of the waiters, he declared a strike.

Grand Hotel was crammed to the roof with guests. Mr. Woodfill tried to substitute with bellboys, but that didn't work. The maintenance crews on the lawns and gardens didn't fill in very well as waiters. The increasing number of complaints from guests forced Woodfill to cave in to the waiters. He agreed that by the next season he would build new living quarters and increase the wage scale.

When the chaos subsided, Mr. Woodfill called the Black strike leader to his office and praised him for his tact and efficiency in conducting the work stoppage. Then Mr. Woodfill said to him, "I know you have one more year at Michigan. What do you intend for a career after you graduate?"

Congressional Chairman Harold H. Velde of the House Un-American Activities Committee; Christopher King; Dr. Carroll Hawkins, Chairman of the Political Science Department, Michigan State University (left to right)

Bounding Sword, a burlesque of Sounding Board by student employees at the Grand Hotel with guest Hon. Harold H. Velde

Getting to Know the Real W.S.

Then Mr. Woodfill offered a proposition to the waiter. "You complete your senior year and pass the entrance examination for the Law School, and I'll pay all expenses at the University of Michigan while you study for your jurisprudence degree. After you pass the bar, I will hire you on retainer to represent Grand Hotel."

Agog with amazement, the Black waiter stuttered, "Mr. Woodfill, I know what you have said, but I don't understand."

Woodfill broke right in, "I have thrown down the gauntlet. You can pick it up or you can walk away. I am doing this with a purpose. You handled the strike so well, I am going to make certain that never again will I face you on the opposing side. So I'm now offering you a chance to pick up the gauntlet and be one of my attorneys on a retainer basis."

The summer of 1953 I did not meet the Black waiter, but I learned the sequence of events. Under Mr. Woodfill's sponsorship, he did attend the University of Michigan Law School, passed the state bar exam, and in 1953 had his own practice in Detroit with Grand Hotel as one of his clients.

During July and August of 1953, I had daily conferences with Mr. Woodfill, either in his office at the hotel or at his home. Occasionally after the business discussion, he would invite me to stay. He loved Grand Hotel. He loved to talk about its beginning and growth just as a parent might proudly relate the progress of a child. I was just as eager to listen as he was to recount the incidents that had led to his success at Grand Hotel. I had often wondered how in the world he could have risen from second cook in a lumber camp to the ownership of the world's largest summer hotel. This is the story he told me.

He was tossing flapjacks and frying bacon and eggs in 1928. The devastating Depression began in 1929. Almost overnight the stately Grand Hotel went into bankruptcy and was on the auction block. A railroad company had owned Grand Hotel. It had transported passengers daily from Chicago and Detroit to the dock at Mackinac City. When the Depression fell over the country like a shroud, people could not afford to vacation at a resort like The Grand.

W.S. Woodfill didn't have much money. With two other investors he bought The Grand at auction. The investment actually was a forty-year-old huge structure with well worn furnishings. Minimal cosmetic decorations were made, and late in March, Mr. Woodfill had the world's largest summer hotel, but no reservations either for conventions or for vacationers.

One April day, two gentlemen arrived at The Grand Hotel and told Mr. Woodfill that their organization would like to engage the hotel for one week. Mr. Woodfill knew, as all innkeepers do, that conventions pay expenses, and summer guests represent the profits. Mr. Woodfill expressed delight and then asked whose convention it would be.

"The Ku Klux Klan," replied the men.

After gaining his composure, Woodfill expressed concern about the title of the organization and made this suggestion, "Gentlemen, if you are willing to change the name of your convention to the annual meeting of the American Southern Historical Society, I would love to have you." The Klan officials consented. Mr. Woodfill had his first convention; moreover, Grand Hotel would be packed for an entire week.

At the Grand Hotel office in Detroit, a contract had been signed for dates immediately following the Klan's dates. The organization was the Michigan Knights of Columbus. Mr. Woodfill could visualize his lobby on the day when the Klansmen were departing and the Knights were arriving. It would be Armageddon.

Getting to Know the Real W.S.

Thereupon Mr. Woodfill wrote memoranda to the Ku Klux Klan and to the Michigan Knights of Columbus stating a new policy. It read, "Because Grand Hotel is so heavily booked each year, it has become necessary to institute a new procedure for the convenience of all guests. The arriving conventioneers will use the elevator in the lobby, and those departing will use the freight elevator in the rear of the hotel."

My reference to Mr. Woodfill as the "reasonable eccentric" was exemplified in innumerable ways. W.S. was well known for his generosity, but one thing he could not tolerate was a waste of time or money. He frequently paid tribute to his Scottish ancestors whenever in conversation, a discussion arose about the dissipation of time or money. There's a tendency in all of us to pull up a chair closer, get comfortable, and engage in trivia. In his office at Grand Hotel, all the chairs were attached to the floor. It was not that he feared someone would steal them, but he didn't want departing guests to drag up a chair close to his desk, to sit back for a chat, and thereby waste his time.

If a person lingered and didn't get the message from the attached chairs, Mr. Woodfill had another way. Under the carpet at his desk was a buzzer. He had written two scenarios which were tacked to the switchboard. When he gave a single buzz, the operator would read the script and carry on a conversation with Mr. Woodfill telling him that there was someone waiting to see him. A double buzz meant the visitor had stayed too long, so the second set of dialogue informed Mr. Woodfill that he was behind in his schedule of appointments. Mr. Woodfill maintained that a person could not effectively fake a telephone conversation when there was no one on the other end.

Another example of Woodfill's reasonable action was the construction of a mammoth swimming pool overlooking

Lake Michigan. He maintained that Paul Bunyan, the gigantic, mythical folk hero of American lumber camps, had put one foot down on Mackinac Island right in front of Grand Hotel when Bunyan had stepped across the Straits of Mackinac on his trek westward. That is where Mr. Woodfill ordered the building of a massive swimming pool to duplicate Paul Bunyan's footstep.

The summer of 1953 at Grand Hotel was an experience full of anxiety, excitement, and emotion. Just as in any other form of show business, there were highs and there were lows. I was always aware that some *Sounding Board* personality might cancel at the last minute. In fact, United States Senator Tobey of New Hampshire died suddenly two days before he was scheduled to appear. Fortunately, Michigan's Governor G. Mennen "Soapy" Williams as well as United States Senators Phil Hart and Homer Ferguson of Michigan were always available in an emergency because they were good friends of Mr. Woodfill.

Then too, there was excitement. Aileen and I were like two kids awaiting Christmas as we marked off the days for the expected arrival of our first child. The physician on the Island, a kindly old gentleman who reminded us of Norman Rockwell's country doctor, would drop by The Grand frequently to see how Aileen was doing. I was nervous, but Aileen kept reassuring me that she never felt better in her life and that she was following in detail every instruction the doctor had prescribed. Later she told me she would have stood on her head if the doctor had suggested it.

Grand Hotel was a majestic stage for an emotional episode I had never anticipated. As we were resting one afternoon, the phone rang and the switchboard operator informed me that there were two gentlemen in the lobby to see me. This was an unusual call because most of the *Sounding Board* arrangements were made by long distance telephone, and an island is simply not a place where people just drop by to say, "Hello."

The elevator door opened. I stepped out to survey the lobby, and there off to the side of the registration desk were two familiar faces. I recognized Paul Anderson and John McEneaney, two of my former classmates at St. John's Seminary, ordained with me in 1943.

The moment they spied me, they walked at a quickened pace across the lobby. Each grasped my hand firmly and exclaimed, almost in the rhythm of Gregorian chant, "Bernie, you will always be our friend."

I stood stunned staring into space. After a few moments, I gained enough composure to say at least, "Paul and Mac, until I recover my composure all I can say is thank you. Thank you so much."

This was the first time I had experienced any contact with friends or classmates from my seminary days. I didn't know why they were there, nor what their attitude would be. For a few moments I felt uncomfortable.

John McEneaney, always the diplomat, broke the ice, "Bernie, I suppose you wonder how we knew you were here at Grand Hotel."

"I have no idea, Mac. I'm so overwhelmed. I . . ."

"Remember? You and I were on the varsity debate team at Holy Cross. When you work together as closely as we did, you get to know a person's speech habits, his stress points, and his tonal inflections. I heard you on WNAC, the Mutual station in Boston.

W.S. Woodfill; Congressman Alvin Bentley, shot on the floor of Congress by Puerto Rican revolutionaries; U.S. Senator Albert Gore, Vice President Gore's father; Christopher King (left to right)

Michigan U.S. Senator Homer Ferguson, Christopher King, Iowa U.S. Senator Guy Gillette (left to right)

Getting to Know the Real W.S.

"But," I interrupted, "you didn't come all the way to an island in northern Michigan just because someone with the name Christopher King sounded like me."

"No," explained Mac. "Through the grapevine I learned you were using the name Christopher King. We were returning from our summer vacation, so here we are."

We reminisced about events over the past ten years, and I unraveled for them the reason for the pseudonym of Christopher King. I told them about the name-change dinner in Wickenburg, Arizona, and said that I use Bernard Kane in teaching and in my private life, but that on the air the name Christopher King is more rhythmic and less guttural than Bernard Kane.

They couldn't stay for dinner, but just before the two priests departed, Mac beckoned me aside and said, "When the baby arrives, let me know and I'll make arrangements for the baptism."

That reunion of us three at Grand Hotel was the beginning. Since then for the last forty-three years, the renewal of solid friendships has been revitalized among most of the priests who were ordained with me in 1943.

Paul Anderson became Bishop of Duluth, Minnesota, and Mac, a Monsignor, visits us in Florida each winter for two weeks of golf. Another classmate, Jack Lawlor, was a chaplain in the U.S. Air Force, and retired as a General. He flies over from Naples, Florida, three or four times each year for an overnight and a couple of rounds of golf.

Even in bringing together old time friends, Divine Providence has the strangest ways. Jim Sullivan, a seminary classmate whom I hadn't seen since 1943, telephoned us in Rancho Santa Fe, California. He and three other priests, called the fearless four, Monsignor Bill Granville, Fathers Lenny Stanton and Frank Connors, had decided to purchase a home in San Diego for their retirement. They were twenty-five years from retirement, but they planned to purchase a house, rent it, and have it available when the time came.

"Bernie, this is Jim Sullivan. Remember me?"

With startling surprise I replied, "Of course, I do. Where are you, Jim?"

"Here in Boston as Chaplain of Nazareth House. It's a stately mansion that a benefactor gave to Cardinal Cushing. Cushing has turned it into an orphanage. Bernie, I have a favor to ask."

"Go ahead, Jim. What are friends for? You know I'll do it if I can."

Jim Sullivan explained that the fearless four were flying to San Diego in three weeks, and that there were two requests. He asked me to reserve a motel for a week and to line up some possible real estate agents.

When I told Aileen about Father Sullivan's call, she chastised me severely, "Don't let those priests stay in a motel. Call Father Sullivan right now, and tell him to bring his friends and stay with us."

The fearless four came, they saw, and they accomplished their mission. Aileen, as she always is, was gracious and hospitable. Over the past decades these and many other seminary friends have been our guests, and their first greeting whenever we see them is, "And how is our blue-eyed blonde?"

At Grand Hotel, decision-time was fast approaching. Within a week it would be the deadline for me to notify Scottsdale High whether or not I would return. If I did return, which resort hotel would be the site of the broadcasts? Would we leave our house unoccupied for a year or more? Then too, I had invited my mother and father to spend the winter with us in warm, sunny Phoenix. But most of all, I wanted Aileen to be in familiar surroundings when the baby arrived. I knew she wished to bring the baby home to our home in Phoenix. I had pretty much made up my mind, but I wanted confirmation from a prudent, thoughtful man like Mr. Woodfill.

Throughout the summer Mr. Woodfill and I had many brain-storming sessions at his study out in the barn, but this one was most important. After all, the future for Aileen and me, and especially for the new member of our family, revolved around the decisions made that second week of August.

Mr. Woodfill was already aware of our major concerns, so he didn't pontificate. He probed with delicate compassion. I began the conversation.

"Mr. Woodfill, I know that you have spent a large amount of money in getting *Sounding Board* off the ground. It would not have been possible without your generosity. How can I repay you?"

"You don't owe me anything," W.S. interjected. "This was not a business investment. I don't expect and I will not accept any financial action in the future of *Sounding Board*. From now on it's your baby, but I will help anytime I can be of assistance."

"But . . . I'm at a loss for words. What can I say?"

"There's no need to say anything." Woodfill broke in. "I had an idea. I researched it. This wasn't any scatterbrained notion. In fact, it was very beneficial by expanding the reputation of Grand Hotel. *Sounding Board* also has added another dimension to its image. Not only is Grand Hotel an ideal vacation resort, but now it is known as the thinking man's hotel."

Then I asked him, in view of the five year contract with Mutual Network, what, he thought, my best options were.

He went on, "It's your life. You and Aileen have many years ahead of you. However, the first consideration is the continuation of *Sounding Board* as well as your obligations under the contract with Mutual.

"And that's what worries me," I interrupted. "Where do I go after Grand Hotel? It takes time to convince an owner that *Sounding Board* is a beneficial proposal, and then on top of that it takes more time to make plans."

"I have anticipated your anxiety," said Mr. Woodfill. "With your approval, of course, I have made arrangements with Mr. Alberding, the owner of Paradise Inn, at Scottsdale to continue the *Sounding Board* series through the winter season and into the spring. His resort is more residential and less commercial than Camelback Inn. That is why I chose Paradise Inn."

Mr. Woodfill's foresight resolved a tremendous uncertainty about the future. He could tell by the relieved expression on my face. Then in his philosophical tone, he offered some judicious advice.

"Don't be steam-rolled by the glamour of *Sounding Board*. It's just another phase of your life. This is my opinion. Go back to Phoenix. Teach another year at Scottsdale High. Resume your television show and, of course, continue *Sounding Board* at Paradise Inn. During that time, evaluate your options. Remember this: you, your family, and *Sounding Board* are welcome next summer at Grand Hotel."

For Aileen, a pregnant mother-to-be, that summer at The Grand must have been an extremely tiring experience. Nevertheless, she exuded happiness, comforted me in moments of discouragement, and always showed a positive attitude in her words and actions. Her resiliency was remarkable as she moved among the *Sounding Board* guests and their wives. She possesses a savoir-faire that seems to be limitless in scope.

However, when a matter of grave importance is a major concern, it is necessary to watch out. She draws a straight line from here to there, and that's the way it's going to be. With about a month to go, she generated vitality and was more beautiful than ever.

W.S. Woodfill could expedite the most minute detail in the operation of a hotel, but he was a kitten when it came to understanding a mother-to-be expecting her first child. Aileen cornered W.S. one day in his hotel office to thank him for the many thoughtful kindnesses during the summer and to inform him that she would be leaving immediately for Phoenix.

He wouldn't trust his secretary with such a delicate mission. He played travel agent himself. Woodfill phoned the doctor on the Island, alerted the U.S. Coast Guard, made a reservation on Capital Airlines from Petosky to Chicago, and on TWA for a connecting flight from Chicago to Phoenix.

He assigned a bellboy to help Aileen pack, called Teddy to get his personal carriage ready, and the next day Aileen took off.

Everything went according to schedule until Aileen arrived in Chicago and went to the TWA desk to confirm her reservation. Imagine her surprise when the young lady informed her that there was no reservation for Mrs. Kane on the plane to Phoenix. Aileen wasn't blaming anyone, but she was determined to get on that plane.

"I just have to get on that plane. Look at me. I'm going to have a baby."

Almost before she knew it, she was in "first class" and was on her way home to Phoenix.

CHAPTER IX

Life is Good and We Love Living It

Before moving on to other events in living our dreams, I must recall a particular episode relating to Mr. Woodfill as the reasonable eccentric. Each winter Mr. Woodfill periodically would ask his valet Mario to drive him on excursions to desolate spots in the Arizona desert. There W.S. would stop the car and interview any old, grizzly prospector walking along the roadside.

This would be Mr. Woodfill's proposal. He would offer to pay all travel costs, all living expenses, and a generous salary for ten weeks at Grand Hotel. In exchange, the drifter would sit in a rocking chair on the sparkling white veranda of Grand Hotel and would spin yarns about the old mining days in Arizona. There were two conditions, however. The prospector must bathe every day, and he must wear freshly laundered old togs. Each summer a different codger would star in the same rocking chair on the veranda of Grand Hotel. Mr. Woodfill didn't believe in reruns.

Life is Good and We Love Living It

The final days at Grand Hotel were hectic. We were making tapes of *Sounding Board* to bridge the interval between Grand Hotel and Paradise Inn. The greatest anxiety of all, however, concerned the imminent arrival of our first child. Every night I phoned Aileen, and every night I asked the same two questions, "How do you feel?" and "When is the baby coming?" Every night the answers were the same. "I feel wonderful." and "The baby's coming the first week of October." I knew nature frequently played tricks on expectant mothers, but Aileen, the consistent optimist, kept repeating, "The first week of October."

The first week of October allowed me sufficient time to return home, to meet my first classes at Scottsdale High School, and to make final arrangements for the first broadcast from Paradise Inn.

The joint annual meeting of the Scottsdale High School faculty and the Board of Trustees was in session the evening of October 6, 1953. A secretary quietly tip-toed to my chair and handed me a note which read, "Please, come home. Now!" I bolted out the door, sped home, and there stood Aileen with suitcase in hand ready to go. We arrived at St. Joseph's Hospital at 9:00 p.m. and the next morning at 11:43 our son was born.

Live Your Dreams

Aileen and I sent out the following announcement:

The producers

Aileen and Christopher

present

The newest and noisiest guest on

Sounding Board

Featuring

V.I.P.

John Christopher

First appearance

Phoenix, Arizona

October 7, 1953

at 11:43 o'clock a.m.

A Christopher King Production

Life is Good and We Love Living It

Former United States Vice President Henry Wallace sent a congratulatory note affirming that October 7th was also his birthday. United States Senator Mike Monroney from Oklahoma sent Chris a life-time pass to the Senate Gallery. Mr. Woodfill, without telling us, obtained an Arizona State Flag from Governor MacFarland, and on October 7, 1953, that flag flew over Fort Mackinac on Mackinac Island.

Sounding Board settled into a routine of extended engagements at these prestigious resort hotels: Paradise Inn and San Marcos Golf and Country Club in Arizona; The Broadmoor, Colorado Springs; The Cloister at Sea Island, Georgia; Wentworth by the Sea, Portsmouth, New Hampshire; and Hotel Del Coronado in San Diego, California.

The 1950's was the period in history of the Communist Iron Curtain and the Berlin Wall. It was then, that Wisconsin's Senator Joseph McCarthy charged onto the Washington political scene supposedly discovering a Communist under every bed and purporting to save Americans from themselves.

McCarthy, in his disheveled clothes, would stand up in the United States Senate, wave sheaves of blank paper, and claim they contained the names of American citizens who were avowed Communists. McCarthy also used the technique of painting with a broad brush. He labeled his political enemies as either Communists or Communist sympathizers or "Pinkos."

Exaggeration was another deceitful ploy in his arsenal of oratory weapons. McCarthy would brand a nation as Communistic if it opposed his policies. He frequently wove the concept of guilt by association into his speeches. This craftiness highlighted one particular *Sounding Board* program.

The Netherlands Ambassador to the United States and California Congressman Pat Hillings, a political ally of Senator McCarthy, appeared as guests. McCarthy in the United

States Senate had tagged Holland as a country of Communist sympathizers because the Dutch were selling their surplus of Gouda cheese to Russia. The simple fact was that the Netherlands enjoyed a plentiful supply of cheese and Russia desperately needed milk products. The ambassador skillfully defended his nation against charges of guilt by association.

The ambassador and his wife remained for a long weekend at Paradise Inn. One day at poolside he suggested, "Would it be possible for *Sounding Board* to originate from the Netherlands? Your description of the Valley of the Sun that went out on *Sounding Board* across the country made me aware that the same kind of publicity would be beneficial for the Netherlands."

"That's an intriguing thought. Let me look into it," was my response.

The Ambassador admitted that he had an ulterior motive. He explained that American tourists going to Europe fly directly from London to Paris. Very few stop in Amsterdam. A few well chosen words like those describing Phoenix could be very effective for the Netherlands.

The Mutual Network granted permission to broadcast from Holland, and the Scottsdale High School Board of Trustees released me from my teaching contract. A detailed agreement with the Netherlands Embassy in Washington eventually was finalized. The agreement specified that we would sail on the *MS Noordam* from Hoboken, New Jersey, and spend March, April, and May in the Netherlands. Each week we would reside at a different resort in various areas of Holland. In return I was committed to produce twelve *Sounding Board* programs.

The ten days aboard the *Noordam* was an experience of luxury and complete relaxation. The Dutch called the *Noordam* the Queen's Ship, and it was truly that. During the

Life is Good and We Love Living It

Atlantic crossing Chris's nanny, Marie, rendered minimal service because she succumbed easily to seasickness. I should mention that a nanny was not a regular member of our household, but the Foreign Office included accommodations for Marie so that Aileen and I would be free to see, day and night, the beauty of the Netherlands.

Mr. Van den Gronden, representing the Foreign Office, welcomed us at the Rotterdam pier. He pointed out the new Cadillac that was to be ours for the duration, and then he introduced us to Hans, our driver. Straightaway we were taken to our first hotel in Hilversum.

Almost two thousand years ago when Julius Caesar was conquering Western Europe, the territory we now call the Netherlands was inhabited by a Germanic, Batavian tribe. The Batavi never gave in to Roman domination. The area became a part of the Charlemagne Empire and later passed into the hands of Burgundy, the Austrian Hapsburgs, and Spain. When Philip II of Spain crushed all political liberties in the domain, revolution broke out led by William of Orange. The result was the Union of Utrecht whereby the seven northern provinces became the Republic of the United Netherlands.

One realizes how low and flat the Netherlands are when he learns that a few hills in the vicinity of Limburg rise only to a height of 300 feet. About half the country's land is below sea level. For that reason, the famous Dutch dikes are a requisite to use the land. Reclamation from the sea through dikes has continued for over one hundred years.

Although the official language is Dutch, students learn English in elementary school. Small countries, as we have observed, require a knowledge of English for survival. In fact, school children in the Netherlands must learn French and German as well as English so that they can compete as adults in the world of trade. The Dutch knew from their world-wide success of the Dutch East Indian Trading Company in the 17th century the inseparable relationship between language and commerce.

Mr. Van den Gronden, our man in the Foreign Office, was skilled in blending business with pleasure. He was most helpful in obtaining prominent personalities for *Sounding Board.* Each day he supplied a news sheet with reports of what was going on in the United States and in Western Europe. He arranged the locations for the broadcasts and made certain a large audience was in attendance. Mr. Van den Gronden also made certain there were social as well as ceremonial events during our visit. The Foreign Office had instructed Hans, our chauffeur, to show us all of the Netherlands, and certainly, he didn't miss many square miles.

Amsterdam and the Hague are like two different branches of the same family. Amsterdam, the canal-cut capital of the Lowlands, revels in its renowned Stock Exchange, the diamond marts scattered throughout the city, and its noisy pubs. On the other hand, the Hague, Amsterdam's neighbor, is stoic, and frozen by hordes of civil servants. The Hague, until recently Europe's biggest village, houses the Dutch government and the International Court of Justice. An impeccable stork walking stately with measured step is the way to picture the Hague.

Breathes there a man or woman who has not planted a Dutch tulip bulb. The ancestry of the Dutch tulip bulb goes back more than 700 years to Haarlem, Holland. Pretty homes, surrounded by brilliant tulips, blanket the landscape of Haarlem. Antique shops, the uniquely quaint market-square, St. Bravo Church, whose famous organ Mozart played as a young man, and the statue of the legendary boy who put his finger in the dike to save his country from disaster, emerge as a scene from a fairy tale.

Life is Good and We Love Living It

Each Friday the bustling Market Square in Alkmaar is taken over by the Cheese Market. Thousands of heads of cheese are stacked up on the cobblestones, to be weighed, to change hands in sales sealed by clap-like handshakes, and then to be carried off on hand barrows by colorfully dressed cheese porters.

As Aileen and I slowly walked on the bumpy street of Alkmaar, we pondered how momentous events in history unknowingly affect our individual lives. The circumstances fall into a natural sequence. The Dutch are enjoying an extraordinary surplus of cheese whereas the Russians are suffering from a lack of milk products. The Dutch sell their surplus to Russia. Suddenly, Senator Joseph McCarthy brands the Netherlands a communist sympathizer. The Netherlands ambassador explains the true situation coast to coast on *Sounding Board*. The ambassador extends an invitation to visit his country. We accept and the result is here we are, enjoying three delightful months in the Netherlands.

Two simple happenings, one in Baarn, and the other in Eindhoven, are etched in our recollections. One late afternoon in March, Aileen and I were enjoying high tea with the managing director of Kasteel de Hooge Vuurschet, a magnificent resort hotel in Baarn. Abruptly he stood up, walked to a huge picture window, and there spotted two young girls skating on the hotel's private pond. The Dutch zealously protect the privacy of their ponds in much the same way Americans protect the privacy of their golf courses. The manager again excused himself and strode directly to the pond.

We watched him through the large window. His walk to the pond was rapid. He stopped at the edge, gazed around and waited for the two girls to skate toward him. Words obviously were exchanged for a minute or two. Then the manager returned slowly to the hotel. The girls continued to

Municipal Reception by Burgomaster
Eindhoven, Holland - March 10, 1955

Greetings to Christopher King for fellow Americans
from President and 150,000 Guild Members - Holland

Guests at Middle Age Flag Waving by Guild at
Best, Holland - March 15, 1955

skate. Today the older girl is Sovereign Queen Beatrix of the Netherlands, and the younger girl, her sister, is Princess of the Netherlands.

One Saturday morning in Eindhoven the burgomaster, or the mayor as Americans call him, hosted a municipal reception for us. He solemnly read a resolution and then handed me the document stating the goodwill of the Dutch people toward the citizens of the United States. The ritual concluded with Middle Age flag waving as performed by Guild members one thousand years ago.

An afternoon tour of Eindhoven's industrialized section completely absorbed our attention. The guide informed us that Henry Ford, after he introduced his Model A, visited Eindhoven and remarked that if the Dutch filled in their canals, they would have excellent parking spaces. I understand the Dutch who heard Ford's comment reacted with facial contortions indicating displeasure.

A festive dinner party climaxed the busy day. Among the guests was the director of publicity for Philip Manufacturing, an international conglomerate headquartered in Eindhoven. Aileen was this man's dinner partner, and I was seated with an alderman's wife at the far end of a long table. It was about midnight when the party terminated. Hans had put in a long, tiring day and evening, but as always, he was ready to drive us back to the Amstel Hotel in Amsterdam.

The next afternoon I was alone in our apartment at the Amstel Hotel. The telephone rang and the caller identified himself as Aileen's dinner partner in Eindhoven. "Everything is set," he announced.

"I don't understand. What is all set?"

"Your trip to Paris. You will take the train from Amsterdam. Philip's representative will meet you at the station in Paris. We have compiled a three day schedule of exciting events."

"Who said we're going to Paris?" I asked.

"Your wife. Last Saturday evening in Eindhoven," he replied.

"Sounds good to me. Paris, here we come."

To me Paris has always been and always will be "Gai Paris." The sword swallowers and the fire eaters on the Left Bank, lovers of all ages walking hand in hand along the banks of the Seine, the red wine, the rich sauces, the zesty cheeses, even the masterpieces in the Louvre seem to silently say, "Life is good, and we love living it."

Today I can visualize that small cafe in Paris where Aileen and I sat one rainy afternoon, forty-one years ago, breaking off pieces of French bread, dipping them in creamy fondue and sipping dry French red wine. It was a simple scene but a dramatic act.

CHAPTER X

A Dream and A Scheme

The road of life like most highways rises and falls against the distant horizon. So it has been with our life. We often relived the pleasures of our Dutch treat, but we also realized our obligation to our son Chris. He was approaching school age; therefore, it became imperative for him to experience a feeling of permanency.

Aileen and I agreed that six years of living at prestigious resort hotels was exhilarating, but we also concurred that our son needed a home atmosphere. This change in our perception meant that on weekends I would travel alone to produce and moderate *Christopher King's Sounding Board* at the various resorts. Each summer, as a family, we lived at the grande dame, *Wentworth-by-the-Sea*, Portsmouth, New Hampshire, where *Sounding Board* originated from the ballroom every Sunday evening.

In the late 1950's most resorts did not provide each room with television. In fact, many did not even have a television room. Whenever a national election, the inauguration of a President, or the World Series occurred, the management would set up a 19 inch television in a small alcove for the interested patrons. As Jack Stewart, the general manager of *Camelback Inn,* had remarked, "Guests come to play and relax." He could have added, "and not to watch television."

In my travels I had observed that most resorts featured some type of stage presentation each evening; it might be medleys from musical comedies, dance ensembles, impersonators, or lecturers. The idea-bulb in my mind lighted. Perhaps I could create a travelogue with a different viewpoint.

After much research and many letters and phone calls, we came up with a lecture, a casual narration with a background of magnificent photography. The presentation was entitled: Little Known People from a Well Known State. The three Kanes would visit fifteen resorts in July and then return to the same inns or hotels in August. In August the format was identical; however, the little known people and the well known state were different. For example, the topic in July could be little known people from Kentucky and in August little known people from Arizona.

I have mentioned magnificent photography, but that statement must be clarified. Neither Aileen nor I possess any talent in shooting pictures. We were at the Pyramids in Cairo when Aileen suggested, "Bernie, why don't you climb to the second level of the Pyramid, and I'll shoot from down here?" As instructed, I crawled through a narrow passageway to the second level and there posed. When the developed film came back, the photograph was extraordinary. It was suitable for exhibition at a modern art show. Really, it was a perfect picture of me from the waist to the bottom of my shoes.

A background of beautiful motion pictures was essential to make the lecture complete. Each of the fifty states through its tourism department makes available a film featuring particular scenes and specific landmarks. The states were very cooperative because I was giving them exposure without any expense. From our viewpoint, these lectures over a period of seven years enabled us to stop in almost every area of New England. Furthermore, our son at an early age learned about New England, its history, its geography, and its literature. Also, I had an ulterior motive, an opportunity to play some of the best golf courses in the Northeast.

The summer lectures had their pleasant moments and also their embarrassing pitfalls. Many of the hotels were no more than 30 miles apart, so we would arrive early, have lunch, maybe a round of golf, a sightseeing tour, or a plunge in the pool. This is called a "working vacation."

As we drove eastward across the country, we stopped at Father Flanagan's Boys Town in Omaha, Nebraska. The brief overnight stay at Boys Town was twofold because not only was it a dress rehearsal for my lecture, but it was also an evening's entertainment of film and stories for the boys. I believe it was Father Flanagan who said that there is no such person as a bad boy, and we support that statement after our observations during six annual visits. I recall one incident when Chris was four years old.

About two hundred boys were gathering in the auditorium for the lecture, and we observed that many of them were nibbling on candy bars. Three teenagers walked over to Aileen and asked if Chris could sit with them. Before long, Chris was chomping on a candy bar which one of the lads had given him. Each ensuing year Chris would renew friendships from the year before, would make new friends, and like all youngsters would swear that the relationships were going to last forever.

Some of the young men at Boys Town were orphans while others had been abandoned, and a substantial number had faced a judge's decision of jail or Boys Town. An amazing number of graduates from Father Flanagan's High School have gone on to college and eventually have become doctors, professors, and lawyers. On the *Six O'clock News* I once interviewed Commander Boucher, a Boys Town graduate, when he and his 83 man-crew of the *USS Pueblo* returned to the States in 1969 after eleven months of incarceration by the North Koreans. The admirable objective of Boys Town has always fascinated me since the time I did considerable research in writing *The Father Flanagan Story* for NBC in 1947.

One of our favorite resorts in New England was the *Waumbeck*, a sedate summer hotel situated in Jefferson, New Hampshire, in the White Mountains. This hotel used to serve a cup of clam chowder in the foyer before guests entered the dining room for dinner. Scrupulous attention to every detail was the way Mr. and Mrs. Kenyon operated the Waumbeck.

Throughout three decades of broadcasting on radio and television, total abstinence from liquor on the day of a broadcast was my steadfast policy. When a performer imbibes, he may think that on the air he appears relaxed, but TV cameras are like x-ray machines, and microphones emphasize every minute nuance of articulation. During the lecture series at New England summer resorts, we relaxed the prohibition on ourselves a wee bit. Aileen and I would enjoy one cocktail before dinner.

One late afternoon in July a guest, his wife, and an entourage of golfers paraded into the lounge where Aileen and I were sipping our cocktails. We had known the couple from previous summers at the Waumbeck. The occasion for the mass parade was a hole-in-one. The celebrant motioned for Aileen and me to join the merrymaking, which we did. We, however, resisted his offer of another drink explaining that one cocktail was our custom before a lecture. The victorious golfer obviously was more absorbed with his first-in-a-lifetime feat than with my explanation, because before we knew it, there were two cocktails in front of us, compliments of our gracious host. Who were we to hurt the feelings of this kind gentleman?

As the minutes passed, I realized that I was not feeling giddy, but I knew that I was happy. No problem, I thought, since the food at dinner will assimilate the liquor, and then too, the lecture was scheduled for 8:30 that evening. Unfortunately, my body chemistry did not act as I had expected, so I visualized myself alone up on the stage at the brink of indignity.

The next morning while Aileen and I were eating breakfast, a bellboy stopped at our table to inform me that Mr. and Mrs. Kenyon desired to see me in their office. My three little words to Aileen were, "This is it."

As I entered the office, Mr. Kenyon was seated behind a large mahogany desk and Mrs. Kenyon, who seldom appeared at that early hour, was in the guest's chair. Mrs. Kenyon opened the conversation, "Everybody is talking about last night. They are saying that the lecture last evening was your best in the five summers you have been coming to the Waumbeck, and I agree with them." With a sigh of profound relief I accepted Mr. Kenyon's check and quickly departed.

Dorset Inn, located on the village green in Dorset, Vermont, was built in the late 1790's and the original structure is still being used. The charm, friendliness, and dignified aura of this wayside inn typify the image of early American history. The owner Fred Whittemore, a crusty yet sensitive Yankee, operated the Inn with a firm but hospitable hand. In fact, Fred told me that when the Hotel Workers Union tried to recruit his employees, he bodily escorted the organizer through the lobby and out the front door. Fred revealed another fact to me, one that is not generally known. Dorset had the first golf course in the United States, named the Dorset Gun and Golf Club.

One lecture at Dorset Inn I will never forget. The general theme concerned the State of New Mexico and specifically concentrated on little-known facts about well-known people and places. My knowledge of New Mexico was adequate because, having lived in Arizona for ten years, we often visited New Mexico and were enchanted by the lore of the Southwest. During the presentation I happened to mention the stalactites and the stalagmites in the Carlsbad Caverns of New Mexico. Stalactites descend from the ceiling of a cave whereas stalagmites rise from the floor. Inadvertently I reversed the direction and at the conclusion, as guests were milling around, a geologist called me to task for the misstatement.

Mrs. Harry Allen was sitting next to Chris and Aileen during a lecture at *Bethel Inn* in Bethel, Maine. Chris was not impressed with his father's kind of entertainment, so he promptly entered the Land of Nod and toppled over into Mrs. Allen's lap. His mother attempted to retrieve him, but Mrs. Allen insisted that he not be disturbed. This was the beginning of a lasting friendship between the Kanes and the Allens. Harry and Adele spent winters at the La Jolla Beach and Tennis Club, and it is interesting to note that Harry Allen was responsible for bringing the concept of the taxi cab meter from Paris to New York City.

Sometimes at the request of an innkeeper my lecture focused on current political affairs. One particular evening at the famous *Wentworth by the Sea* in Portsmouth, New Hampshire, I was comparing Presidents and happened to mention that Dwight D. Eisenhower was a good, kindly, and effective

A Dream and A Scheme

President but not a great President. After the lecture, a gentleman came up and asked me in a friendly manner to clarify the statement about President Eisenhower. After I finished explaining the meaning of my statement, the gentleman introduced himself as Milton Eisenhower, brother of the President.

As smog falls upon our white shirts, as pollen settles on our eyes to cause tears and swelling, as some unforeseen event brings sadness or joy, so do many of our dreams reach fulfillment from sources unknown and unexpected. *Narragansett by the Sea* at Kennebunkport, Maine, always scheduled two lectures each summer. When I think about this particular resort, I remember Ken Takashima, a Japanese student in my college Shakespeare class in San Diego.

One day at the end of class I asked Ken Takashima to remain for a few minutes. I wondered why he spoke such fluent English, how long he had been in the United States, and especially what he planned for a future career. Apologetically, I said to Ken, "Forgive me for seeming to pry, but I am curious about your life in Japan, and what you anticipate for the future."

Somewhat reluctantly Ken recounted that his father, a doctor, was killed in the war sixteen years before. His mother, also a doctor and strong believer in a good education, had done everything to make certain that Ken received a broad education. This is the reason she had sent Ken to America. Ken's dream unfolded one episode after another. In contrast, Richard Hatherway's devious plan, to which I shall refer later, was a scheme, not a dream.

Ken related that eventually he hoped to work at the United Nations. In 1960, however, only fifteen years after Japan's surrender, there was still a silent stigma in America against Japanese citizens. I asked him how long he had been in the United States. Ken stated that he had flown from Tokyo to San Francisco, immediately had boarded a bus in the Bay city, and with overnight stops at Monterey, Los Angeles, and San Juan Capistrano, had arrived in San Diego six weeks earlier.

"My allowance for the trip," he said, "was running low, so there was not the money for sight-seeing." As Ken described his aspirations, I thought to myself that this is a young man with a dream. I could picture myself ten years earlier when I also had a dream and very little money.

Through casual conversations Ken's fluency in English became obvious. He told me that he had earned a baccalaureate at Japan's Sophia University where he had taken as many English courses as possible. Often Ken would express a desire to see more of America, especially the Midwest, the South, and the East Coast. It was a remote desire because financial circumstances forced him to get a busboy's job while attending Mesa College in San Diego.

Since I spent summers in New England giving lectures at prestigious resorts, the thought occurred to me that Ken could be a busboy at a New England hotel, and at the same time he could see America en route to his job. Ken enthusiastically reacted to the idea; however, he questioned, "How can I do this?"

Over the years I had developed a friendship with some of the managers and owners of resort hotels; therefore, I felt free to make a request for Ken. "Tell you what I'll do, Ken. I'll write seven letters, list your qualifications, and ask that they consider you for a position as busboy. I can't guarantee you anything."

"Thank you, Mr. Kane. I'm deeply appreciative."

The letters were basically the same with a few different personal remarks in each. Intermittently, the replies came back: six rejections for one reason or another. Some, although

136

A Dream and A Scheme

impressed by Ken's qualifications, were hesitant to have an employee of Japanese origin. The seventh reply was from Owen Wentworth, the owner of Kennebunkport's *Narragansett by the Sea*. Between the lines, I could read that Owen was not completely sold on the idea, yet he was willing to take a chance.

The next hurdle was to get Ken across the country. At my suggestion, he placed a classified ad in the *San Diego Union* offering to drive a car to the East Coast. The first day the ad appeared, an elderly gentleman who wintered in La Jolla expressed interest in Ken's proposal. They met and Ken agreed to drive the man's Nash Rambler to Pennsylvania.

Ken took off for Kennebunkport, Maine, in the sporty Rambler. There were no interstates in those days, so the route across the United States was peppered with hamlets, villages, towns, and cities. It was a good way to see America.

While he was driving through Phoenix, a deafening racket developed under the hood. Ken stopped, raised the hood, and to his dismay found that two pistons had broken loose. He phoned the elderly gentleman in La Jolla and was instructed to have the engine repaired at the owner's expense. There was a three day delay, so Ken took bus trips sightseeing in the Valley of the Sun. One day he visited the campus of Arizona State at Tempe, went to the student affairs office, and inquired whether a student might need a ride to the East Coast. The clerk glanced down a list, stopped with a quizzical look at one name, and said, "This might be the student you're looking for. He needs a ride immediately to the Philadelphia area." Ken made the contact and the two young men were on their way. With two instead of one traveling in the Rambler, expenses were cut in half.

The two students drove through Sedona's spectacular Red Rock area to Flagstaff and then directly eastward across the Navajo and Zuni Indian Reservations. In Santa Fe, New Mexico, the two travelers absorbed the Spanish Colonial heritage as they walked across shaded plazas and meandered through winding alleys.

Santa Fe's centerpiece is a charming plaza, laced with flagstone walks and sheltered by arching trees. The Palace of the Governors, on the north side of the plaza, is the oldest continuously occupied public building in America. The two young men ambled over to the Governor's Mansion, where in the 1870's General Lew Wallace, the territorial governor, was writing *Ben Hur*. Governor Wallace had previously offered amnesty to Billy the Kid if the gunman would surrender his weapons. Billy defied the Governor and vowed to kill Wallace. Billy, however, was thwarted because each evening, as the sun was going down behind the Sangre de Christo Mountains, Mrs. Wallace would close the ceiling-to-floor shutters to protect her husband as he worked on the manuscript of *Ben Hur*.

As one drives across expansive, sparsely populated Texas, time seems to stand still, especially to a Japanese motorist who is accustomed to people stacked one on top of another. Once when Ken and I were reminiscing about his original trip across the United States, he said, "In Nebraska and Kansas we saw nothing except corn and wheat fields. It seems the United States feeds the world."

"We do," I replied.

From sod houses to baronial mansions, from watery bayous to peaceful pasture lands, from the plains of Oklahoma to the rolling hills of Missouri, the heterogeneity of the Midwest is obvious. Ken was bewildered that within a half-hour's drive from Chicago he was gazing at sweeping farm acreage.

Finally the two travelers reached Washington, Pennsylvania, delivered the Rambler to the owner's son, and immediately boarded their respective buses to Philadelphia and Kennebunkport, Maine. The cross-country trip, especially the sight-seeing, had nearly depleted Ken's funds. He realized that he did not have the cab fare from the bus station in Kennebunkport to the hotel in Kennebunkport, a distance of about eight miles.

As Ken alighted from the bus, his eyes focused on an old red, brick building with *Kennebunkport Bank* chiseled in granite above the entrance. He opened the highly polished door, strode past the tellers' cages to a gentleman seated behind a railing at the far end of the room.

"I wish to speak to the manager," Ken said.

A slim, somber, grave-looking man replied, "I am the vice-president. May I help you?"

"I need to borrow one hundred dollars for one month," Ken stated.

"Do you regularly bank with us?" the vice-president inquired.

"No, sir."

"Where do you bank?"

"Tokyo. I am reporting to *Narragansett Hotel* where I have a position as busboy for the summer."

The gentleman lost his composure for a few moments. Then excusing himself, he walked briskly to an inner office. The banker telephoned Owen Wentworth, owner of *Narragansett by the Sea*, and related the incident.

"Oh, my God!" exclaimed Owen Wentworth. "Give him the money."

When Ken arrived at *Narragansett by the Sea*, Mr. Wentworth, without referring to the phone call, outlined Ken's precise duties as a busboy. "You will be a kitchen busboy. That means you will not enter the dining room while any guest is present. Am I clear?"

"Yes, sir."

Ken followed the instructions with rigid exactness, paid the loan plus interest on the specified date, and occasionally socialized with other college students working at *Narragansett by the Sea*.

One evening six guests were tarrying at their table long after all the other diners had departed. Ken did not see the lingering guests as he entered the dining room to clear some tables. A male voice called out, "Young man, will you kindly bring us some coffee?"

As Ken was pouring the coffee, the man inquired, "What is your name?"

"Ken Takashima," was the reply.

Then a lady among the six asked, "Do you know Kabuki?"

"Yes ma'am, I do. I took two terms of performing Kabuki drama at Sophia University in Japan."

"Would you be willing to show us a simple Kabuki?" the woman pressed on.

The six dawdling guests were electrified. They were enraptured by the presentation. Kabuki is a popular Japanese drama, incorporating song and dance, and performed solely by men. It originated in the 17th century as an offshoot of *No* drama and is characterized by exaggerated highly stylized acting, elaborate scenery, and heavy makeup.

At summer resort hotels news spreads quickly over the grapevine. The next day guests were chatting about the Kabuki dramatic dancing. They started asking Mr. Wentworth where they could see it. A basic axiom of the resort business is to listen to the requests of guests.

A few days later Ken was called to Mr. Wentworth's office. He went with fear and trembling, feeling quite certain that he would be fired for disobeying Mr. Wentworth's instruction.

With a stern, solemn face and a foreboding monotone in his voice Mr. Wentworth began, "Mr. Takashima, you have raised havoc with my guests. Everyone is talking." Then with a broad, pleasant smile Owen Wentworth continued, "And I love it. We must be the only hotel in Maine with a Kabuki dancer. There is, however, a problem. It seems now that most of our guests are requesting the second seating."

"I'm sorry, Mr. Wentworth," Ken broke in.

"You have nothing to be sorry about, Ken. I have a solution if you are willing. We'll move the Kabuki to the lobby after dinner. Do you agree?"

"Yes, Mr. Wentworth. I am most fortunate."

Kabuki was the word that season in Kennebunkport. As the summer drew to a close, Mr. Wentworth once again summoned Ken to his office.

"Ken, *Narragansett by the Sea* has been serving vacationers for over fifty years. Never, in all that time, has there been so much excitement not only at our hotel, but throughout Kennebunkport. Would you consider this proposal for next summer? You would perform Kabuki in the lobby and become the maitre d' of our cocktail lounge. These two positions could be very rewarding financially."

"Mr. Wentworth, your offer is flattering. I thank you. If I give you an answer before Christmas, is that time enough?" Ken was reluctant to commit himself for the next summer because he had been negotiating to work at the United Nations in New York. That was his dream.

A classified ad offering to drive a car eastward worked in June. Why not an ad to drive a car westward? Ken placed a classified ad in the Kennebunkport newspaper. The owner of a neighboring inn, who wintered in La Jolla, California, wanted his new Thunderbird driven to the West Coast. An agreement was reached and three students, returning to colleges in California, joined Ken for the westward journey.

Ken received a letter in November advising him of an appointment as an aide at the United Nations. Ken Takashima had a dream; Richard Hatherway had a scheme.

"What beautiful trees," remarked Richard Hatherway as he viewed the bucolic eucalyptus grove from our patio. "I haven't seen such magnificent trees for quite awhile." Little did I know that Richard Hatherway's remark about the trees was foreboding. Neither did the real estate agent, who had brought Mr. Hatherway, realize the significance of that remark.

Our home was located in Rancho Santa Fe, a California village four miles from the Pacific Ocean and twenty miles north of the city of San Diego. The present covenant of 4,400 residents traces its history to 1769 when Juan Osuna came to San Diego as a Spanish soldier with an expedition whose mission was to establish Spanish outposts. Rancho Santa Fe is still a quaint Spanish village with winding rural roadways and rolling hills. Magnificent homes are tucked away among the eucalyptus trees.

Both Aileen and I had just been notified that sabbaticals had been approved by our respective academic boards of trustees. Since we would be traveling in Europe, our home would be unoccupied for a long period of time. For reasons of security it seemed prudent to lease it.

A new Lincoln Mark IV came slowly up the serpentine driveway. Two men stepped out, Mr. Hatherway and his attorney Sal Maroni. The real estate agent led the two men into the house while Aileen and I remained on the lawn. In less than ten minutes Hatherway emerged and stated, "I'll take it."

Such a quick decision truly amazed us, but we assumed the realtor knew her client. Richard Hatherway, an athletic man about forty-five, possessed a pompous demeanor, the kind of personality one is predisposed to dislike. Hatherway signed the contract and informed us that the whole six months rent would be paid in advance from a trust fund held by his attorney Sal Maroni. Then he began to enumerate his demands.

"Mr. Kane, I request that you remove all appliances that are not permanently attached. My new bride wishes to use her own very expensive appliances. May I place them in the garage before we occupy the house in a week?"

"Of course. I'll make certain nothing happens to them."

Aileen and I made the house ready for Mr. Hatherway. Immediately we rented a condominium for ourselves on a monthly basis in a neighboring community until our sabbatical began. At the time, our son Chris was a senior at the University of Notre Dame in South Bend.

One morning a new Lincoln Continental turned into the driveway and two gentlemen, Mr. Hatherway and another man, stepped out. "Mr. Kane, this is Mr. Wagner, my vice-president."

Hatherway continued, "Since we'll be living in your home for at least six months, I thought Mr. Wagner and I should look around the village plaza for the market, the pharmacy, and especially the library. I've become an avid reader. Will you escort us?"

At the combination pharmacy-liquor store I introduced Hatherway, showed him throughout *The Inn* as well as the library, and took him to the market, the only one in town, where I acquainted him with the owner. Unknown to me, of course, Mr. Hatherway was making mental notes whenever a customer would say, "Charge it." For Ranch residents it had been a long time policy to charge all merchandise and services.

On the appointed day Mr. Hatherway and Mr. Maroni arrived in a new Cadillac. There was no luggage, just a few clothes hanging on hooks in the rear of the car. I guess Mr. Hatherway observed my apprehensive look because he said, "My bride will be coming from Las Vegas in a few days. I want this to be her doll house."

That day as Aileen and I were settling into the condo and unpacking a few items, she firmly said, "Do you realize, Hatherway has not paid us one cent and he's living in our home?"

"But dear, the contract states explicitly that the rent for six months will be paid in advance from Hatherway's trust, held by his attorney Maroni. If it will make you feel better, I'll phone Maroni right now."

The call made it very clear that a cashier's check for the entire six months rent must be deposited in our bank account by noon the next day or I would have the police physically evict Hatherway from our house. I phoned the bank at eleven forty-five the next morning. The check had been deposited.

Our twenty-fifth wedding anniversary would be in eight months after we had returned from our sabbatical. It was prudent to make plans before we departed for Europe, so my blue-eyed blonde and I went to *The Inn* at Rancho Santa Fe to make arrangements for the reception. After the reservation was made, we dropped into the Vintage Room at the Inn for a Bloody Mary. Except for one couple seated at the far end, the lounge was empty. On closer inspection I recognized the gentleman as our tenant Richard Hatherway. I walked over, extended my hand and as Hatherway stood, so did his female companion. "Sit down," he said sharply to her. Thereupon in a commanding tone he addressed me, "I want to talk with you in the lobby." We walked to the lobby and there he outlined his project.

"I intend to purchase the Whispering Palms Golf Club across the road from your house. The price will be about three million. Of course, Frank will help out financially. He makes that much in a three week stand at Vegas." I wasn't sure of Frank's identity, but I later learned that the reference was to Frank Sinatra.

Mr. Hatherway asked me if I would be willing to put in a good word for him with some members of the board of governors at Whispering Palms. I respectfully declined, explaining that any transaction he would have with Whispering Palms was his business and not mine.

Two weeks had passed since that meeting with Hatherway at *The Inn*. I was teaching a Shakespeare class when the college president's secretary gently knocked on the door. It's kind of an unwritten policy at Mesa College: if the president's secretary comes with a message, it's usually a death in the family; if a clerk comes, it's important but not immediate; otherwise, a memo is placed in the faculty member's mailbox.

At the door the secretary declared, "Mr. Kane, there's something very serious at your home. A real estate agent wants you to call her right away. She's at this number."

The agent would not tell me what the particular problem was, but she insisted that we should meet with her and the lawyer Sal Maroni at our house that afternoon at four o'clock.

"We have no right to go into that house without Hatherway's permission," I protested.

"I would not be concerned about that," the agent assured me. "We'll meet at four."

The realtor was waiting in her car when Aileen and I arrived. Attorney Sal Maroni drove up shortly afterward. With somber earnestness Maroni began. "Mr. Hatherway has fled and I wish to negotiate the six months advance rent which has been paid." I quickly informed him that there were no grounds for negotiations.

"You don't understand, Mr. Kane. Richard Hatherway had no trust account with me, and I used the firm's trust account to pay you. All I want is to split the difference."

The real estate agent intervened, "Mr. Maroni, a deal is a deal. Mr. Kane signed a contract in good faith. We expect Mr. Hatherway to honor that contract."

"Let's go inside and look around," I proposed.

The house as well as the furnishings did not appear damaged in any way. When we, however, opened the liquor cabinet, it looked like the *Ritz-Carlton* bar with the most expensive brands of every alcoholic beverage. Then we pulled open the refrigerator door, and in the freezer compartment were about twenty pounds of filet mignons.

"Get the steaks and liquor out of here," I ordered Mr. Maroni. "I don't want them in my house."

Sal Maroni was still hoping that I would split the advance rent; on the other hand, I was eager to learn what had happened to Richard Hatherway. Maroni knew that as long as he kept me in conversation, there at least was a slim chance I might refund half the money. So he suggested that we all sit in the living room, and he would unfold the story of Richard Hatherway.

A Dream and A Scheme

From Mr. Maroni's narration, we learned that Richard Hatherway had escaped from a federal prison. He had been convicted and sentenced for transporting stolen property across state lines. Hatherway was a skilled con man selling stock in non existent investments to gullible buyers. His *modus operandi* was twofold. He would wine and dine grieving widows who had inherited life insurance money. Newspaper obituaries were his source of information.

His other method was to burrow his way into a foundering commercial enterprise and to bandy Frank's name around, as a means of gaining the executive's confidence. Desperate businessmen, facing bankruptcy, often grasp at straws. Richard would convince the officers of the faltering company to authorize a bank loan in his name. As soon as the loan was processed, he would abscond with the money, and the company would have another debt in its mortgage portfolio. Hatherway had bilked quite a few people as well as prominent businesses.

It was a balmy California afternoon when an automobile occupied by four men drove very slowly, on the wrong side of the country road, along the white horse fence which encircled our property. Richard Hatherway recognized one man, an FBI agent who had been a witness at his trial. As soon as the FBI car passed out of sight, Hatherway leaped into his Cadillac convertible and sped away leaving the lady companion stranded in our house. As Sal Maroni told us, she was on probation, and because she was consorting with an escaped felon, she did not dare to call the authorities for help.

Now we better understood some of Richard Hatherway's remarks. As a rule, there are no trees in a prison yard and there is plenty of time to read. Richard Hatherway was selling a bogus gold mine to a group of Palm Springs widows when the FBI captured him.

No man is an island unto himself. Whether we are plotting a scheme or living a dream, we touch the bystanders on our passage through life. Richard plotted his scheme; Ken pursued his dream, and we as bystanders felt their presence.

CHAPTER XI

Preparing for the Unexpected

Frequently college students have asked, "How can I fulfill my dream of getting into radio or television? That's what I desire most for a career. Should I take a heavy load of communication courses?"

I advise them to take many English courses, a smorgasbord of philosophy, and a general survey of world history with concentration on American history. A fundamental course in communications is helpful if a person speaks too fast or too slowly, has a minor speech impediment, or experiences trouble with enunciation. Most large radio and television stations project their own special style of communication; therefore, sometimes it will be necessary to adapt to their method in order to survive. The most important factor is to be on the scene with the ability when the opportunity arises. I am reminded of Bob Eliot and Ray Goulding, the famous Bob and Ray comedy team. Bob Eliot and Ray Goulding were staff announcers at WHDH in Boston. One St. Patrick's Day—

that's the day when all nationalities in Boston are Irish—the host of *The Farm and Home Hour* went to South Boston to view the annual spectacular parade. He did not return in time for his show at 12:30, so the station manager said to Bob Eliot and Ray Goulding, "Go in there and fill the next hour with anything you can think of." Bob and Ray with unusual humor and satire described an imaginary St. Patrick's Day parade from behind an imaginary high brick wall in South Boston. As a result of being on the scene with the ability when the opportunity arose, this comedy team went on to exceptional national popularity.

A friend of mine, a dean at a San Diego community college, a man about forty-five, was physically burnt out climbing the administrative ladder. He confided to me one day that administrative work was wearing him out. His nerves were frayed and he was getting harder to live with. He thought he would like to go into radio broadcasting but didn't know where to begin.

My suggestion was to get a summer job even if it's menial, in a large radio station; then he would be able to observe first hand the duties of various personnel. If he were lucky, when an emergency occurred—and they do—he would be on the spot. He did as I proposed. After a summer of working at a large radio station, he resigned his deanship and went on to a lucrative career in radio. The secret again was to be in the right place at the right time with the right equipment.

The time-honored debate between the proponents of a liberal arts education and the advocates of occupational training continues. By occupational training I mean specialization, whether it be medicine or auto mechanics or anything in between. To make life meaningful, a liberal arts background is the foundation upon which a profession or occupation should be based. In recent years it is startling how many dentists, doctors, and lawyers are abandoning their chosen professions for endeavors entirely diverse from their chosen careers. One hears expressions such as, "I'm in a rut. There's more to life than just making money." These men and women who hope to change their careers have an added advantage if they possess a broad liberal arts background.

After appearing on Johnny Carson's *Tonight Show*, Lewis Grizzard wrote in one of his columns that he was greatly impressed by the kindness of the host. He mentioned that Johnny Carson had made a lot of people's careers, but never had he broken anyone's career. Grizzard's observation is valuable to a young college student aspiring to a livelihood in radio-television journalism.

At no time on TV or radio have I intentionally insulted, ridiculed, or lampooned a guest; however, there have been incidents, when guests have stumbled over their own inordinate remarks or tempestuous actions. I recall two occasions in particular, one involving a politician and the other, an Air Force General.

In San Diego during local elections, it was the policy on *VOX POP*, my nightly talk show, to allot one entire program to each qualified candidate running for office. Those were the days of strict equal time for all political hopefuls. In general, it meant that if a TV or radio station granted free time to one candidate, then it must allow the same amount of time to all candidates vying for the same office.

Harry Scheidel, an incumbent city council member, was being challenged by Martin Montroy, a city council gadfly. The radio station, to protect itself, followed this procedure: a registered letter was sent to each candidate requesting a personal signature of the addressee. In this way, there was proof that the campaigner had received the invitation. Thereupon a secretary would phone the candidate to confirm a date. Very seldom did an aspirant refuse, especially since a free hour on the *TIME-LIFE* station was money in the bank. Harry Scheidel had filled his date on *VOX POP*. On this particular night it was Martin Montroy's turn. About half an hour before air time, Harry phoned and said that he had just come from a home rally where Martin and he had appeared. Martin told Harry that he was not going down there to be cut up by Christopher King.

At the stroke of ten the engineer was at the console. I was at the microphone. "Good evening. This is Christopher King with *VOX POP*, the voice of the people. Our guest tonight is Mr. Martin Montroy, who unfortunately has not yet arrived. I'm sure he'll be here momentarily." The minutes were ticking off. I was killing time with chit-chat. The engineer was running extra commercials, and yet Mr. Montroy had not appeared.

About twenty minutes into the hour, Harry Scheidel quietly opened the door of the closet-size studio and handed me the phone number of the house where the rally was being held. Then Harry quietly closed the door and departed.

On the air I dialed the number and asked for Mr. Montroy. A lady answered, inquired who it was and then yelled, obviously to the back of the room, "Martin, it's for you. It's Christopher King."

Faintly in the background I could hear, "Tell him I've gone."

"But he insists on talking to you," the woman continued.

"Tell him I'm not here. I don't want to talk to him." All of this telephone conversation was going out over the air.

Preparing for the Unexpected

At about twenty minutes to eleven, the studio door burst open, and in walked Martin Montroy with his two daughters, who, I had heard, were professional models.

"I want to make a statement," Montroy barked.

"I'm very sorry, but these eight telephone lines have been lighted since we went on the air forty minutes ago. These callers want to talk to you. Hello, you're on the air." For the next nineteen minutes we heard a barrage of "Can't you tell time, Martin?" "If you can't make a radio broadcast, you'll never be on time for council meetings." "You had my vote, but not now."

The bombardment of derogatory remarks went on until I said, "That's it for . . ."

His face raspberry red, his muscles taut as iron, Montroy bellowed, "I want to make a statement."

"Thank you, Mr. Montroy. Our time is up. Next, NBC news."

Whereupon the light indicating we were on the air went out. Martin Montroy evidently saw the light go out because with uncontrollable rage he stood up and hollered at me, "You goddamn, Red professor!" True, the bulb had burned out, but we were still on the air. Martin Montroy, indeed, had made a statement.

There is another vignette about the equal time law with quite a different twist. George Murphy, the song and dance man and the guy, who in the movies, never got the girl, and Pierre Salinger, President Kennedy's Press Secretary, were running neck and neck for a seat in the United States Senate. The California race, apart from exciting politics, glittered with the klieg-light glare of spectacular theater. So the executives of *TIME-LIFE* Broadcast in San Diego decided that an hour's debate on TV between George Murphy and Pierre Salinger would be a good marriage of theater and politics. *TIME-LIFE* offered the program to other California stations who readily accepted.

No sooner had the debate gone off the air than *TIME-LIFE* Broadcast received phone calls from other qualified candidates who were seeking the same Senate seat. The other campaigners cited the equal time law and demanded the same amount of time. Since George Murphy and Pierre Salinger had used an hour between them, all other candidates in the same race were given one-half hour of free time. There were ten of them. One suffered from microphone fright. Another presented a medley of songs and dances. It was an amateur hour never meant to be.

Now and then there was disagreement between the news department and the executive department of *TIME-LIFE* Broadcast concerning a particular news story. Such pertained to a taped interview with Air Force General Curtis LeMay. Within the week General LeMay had retired as head of the Strategic Air Command, the air group responsible for retaliation in the event of a nuclear attack. Within that same week newspapers were speculating about General LeMay running for a seat in the United States Senate. These speculative newspaper reports are circulated, many times by the candidate himself, to test voters' reaction. Candidates usually deny any remote responsibility.

General LeMay, accompanied by a man whom I recognized as a political consultant, arrived at the studio for an afternoon taping session. The segment was to be aired on the *Six O'clock News*. I wondered why a political image-builder was traveling with a retired general. The two gentlemen were introduced to me, and straightaway the consultant handed me a printed list of questions to ask General LeMay. Immediately, I apprised the gentlemen that never had it been and never would it be my policy to accept written questions from the guest.

My first questions concerned the Vietnam War. General LeMay answered with clarity and knowledge. Then I queried, "Do you intend to challenge United States Senator Thomas Kuchel in his bid for reelection?"

"No comment," was the reply.

Thereafter I alternated questions about Vietnam and LeMay's possible role in the upcoming Senate campaign. Suddenly it became obvious that my political questions irritated the General. The uneasiness of his demeanor indicated that the questions did not synchronize with the answers he had already rehearsed with his consultant. Tension was building. General LeMay's face reddened. He squirmed toward the edge of his chair. Abruptly, he stood like a ramrod, eyed the nearest studio exit, and then stomped off the platform toward the doorway. In his rage the General had forgotten that around his neck hung a lavaliere microphone attached to a long cord securely fastened to the wall. When he reached the end of the cord, his neck snapped backward. Embarrassed, the General stared at the exit. A TV camera recorded the histrionics.

Many of us believed that the interview was legitimate, and, therefore, should be broadcast at six o'clock. Although the executives of *TIME-LIFE* Broadcast admitted that General LeMay had revealed a short temper and a cavalier attitude, they overruled the airing of the segment. Their reason was sound and thoughtful. They said, "The reputation and the tradition of the United States Air Force is more significant than the action of one person."

A particular subject for a talk show program can be solemn and profound, yet the background research can lead to unexpected and bizarre events. This was true when I chose the timely topic: What is the difference between pornography and art?

Since 1788 when the United States Constitution was approved, the First Amendment has been the keystone of our American democracy. The Supreme Court for over two centuries has zealously protected the First Amendment against a barrage of onslaughts. Chips in the keystone, as the Justices well knew, could eventually cause cracks in our democratic way of life.

Time and again the nine judges have been asked to say how free is free speech. In the 1960's the same brouhaha swept across the land until the Supreme Court finally agreed to define pornography and art. *Playboy, Playgirl, Hustler,* and *Penthouse* were adding fuel to the fire each month when they published a new issue. Nudist colonies and advocates of nude beaches became minor players in the controversy. The *Macbeth* witches were constantly stirring the cauldron.

G. Walter Baynes was the owner of Sun Island, a nudist colony nestled among the hills of Escondido in southern California. I phoned Mr. Baynes inviting him to appear as a guest on *Christopher King's VOX POP.* G. Walter Baynes assured me that he would be willing to appear, but he added a proviso, "I'll be happy to join you, but you first must do your homework at Sun Island." In my journalistic career I had done innumerable background researches but never at a nudist colony. Baynes set the time for the visit and then questioned, "Do you have a wife and any children?"

"Yes, I do, a wife and one son, eleven years old."

"Bring them along. It will be a learning experience."

My reaction was automatic, "I'll bring my wife provided she doesn't have to disrobe. Our son has another engagement."

Preparing for the Unexpected

Aileen alerted me that the appointment at Sun Island might overlap an invitation to a dinner party at John Quarty's summer home in La Jolla. John Quarty was the owner of San Marcos Resort and Country Club, south of Phoenix. At the time he was talking with American Airlines about selling his hotel.

I phoned John and he assured me, "Don't worry. Come whenever you can. In fact, I'll inform my guests where you and Aileen are. It will make exciting and exotic conversation."

With an apprehensive voice Aileen asked, "Do you think it would be better if you went alone? After all, this is an assignment like any other."

"No. I've already committed you. At least, I prudently excused Chris."

According to the directions we drove on the main highway to an intersection where a one-lane dirt road led into an overgrown wilderness. The only indication to show that we were following the directions was a small arrow marked Sun Island. We drove about eleven miles along the rutted lane.

"These people really like privacy," observed Aileen.

"Indeed, they do."

"What do you really think it will be like?" she questioned.

"I don't suppose it will be much different from bikinis and men with bare hairy chests at any beach. Quite often the public exaggerates what it doesn't know. We'll see," I said.

"We certainly will," Aileen prophesied.

Finally we reached the entrance. A large arch spanned the driveway and at the side was a sentry box. Out walked a lady clad only in sneakers.

The lady leaned in the window opening on the driver's side and inquired, "Are you Mr. King?"

"Yes, I am."

"Mr. Baynes is expecting you," she announced pointing out directions to Baynes' office.

As we drove from the gate, Aileen and I glanced at each other. Aileen blurted out, "I wonder how Baynes will look."

In the office parking lot we alighted from the car, braced ourselves, squared our shoulders and with measured step approached the office door. Through a half-opened door a powerful voice resounded from within, "Welcome to Sun Island." There stood G. Walter Baynes attired in a Brooks Brothers suit, a buttoned down oxford shirt with a regimental tie, and alligator loafers.

After introductions and a few words of greeting, Baynes indicated two chairs as he ambled to the leather high-back chair behind the desk. Our host easily saw through the puzzlement on our faces because he remarked, "You are surprised, I noticed, that I am clothed. I have done this in deference to Mrs. King. At Sun Island male guests must disrobe after two visits and ladies, after three.

I was anxious to divert the subject, so I asked Mr. Baynes, "When and how did you become interested in nudism?"

"It's philosophical with me," he began. "The creation of the human body is a masterpiece of mystery and beauty. You don't cover an invaluable painting, a priceless sculpture, or Dresden china. So, why should you cover the human body?"

"Interesting," Aileen and I replied in unison.

"There's also a geographical reason why I endorse nudism. In Germany where I was born and spent my childhood, people are much less prudish about the naked body. We must remember that the original Olympic athletes contended in the

158

nude. Would you like to take a look around? We can continue the conversation as we ride in the Jeep."

It was a bucolic setting. Towering eucalyptus trees, grassy knolls, and patches of wild flowers, were scattered over the landscape. A mother and father with two children, all completely nude, were playing volleyball; a couple holding hands were strolling among the trees; a male and female were sunning on a blanket.

"How do you control Sun Island?" I asked. "It seems to me that so much freedom would be unmanageable."

"We are very, very strict," Baynes emphasized. "A true nudist community is founded on a philosophical concept, as I have stated, not on erotic exploitation or distasteful exhibitionism." Mr. Baynes went into detail, "Not only is liquor forbidden, but any member with even the smell of liquor on him is asked to leave. Sightseeing is banned as, of course, anyone would expect."

When we passed by the members' parking lot, I was astonished to see so many Fords, Chevrolets, and Pontiacs. I anticipated a parking area full of Lincolns and Cadillacs. My remark that I always thought nudism was a sport of the rich evoked a mild rebuke from Baynes. Choice of the word "sport" hit a tender spot.

"Nudism, Mr. King, is not a sport; it's a way of life for rich and poor. The demographics of American society are responsible for nudist colonies springing up everywhere. The rich can purchase acreage, build a high wall around the perimeter and practice nudism. The size of subdivision lots, zoning, and a myriad of restrictions force the average American into a nudist compound. It's as simple as that."

The Jeep ascended the hillside until we reached a plateau from where we could see the Pacific Ocean twenty miles away. "This is spectacular," I exclaimed.

Live Your Dreams

"That's just the point," Mr. Baynes interrupted. "This promontory is valuable for a resort where tired executives could completely relax. Permit me, if you will, to expound."

"After my graduation from M.I.T., I became Far Eastern sales manager for IBM. My wife and I lived comfortably according to Asian standards; however, I was paid according to an American wage scale. We put all that extra money into cheap, raw land which now is Sun Island. Although I am a devotee of nudism, I established Sun Island to pay the property taxes. Some day I hope to sell this land to a national corporation."

After driving over the bumpy mesa and since it was late in the day, Mr. Baynes suggested that we stop at the pool to observe how normal and natural the nudist lifestyle is. We were greeted at the pool by a female manager clad only in sneakers. Around the pool were men, women, and children of all shapes and sizes. Some were sun bathing. Others were playing cards. A few were sitting on the side dangling their feet in the water.

Aileen and I arrived late at John Quarty's home. No sooner had we entered the doorway than a shower of questions inundated us. "What's it like? Did you feel uneasy? Do they really romp in the nude?"

At the time we were departing, John invited me into his study. "Do you think, Chris, you could arrange for Angèle and me to visit Sun Island? As you know, I've been around, but I've never been to a nudist colony."

"There's one big hornet's nest, John. If they think you're sightseeing, they'll throw you out bodily. Nudism is serious business with them."

"I understand," John murmured.

Preparing for the Unexpected

"On second thought," I reflected, "there might be a possibility. Mr. Baynes plans to sell the property, which by the way is magnificent, to a large corporation. He envisions a resort for tired executives. Your experience at San Marcos may interest him."

The night of the *VOX POP* show I mentioned to Mr. Baynes the success John Quarty enjoyed at San Marcos Resort and Country Club, and that the two men might have a common interest in exchanging ideas.

"Indeed, I would," responded Baynes. "Bring him and his wife any time it's convenient."

On the appointed afternoon John and Angèle picked us up en route to Sun Island. It seemed a good idea to forewarn the Quartys about what to expect.

"The place is not walled. It's wide open," I began. "You will be stopped at the gate by a female sentry wearing only sneakers. We shall proceed to Baynes' office where he may or may not be attired. From then on you're on your own with guarded glances."

John drove up to the gate. A female sentry approached the car. She was wearing a sweater, slacks, and sneakers. It was a cool day, and the sentry was dressed for the weather. In his office Mr. Baynes projected the same Ivy League image as on the previous occasion. After explaining his future plans for Sun Island, Baynes directed us to a six seater Jeep for the tour.

A fully clad foursome was playing volleyball. Now and then, a fully dressed couple was strolling among the eucalyptus. Even sun bathers looked like ordinary people on a cold day.

Unobtrusively, John Quarty poked me in the ribs and whispered, "Where are the nudes?"

Live Your Dreams

It was a comical situation as we rode along the dusty, rustic cow paths full of deep pot holes. Mr. Baynes was extolling the extraordinary beauty of the landscape while John Quarty was beholding fully-clothed fellow Americans.

Finally Mr. Baynes asked, "Would you like to see the pool?"

"Let's go," said John.

The same pool manager dressed in a jump suit greeted us. Around the pool were groups of men, women, and children all bundled up because it was an unusually cold day.

Eight months later Aileen and I were luncheon guests at Mr. Baynes' home. His residence was not in the area of Sun Island. The day was quite warm and very humid.

During the dessert course, Mr. Baynes leaned over on his right toward Aileen and said, "Would you like to go in the pool?"

"Oh too bad! We didn't bring our swim suits," Aileen informed him.

During conversations with young people about their dreams of entering radio or television, I have always emphasized that on unrehearsed programs like talk shows and live interviews a statement can sound differently the second time around. I recall a *VOX POP* show about credit cards when they first appeared on the American scene.

One morning I entered the mail room at Mesa College and to my surprise saw identical envelopes in every box. At first, I thought it might be a general faculty invitation to some special event. When I opened the envelope, I realized it was an unsolicited credit card from Richfield Gasoline. Evidently, it was a mass mailing of credit cards.

This struck me as a dangerous procedure. Anyone could walk through the college mail room, grab a fistful of credit

162

cards and charge hundreds of dollars of merchandise before the addressee knew what had happened. That evening I changed the scheduled subject and asked the audience for their reaction to unsolicited credit cards.

During the hour I happened to mention that credit cards can impoverish those financially undisciplined. I remarked, "Beware. If you don't pay on time, Richfield can be a Shylock demanding a pound of flesh." That comment did not endear me to a Richfield executive who was driving on the Santa Ana Freeway in Los Angeles.

Three days later Wilson Edwards, manager of *TIME-LIFE* radio in San Diego, phoned my home and demanded that I be in his office within the hour. He said somberly, "It can mean the survival of *VOX POP*."

Wilson Edwards' office had no windows. There was a divan, two occasional chairs, a standing lamp and a desk lamp. A recording machine was set up beside Wilson's black leather chair. Wilson Edwards introduced me to the two men sitting on the divan. Then in a very serious tone he asked me, "Have you ever heard this before?" as he played the tape comparing Richfield to Shylock.

Immediately I realized the metaphor offended the Richfield Gasoline Company, but now the question was how to mend fences quickly and prudently. After all, the two men on the divan were state and regional executives of Richfield.

"Gentlemen, in retrospect, I now am aware that my remark was cruel and thoughtless. For it, I am truly sorry. If you wish, I shall apologize publicly on the show tonight."

I could see a gradual relaxation in the facial expressions of the two men. The older of the two spoke. "We all make mistakes. It requires courage to admit them. We accept your apology on behalf of Richfield."

"Thank you, Sir."

Then the man strongly advised, "Please don't apologize publicly. It will just reinforce the comparison in listeners' minds."

After the men departed, Wilson informed me that Richfield a few days before the incident, had bought $50,000 worth of spots to promote Boron gas.

CHAPTER XII

Meanwhile, Back on the Ranch

When we built our home in 1960, Rancho Santa Fe, California, was a village of two thousand residents twenty miles north of the City of San Diego. The San Diego area at that time was a sleeping giant. So nondescript was this area, that *TIME* magazine in 1960 ran a cover story with the headline: San Diego—Bust Town. The city had unlimited potentiality, but the elected officials continually had wavered between smokestacks and geraniums. A substantial number of the voting public supported industrial development, whereas about the same percentage recommended a resort city. A compromise between the two factions has resulted in a beautiful city, the sixth largest in the United States, where clean, scientific industries such as medicine, computer sciences, and higher education now exist side by side with resorts.

Sometimes we are so close to the daily details of modern development that we overlook the priceless heritage of a particular geographic area. The name California was given by the Spanish Conquistadors, maybe even by Cortez. California is the name of an imaginary island, an earthly paradise in *Las Serges de Esplanda*, a Spanish romance written by Montalvo in 1510. The original settlement was the Spanish Alta California mission at San Diego established by the Franciscan Padre Junipero Serra. Each mission was separated by the distance of a twelve-hour horseback ride. The Spanish pioneers firmly entrenched themselves on California soil by building the missions along the Pacific coast and then by creating ranches inland.

American traders and entrepreneurs, mixing with the Spaniards and Mexicans, arrived in the early 19th century. United States military forces occupied California in 1846, and at the end of the Mexican War in 1848, Mexico ceded the territory to the United States.

The Gold Rush began in 1849 and from then until the Civil War, California exploded with adventure, commerce, and speculation. San Diego was in the midst of all the excitement. Each year more than a hundred sailing ships laden to the gunwales with heavy farm machinery, rugged furniture, and building supplies made the trip from Boston around Cape Horn to San Diego and then on to San Francisco. After unloading the weighty cargo, the crew would reload with carcasses which had been transported on wagons from the inland cattle ranches. Then the ship, stacked with skins, would make its way down the Pacific coastline to San Diego.

Since San Diego enjoys constant sunshine and minimal rain, the carcasses were laid on the beach to dry with the result that the maximum of skins and the minimum of weight posed a problem for the treacherous journey around Cape Horn. So just before weighing anchor, the seamen would gather boulders on the shore and pile them in the hold of the ship for ballast on the return trip around Cape Horn. The Bay State and San Diego shared a mutual interest. Boston was the shoe manufacturing capital of the world and California was the largest producer of hides in the world.

Rancho Santa Fe, translated from the Spanish means Ranch of the Holy Faith, is a village where the residents pride themselves on the obscurity of their community. It is a protective covenant with three acres as the minimum lot size; there are, however, mansions located on ten, fifteen, and even twenty acres. The general philosophy of The Ranch is privacy with independence or to paraphrase the rallying cry of the Three Musketeers, one for all and all for one. When Aileen and I built our home in Rancho Santa Fe, many of our San Diego teaching colleagues, who lived only twenty miles away, did not know where The Ranch was, but in Switzerland a lady we met spoke about our little village as if it were next door.

One late Saturday afternoon, Aileen and I a bit weary from mountainous driving stopped for the night at a small Swiss inn on the shore of Lake Lucerne. When registering, I wrote San Diego, California, as the place of residence because I was certain that very few Europeans had ever heard of Rancho Santa Fe. Then I handed our passport to the desk clerk as required by law.

Everything in Switzerland seems so neat, so clean, so attractive. Freshness permeates the whole atmosphere. It is the Heidi story revisited.

The name of the village on Lake Lucerne escapes my memory, but the scene is vividly etched in my mind. The village green projecting the image of a cartwheel with spokes of houses and tiny shops is overpowered by a majestic, stone church. The hotel was so near the water's edge it seemed that we were looking out a picture window on an ocean liner. While

Live Your Dreams

Aileen and I were surveying the landscape from the window, the church bells began to peal. Suddenly the doors of the houses opened and people from all directions were scurrying to the church. It was about five minutes before we realized that the houses were empty and the church was full.

The large room decorated with old weighty furniture and Alpine antiques possessed two definitely Swiss luxuries, very soft down pillows and a soft down comforter as well as a candy dish heaped with Swiss chocolates. C'est la vie!

The next morning at breakfast a lady stopping at our table, introduced herself as the owner's wife and then inquired, "Are you from Rancho Santa Fe?" After affirming that we were, she with a tone of uncertainty asked, "Are you, perchance, Chris Kane's parents?" Thereupon she explained that the previous evening while she and her husband were reviewing guests' passports, she was astonished to find Rancho Santa Fe on ours. She went on to tell us that many years before, in her early twenties, she had been a nanny for a family on The Ranch. One of her chores was to drive the boy to Little League practice and occasionally on the way she would pick up Chris. With a certain pride she said, "I know exactly where you live."

For thirty years we lived in Rancho Santa Fe, and as we sometimes have looked back on our married life together, three categories loom prominently. The ten years in Phoenix, Arizona, were an adventure; the thirty years in San Diego was a time of establishing security; and the fifteen years of retirement have been a period of immense enjoyment and reflection.

The year was 1959, a time for serious decisions. Every week-end I was flying to a resort for the broadcast of *Sounding Board*; Aileen was teaching school in Phoenix; and Chris was a first grader. Aileen and I were well aware that a family,

168

like a tree, cannot develop a strong trunk when the branches are never trimmed. We decided that I would seek a position in the English Department at San Diego City College and that Aileen would apply to teach English and Latin in the San Diego School District which possessed an excellent academic reputation. Thereby permanence would be added to our lives and Chris would sense a greater stability as he progressed through elementary grades. Hotel Del Coronado in San Diego had already agreed to host the *Sounding Board* programs on Sunday evenings for a year.

My two letters within three months resulted in the same response from Dr. Howard Croft, personnel director of San Diego City College as well as the San Diego High School District. The same formal reply stated that it was the policy to promote individuals to the college from within the school district. There was, however, a handwritten addendum stating that Dr. Croft would be available for interviews in Phoenix on certain dates at a particular hotel.

During the interview, Dr. Croft, a kindly, considerate man, listened graciously to my narration of achievements, but he obviously was not impressed. He continually repeated the policy of promoting within the system. With a diplomatic transition he turned to Aileen and questioned, "What do you do?"

"I teach high school English and Latin."

Immediately he focused his full attention on Aileen while I sat and listened to her responses to his queries about her educational background. After she very succinctly informed him about her Bachelor of Arts degree from Trinity College and her Master's degree in the teaching of English from Harvard University, Dr. Croft, with upturned eyebrows and a slight smile remarked, "This certainly is a coincidence.

169

Harvard is where I earned my Doctorate. I'm very sure we'll have a place for you in one of the high schools. I'll contact you in a day or so."

That very night Dr. Croft phoned to offer Aileen a position teaching English and Latin at Clairemont High School in San Diego. She politely thanked him, but explained in no uncertain terms that she could accept only if I were offered a position on the college level. The next day Dr. Croft called to announce that quite unexpectedly a place for me in the English Department at San City College had opened up. Through the ensuing years, Dr. Croft and I became good friends; in fact, his son was a student in my American Literature class for one semester.

All aspects of the relocation to San Diego fell into place, and I might add quite pleasantly. TIME-LIFE Broadcast aware of my *Sounding Board* programs from the Hotel Del Coronado inquired if I would be willing to inaugurate the first talk show in Southern California. It was entitled *Christopher King's Vox Pop*, the voice of the people, and was slotted five nights a week, Monday through Friday, from ten to eleven. Soon after *Vox Pop* had built a listening audience, *TIME-LIFE* proposed that I present on television an interview or commentary five nights a week on *The Six O'clock News* immediately preceding Huntley-Brinkley on NBC.

Each of these three new segments of my professional life was different, and to the extent each was different, there was a variation which made the enterprise exciting. College teaching has its minimum of humdrum, but on the other hand, one's realization that young minds are exploring new worlds is a gratifying reward. On the talk show *Vox Pop*, the unexpected was the usual. The M.C., Art Linkletter, wrote a book titled *Kids Say the Darndest Things*. After a few nights as moderator of *Vox Pop*, I can expand Linkletter's remark with the pronouncement, adults also say the darndest things. Then there was the nightly television interview or commentary which enabled me to feel the pulse of San Diego, to know intimately which way the civic wind was blowing.

San Diego was where we pursued our livelihood, yet Rancho Santa Fe was where we lived our family life. The Rancho Santa Fe Protective Covenant, through its legally written words, spells in detail what property owners can do and what they cannot do. In return, all owners place their private property forever under the regulations and restrictions of the Covenant. These governing principles make it possible for human beings and nature to live peacefully together without intruding on each other.

Although the San Diego County population at the present time is expanding in all directions, The Ranch, basking in its effortless beauty, reflects the style and grace of a time past. The village plaza, a myriad of vivid, colorful flowers and shrubs, possesses a muted charm. There are no chain stores and only one gasoline station. The banks are not ostentatious. The complete aura among merchants seems to be that they are there to serve, not to sell.

The Atchison, Topeka, and Santa Fe Railroad in 1922 had obtained the 6,600 acres which now comprise the Covenant of Rancho Santa Fe. At the time it was a sleepy, Spanish village until Bing Crosby in 1932 purchased fifty acres and commissioned an architect to construct a mansion harmonious with the adobe hacienda already on the property. The famous Bing Crosby Clambake, the golf tournament now known as The Pebble Beach Championship, originated and was held for ten years at The Rancho Santa Fe Golf Club. Golf tournaments under the supervision of the PGA were suspended in 1942 because of World War II. After the war, Bing moved to the Bay Area of Northern California and his Clambake moved to Pebble Beach.

During a reception honoring Sam Sneed at our present country club in Florida, he graciously asked Aileen where we were from. When Aileen said Rancho Santa Fe, Sam immediately reacted and declared, "That's where I won the Bing Crosby Clambake two successive years in 1940 and 1941."

The Atchison, Topeka, and Santa Fe originally purchased the acreage to grow cucalyptus trees for the production of railroad ties. These trees, natives of Australia, adapt very well to Southern California climate and furthermore, grow very tall very quickly, a matter of economic concern to the railroad. So the Atchison, Topeka, and Santa Fe imported three million eucalyptus saplings and planted them in systematic rows at Rancho Santa Fe. The railroad executives, however, learned one essential fact. Eucalyptus wood is as hard as marble, and when it is pierced by a spike or heavy nail, it shatters like glass. As Ranchoites reminisce about the history of their little village, they chuckle at the thought that their community resulted from a grievous mistake.

These eucalyptus trees have a special meaning for us. The shade from the towering eucalyptus trees on our three acre site was beginning to overwhelm the house. After obtaining several estimates, we realized that the price to remove some of the trees was going to be staggering. But, fortunately or unfortunately, nature took care of our dilemma. One cloudy afternoon a strong wind came up and grew progressively worse until all of a sudden we were in the midst of a full blown tornado. In thirty seconds we lost eighty-four, one hundred foot eucalyptus trees. I know the number because I personally counted them for the insurance company.

Meanwhile, Back on the Ranch

The miraculous part of the whole disaster was that not one tree hit the house. After Bing Crosby's relocation from Los Angeles to Rancho Santa Fe, many celebrities in the entertainment industry built homes and settled in The Ranch. Among the early stars were Douglas Fairbanks and Mary Pickford who owned large acreage adjacent to the Covenant, George Brent and his family, and Victor Mature. Even today Victor Mature, in his special fire-engine red golf cart, can be seen driving up to The Ranch Golf Club. Robert Young and his wife Betty, as grandparents, moved to The Ranch and, like the neighborly Dr. Marcus Welby, exchange friendly greetings with everyone they meet at the market and the post office.

Milburn Stone, Doc on *Gunsmoke*, one day at The Ranch post office motioned that he wanted to speak to me. He was very gracious in praising an interview I had recently done on the *Six O'clock News* and then went on to expound some of his philosophy concerning the state of television. He declared, "In the early fifties when Westerns became popular on TV, there were subtleties in the plots, the language, and the action. Today television is like an x-ray lab where nothing is left to the imagination. It's about as glamorous as a printout from a machine."

Patti Page became a popular resident of The Ranch. A close friend of ours from Tulsa explained how Patti acquired the stage name of Page. At the time of the name change, our friend was a time salesman for a radio station in Tulsa, and Patti was a high school teenager with a lilting voice. The Page Milk Company of Tulsa was seeking a female singer to represent the company on radio. Our friend sold Patti's first show as the Page Milk Girl and she has retained the name Patti Page to this day.

It is difficult to miss Dick Enberg, another Ranch resident, on NBC Television any Saturday or Sunday afternoon during the football or tennis season. Another Rancho Santa Fe neighbor, Pete Rozelle, who recently passed away, pioneered *Monday Night Football* and many claim that he is the man who made football what it is today.

Although Jimmy Durante and Desi Arnaz did not live in Rancho Santa Fe, I feel justified in relating this amusing vignette. Rancho Santa Fe did not have a Catholic church, so residents of The Ranch attended Mass at St. James in Del Mar, an adjoining town where Jimmy and Desi lived. The major attraction each week in the little community of Del Mar was the eleven o'clock Mass at St. James. There were as many non-Catholics in attendance as Catholics because Jimmy Durante and Desi Arnaz always took up the collection. People came to see the comedy team of church ushers. Furthermore, during Racing Season, the pastor would announce that winning tickets were just as acceptable as cash in the collection basket. Monday mornings the pastor could be seen at the racetrack cashing all the offertory winning tickets.

These were some of the celebrities who lived in Rancho Santa Fe and environs, but the celebrity who most influenced our lives was His Excellency Francis J. Furey, Bishop of San Diego. The Bishop and I became friends because I frequently interviewed him on the *Six O'clock News*. Bishop Furey was exceptionally interested and involved in the civic as well as the religious welfare of San Diego. The *TIME-LIFE* station in San Diego was planning to televise, for the first time, a Christmas Midnight Mass from Mission de Alcala, the first of the many missions that dot the coastline from San Diego to San Francisco. Bishop Furey requested the station management to have me do a running commentary as the Mass proceeded. It was an historic event and I was privileged and honored to be a part of it. Bishop Furey, through the grapevine, had learned that I had once been a Catholic priest. He called me into his office one day and without much ado asked if Aileen and I would like to be married in the Church. I assured him that we certainly would. The Bishop went ahead with his plan and sometime later he married us in his office in a simple, but emotional ceremony.

One balmy California afternoon, Aileen and I were lounging on the patio. Rather casually I asked her, "Do you ever think of the years when we'll be sixty and seventy, God willing?"

"Yes, I do," she replied. "Some of my friends don't think about those future years. They don't want to. Then suddenly the years creep up on them, and whoops, it's later and more serious than they thought. I suppose regular days for golf will be important to you in retirement."

"Sure," I interjected, "golf is fun, but man doesn't live by golf alone; it's just a part of retirement. In fact, I'd like to own a bookstore and travel agency. Then I could wear Harris tweed jackets, tan poplin trousers, and read all the best sellers before I sell them."

Aileen broke in, "Do you realize it takes time and constant effort to build a reputation as a bookseller? It takes even more time to establish a list of loyal clients who have the time and money to travel."

For three months we discussed the idea. Finally, Aileen and I agreed to establish a combination bookstore and travel agency with the help of a bank loan. As absentee owners, we would nurture the enterprise along so that the business would be financially stable when the retirement years became a reality.

Live Your Dreams

We were ambitious but not very prudent. Although the idea was good, Aileen and I learned some very practical lessons. Absentee ownership can be fraught with all kinds of problems. Under-capitalized ventures very seldom are successful, and loyal employees are hard to come by.

One of the benefits of owning a travel agency is that steamship lines and airlines offer extraordinary air travel, hotel accommodations, and steamship cruises at a minimal cost. I recall one exceptional offer; it was a two week cruise, all first class, through the Polynesian Islands for two hundred dollars. Aileen and I could not take advantage of incentives like that because she was committed to teaching and I had an obligation to broadcasting as well as teaching. Eventually, we separated the bookstore from the travel agency and sold each as an independent entity. Even today, thirty-eight years later, I occasionally wear a Harris tweed sport coat with poplin trousers and still reminisce about the bookstore and travel agency and what could have been possible in our retirement years.

The original building on the plaza of Rancho Santa Fe was completed in 1923. The one-story complex, divided into four separate sections, was made of stucco with a narrow roof edge of red clay tiles. Each recessed floor-to-ceiling window is encircled by an arch and on three corners of the building are mounted miniature domes. Owners since 1923 have retained the same image with the result that the structure is the cornerstone of the village and is noted in the National Register of Historic Places.

A small section in later years was converted into an apartment consisting of a living room, dining room, kitchen, and bath. It was my good fortune that the apartment in this historic edifice was vacant in 1961 when I was looking for a location to house a bookstore and travel agency. Every phase

Aftermath of Rancho Santa Fe tornado

Opening day at Christopher King's Book Stall

of planning the enterprise seemed to fall into place. Dick Lipke, an outstanding set designer and a colleague of mine at the college, produced a spectacular design. Although the bookstore physically was entirely within the living room of the apartment, Dick created the illusion of a book stall extending outward from the exterior of a French boutique. The setting looked so authentic that people often came to view the artistry and forgot to purchase a book. Dick also remodeled the old kitchen as a travel agency office with the same French flair, thus creating a completely genuine Parisian atmosphere.

When I rented the property, there was an old one-car garage on the site. Dick Lipke continued the French motif by making the garage into an art gallery where we sold the paintings of local artists. Dick's scenery of that old garage would easily convince a browser that he or she was strolling along the Seine in springtime.

One story concerning the bookstore I remember vividly and recount often. Now and then, I would purchase a commercial for the bookstore on my own talk show *Vox Pop* aired five nights a week. It was a Friday night when the commercial was read. The next morning the sales lady at the bookstore phoned my home and said, "The chaplain on the Kitty Hawk just called and asked for your unlisted number. I gave it to him. I hope it was all right."

"Of course," I replied. "I wonder what he wants."

"I don't know. He didn't say."

No sooner had I put down the receiver than the phone rang again and a deep, masculine voice announced, "This is Captain Sullivan of the Kitty Hawk. Is this Bernie Kane?"

After I acknowledged my identity, the story started to unfold. Captain Mark Sullivan, chief chaplain of the Kitty Hawk, had been a classmate of mine at Holy Cross College twenty-five years before. He informed me that he had heard

Meanwhile, Back on the Ranch

Christopher King's Vox Pop as the ship was approaching home port.

Puzzled I asked him, "Since the name Christopher King didn't mean anything to you, how did you know it was I?"

"Listen Bernie, when I heard, 'This is *Vox Pop* with Christopher King,' I recognized that voice, even fifty miles at sea. It's been twenty-five years since I have heard that voice, but it sounded the same as it did when you played Malvolio in *Twelfth Night* at Holy Cross."

After the bookstore sale, Aileen and I did not forsake our dream of a financially secure retirement. Merely, the tack of our sails was changed. We decided to invest all Aileen's teaching salary in multiple rentals and land in California. First, we purchased an older triplex and then a few years later bought a building with six apartments. Real estate does not produce a fast profit, but over time its value usually increases. After all, there's only so much land on this earth, and each year more people are inhabiting it.

For Aileen and me, our first sizeable acquisition was a 160 acre ranch of unimproved land at the foothills of Mount Shasta in northern California. The purchase was made at a bankruptcy land auction. For ten years we did nothing with the land except to pay the taxes; however, the owners surrounding us were building landing strips for their private planes as well as developing ten acre ranchettes. A Los Angeles entrepreneur one day flew into his friend's landing strip, saw our acreage, phoned us in Rancho Santa Fe, and made an attractive offer.

The foothills between Mt. Shasta and Mt. Lassen are truly beautiful. In July a person can stand in those foothills and looking northward he can view snowcapped Mt. Shasta. He need only to turn slightly eastward and there before him towers Mt. Lassen with its mantle of snow. The setting is bucolic, but not wild. Nature has supplied the land, and human beings have been discretionary in their use of it. Mt. Shasta and Mt. Lassen, their peaks shrouded with snow year round, stand tall, protecting the landscape below.

The first time we walked around our 160 acres, I observed that our property as well as many other parcels were enclosed by stone walls. I asked a native to explain. He said with authority, "In the early 1900's Mt. Lassen blew its top. The distance, as the crow flies, between Mt. Shasta and Mt. Lassen is 50 miles; boulders sailed through the air as far as thirty miles. Huge rocks were strewn all over this ground where we are now standing." He further explained that ranchers were forced to clear the land so that their cattle could graze, and yet they couldn't throw the boulders on a neighbor's property. That's why the stone walls were built.

It is interesting how history repeats itself. In the early 1700's the farmers of Concord and Lexington cleared boulders from their land so that their cows could graze. They piled rocks upon rocks to build stone walls. Those stone walls in 1775 played a critical role during the Battle of Concord and Lexington. Against superior military forces, the Minutemen hid behind those stone walls and fired relentlessly through the gaps in the stone walls at the British troops marching in formation. Eventually in disarray the Redcoats retreated to their ships in Boston Harbor. In the words of Ralph Waldo Emerson, "Here once the embattled farmers stood, and fired the shot heard round the world."

Since horses would be expected on The Ranch, many beautiful breeding and training stables are scattered throughout the 6,600 acres. Young people, especially girls, learn to ride at an early age and as a result they win state and national honors in their teens.

Meanwhile, Back on the Ranch

The interest of the Kane family, however, leaned toward dogs. In our thirty years at Rancho Santa Fe, Aileen had three successive, white miniature poodles, always meticulously groomed, while Chris and I had successively two fawn, AKC registered boxers. As one would expect, the poodles were prim and proper, but the two boxers were as different in their behavior as night and day.

Hildegarde, the first boxer, was a feisty female whereas Franz, the second boxer, was a loyal docile male. Hildegarde kept us alert every minute. It was an automobile vacation trip to Cape Cod when Hildegarde, on four occasions, showed her bravado.

After leaving Rancho Santa Fe, we stopped in La Jolla, California, for a last minute item. Hildegarde bolted from the car and for two hours played tag with us, the merchants, and the elderly residents of La Jolla. She would whisk across the busy main street with us chasing her, and then when we reached the other side, she would play hide and seek among the parked automobiles. Hildegarde began to draw an audience and as the onlookers multiplied, she became more difficult to corner. Merchants would come out of their stores with goodies to entice Hildegarde, but as soon as they were about to grab her collar, she would shoot like lightning into an alley. After two hours of running, dashing, and playing hide and seek, her energy finally gave out. Like a mischievous child, she meekly returned to us and snuggled up as though nothing had ever happened.

The next three escapades were intercontinental, taking place in New York City; at Migis Lodge on Lake Sebago, Maine; and along the countryside of downstate Illinois. In New York City, I was checking into the hotel while Aileen was showing the bellboy the particular luggage to be carried in. When the bellboy opened one of the rear doors, Hildegarde scooted out and made a beeline for the opposite side of the street with Aileen running after her. Brakes were screeching, drivers were yelling obscenities, and finally, a kindly cop at the corner intervened. I don't know how Aileen and Hildegarde made it back to the car, but thank God they did.

At Migis Lodge the chef was preparing for the dinner hour, so on a large butcher block he had placed the T-bone steaks to be seasoned later with spices. Hildegarde smelled them from afar and somehow made her way into the kitchen. The chef tried to save his steaks, but one must be very quick to get ahead of Hildegarde.

During the return trip to Rancho Santa Fe, we stopped for gas in down-state Illinois. It was a small country town and from the appearance of the station I presumed that it had been there many years. While I was telling the attendant which parts of the car to check, Aileen led Hildegarde on a leash to a faucet on the side of the building. As Hildegarde was lapping the cool water, she spied some chickens across the road. She jerked the leash from Aileen's hand, raced across the street, and ran after the chickens. Feathers were flying in every direction; Aileen was trying to get across the highway to retrieve her dog; and the farmer, screaming profanities, was endeavoring to corral his chickens. It was a brief encounter because the farmer was not interested in listening to Aileen's apologies.

The permeating aura of The Ranch profoundly influenced our son and only child Christopher in numerous subtle ways. In his childhood, during the teen years and until he left our home with his lovely bride, The Ranch was continually making an impact on him. It was a soft, subdued impact, but it was fiercely effective.

Meanwhile, Back on the Ranch

The legal three acre lot size in a way was responsible for the low enrollment in the elementary school with the result that the relationship between each teacher and each student was exceptionally productive. Each classroom atmosphere, because of its size, induced creativity.

This brings to mind an entrepreneurial enterprise which occurred during the sixth grade. Chris happened to be editor of the school newspaper and each week he was turning out a typical elementary school paper. At that time, there was no television set at the school and Chris believed that some of the Public Television programs would be beneficial to the class as a group for discussion. He, therefore, proposed to the principal that if they published a school newspaper to appeal to adults as well as to students, they could sell copies each Saturday morning outside Ashley's, the only meat, grocery, and produce market in town. They charged ten cents a copy; circulation soared; and at the end of the year the newspaper presented a color television to the school. It was a quiet enterprise demanding responsibility from the newspaper staff, support by all residents, and a little excitement for the usually subdued Ranch.

Since there was no junior or senior high school in Rancho Santa Fe, Chris attended the seventh and eighth grades at a junior high school in Solana Beach about four miles away. This was a wonderful, different opportunity for him. At the junior high the Mexican-American student population was around thirty-five percent. Chris not only studied Spanish, but also polished his conversational Spanish on the athletic fields as he played baseball and other sports with his friends. In Little League, The Ranch team and the Solana Beach team were fierce competitors, yet after the game many players of both teams accompanied by their parents would gather at *Tony's Jacal* for a Mexican dinner.

Live Your Dreams

At University High School, a part of the University of San Diego complex, Chris not only served on the staff of the school newspaper, but also played varsity singles on the tennis team. From freshman year the honing of his tennis skills was very important because Chris was hoping to win a college tennis scholarship. The summer following his junior year we made a tour of eastern college campuses. Our first stop was the University of Notre Dame and from there we went on to Dartmouth, Williams, Harvard, Columbia, Princeton, and the last one was Annapolis.

The environs of Annapolis are stately and yet not severe. Among the personnel a spirit of friendliness blended with pride pervades the entire atmosphere. Mr. Bayliss, the tennis coach at the Naval Academy, encouraged Chris to apply for admission. As much as the Academy impressed Chris, he was aware that the curriculum at Annapolis emphasized engineering and the sciences. He, however, left the door open.

Although football is the keystone of Notre Dame's athletic tradition, individual sports like tennis, golf, and fencing fill their particular niches in the whole athletic program. Tom Fallon, the tennis coach of The Fighting Irish, showed some interest when he read Chris's list of victories, including three United States Tennis Championships and fifteen State Championships. Coach Fallon, nonetheless, was noncommittal about a tennis scholarship. Chris not only took the exams for the Naval Academy but also applied for early admission to Notre Dame.

It really was a toss-up for Chris because he had an equally high regard for both institutions. Basically it was a decision between a science and a liberal arts course of studies. In January of his senior year, Chris received a letter from the Secretary of the Navy stating that he had been accepted at Annapolis. It also requested that he sign a letter of intent within three weeks. Immediately Chris phoned Coach Fallon and informed him about the good news. Naturally the Coach was not ecstatic; however, he requested that Chris delay his signing of the letter for a week. Within seven days the offer of a scholarship to Notre Dame arrived in the mail. It must have been his parents' liberal arts genes that influenced his decision. September marked the beginning of an exciting and profitable four years at Notre Dame.

Meanwhile Aileen and I, like so many other parents, were adjusting to the empty-nest syndrome. Although our workday schedules prohibited us from participating in many of the charitable fund raisers on The Ranch, we enthusiastically supported them. Preeminent among these events is the Annual Rummage Sale held early in May. Volunteers, both men and women, for an entire year work one day each week collecting, sorting, and pricing the used merchandise. It is a badge of distinction to work for the Rummage Sale; moreover, our friend Carolyn, who has been in charge of shoes for many years, calls it friendly fun. For three days Thursday, Friday, and Saturday, once a year, people come from distances of over one hundred miles, even from Los Angeles. The last Rummage Sale produced a profit of more than $72,000.

Carolyn would alert us when something exceptionally nice came in for The Rummage. Each alternate Christmas Aileen and I spend ten days with Chris and his family who live in Barrington Hills, a suburb of Chicago. The Christmas season, as everyone knows, can be cold and snowy in Chicago. During our forty-eight years of married life, Aileen and I have always lived in a warm climate, Phoenix and San Diego. For this reason I did not own an overcoat and furthermore I was unwilling to spend eight hundred dollars for a winter coat to be used only ten days every other year. Carolyn was aware of my plight, so one day she informed Aileen that a stylish Harris tweed, Brooks Brothers topcoat had just come in. She told Aileen on which rack it would be located and suggested that Aileen be at the Rummage Sale early on opening day to look at the topcoat. It was my size and Aileen paid ten dollars for it. Dry cleaning of the coat cost five dollars.

Later we learned the story about the Brooks Brothers topcoat. A retired couple from New York had recently built a home in Rancho Santa Fe and immediately before leaving New York, the gentleman had purchased the topcoat for protection on an occasionally chilly day in Southern California. Sadly as soon as the couple moved into their new home, the gentleman died. The widow had given the late husband's clothing to The Rummage.

We enjoyed many pleasant friendships on The Ranch and one in particular began in the most extraordinary way. It originated in my Shakespeare Class at the College. On Friday during the first week of the semester, I assigned a critique of *Hamlet* starring Maurice Evans which was scheduled on Public Television the following evening. My assignment requested the students to note Hamlet's tragic flaw and then to show how that weakness was woven throughout the plot. Saturday night I turned on my TV at home to view the rendition of *Hamlet* when all of a sudden an explosion in the picture tube ignited the television set. We quickly doused the fire, but of course I was unable to watch *Hamlet*.

Monday morning I apologized to the Shakespeare Class explaining the mishap to the TV set. As the students were leaving after the session, one young lady who lingered in the background until all had departed stepped up to me and said, "I'm Donna Rosen and I'm a neighbor of yours. I know exactly where you live." With the air of having something important to say she continued, "I go by every day and I always see your fawn boxer outside your house. I'm sorry you weren't able to see *Hamlet* on TV, but it just occurred to me that if you want to buy a new TV, my father can get it for you whole-sale."

Mr. Rosen called me that evening and made arrangements to have a new set delivered the next day. This was the beginning of a wonderful friendship between the Rosens and the Kanes.

During the thirty years we lived in Rancho Santa Fe, two dates especially are etched in our memories, November 1974 and May 1984. November brought joy and happiness into our lives whereas May shadowed our lives with grief.

I remember the day in November very well. It was a Saturday evening when Chris phoned from South Bend. He called frequently to tell us the news on campus as well as to inquire about the happenings in California, so the phone call was no great surprise. The question he asked to open the conversation was more than a surprise. "What are you going to be doing on June 7th?" he asked.

We immediately surmised what he was going to tell us since we had been hearing a lot about Susan and we knew that he had recently been visiting her parents in Lincolnwood, Illinois. Susan was a student at St. Mary's just across the street from Notre Dame. Her folks owned a condo in La Jolla and spent winters there. During that time we spent many days and evenings with the Skowrons and already felt that they were family.

We were busy on June 7, 1975. That was the day Susan and Chris were married at All Saints Basilica in Chicago at a beautiful wedding ceremony. It is strange how numbers play a role in our lives. We were married in 1950, and Chris and Susan were married as we celebrated our twenty-fifth wedding anniversary. And so it follows that in two years Aileen and I will celebrate our fiftieth anniversary while Chris and Susan will observe their twenty-fifth.

May 1984, on the other hand, was an ominous month. Aileen had gone to our regular doctor for her routine yearly physical. A mammogram showed a very small lesion in her breast, so our physician referred her to a surgeon for a biopsy. The results indicated that Aileen did indeed have a cancerous growth. Needless to say, we were devastated, but the final outcome after the mastectomy calmed all our fears because she has been cancer free for fourteen years, thanks to early detection and excellent surgeons.

The sequel to the tale of Richard Hatherway, the schemer, is a bizarre episode. After Richard Hatherway and his female companion had fled from our home, it was imperative that we immediately rent the house especially since all the arrangements for our six month sabbatical were in place.

A sabbatical project must be approved not only by the administration but also by a committee of faculty peers. Aileen and I were able to submit identical proposals because we taught the same subjects, but in separate educational entities. This circumstance made it possible for us to work together. Our plan was designed to produce interviews on tape with relatives, friends, and neighbors of well known American and British authors. Among the personalities interviewed were the granddaughter of Charles Dickens; Madrid's leading newspaper publisher, who as a boy often sat and listened to Ernest Hemingway when Papa would visit the family home in Spain; and John Kieran, the New York Times columnist and author. Then too, there were others like Gregory Mcdonald, a former theater critic for the Boston Globe and author of the *Fletch* series of books and movies, as well as John Updike's neighbor who could identify many of the characters masqueraded by Updike in his novels.

The sequel of Richard Hatherway's escapade continues when a real estate agent brought two young men, the Lewis brothers, to view our home. They were in their late twenties, clean shaven, gentlemanly, the All American boy type. The real estate agent revealed that a wealthy uncle from the Pacific Northwest, whose fortune was amassed from timber, had recently passed away and the Lewis brothers were his sole inheritors. The brothers signed the lease, paid the entire rent in advance, and informed us when they would occupy the house.

In London on March 19th, the day each year when the swallows return to Capistrano, California, we stopped at the American Express office to pick up our mail. The letter marked Special Delivery we opened first and our jaws dropped. There had been a fire at our home. Fortunately, the blaze had damaged only the family room, and the real estate agent already was arranging for complete renovations. The Lewis brothers had fled.

Even though speculation about the Lewis brothers surfaced throughout The Ranch, it was not until July that we heard the true saga. A Volkswagen Beetle motored up the drive, a six-foot male, clad in cowboy regalia alighted, ambled up to the door and flashed a badge identifying him as a Federal agent of the Bureau of Alcohol, Tobacco, and Firearms. Under his arm he carried what appeared to be a large photo album. He asked if he might come in to talk with us about the Lewis brothers. As the conversation ensued, he opened his album and asked if we would try to identify the Lewis brothers.

I had not met the Lewis brothers, since our real estate agent had handled all the details. Aileen was sure she would not be of any help because she had met the gentlemen only once and it was a very brief encounter. At the Federal agent's urging, however, she opened the album and started turning pages when all of a sudden she pointed to two pictures and quietly remarked, "There they are." In contrast to their appearance when they had first come to our house, they were heavily bearded and looked disheveled and dirty.

The agent apprised us that the statute of limitations was running out and for that reason the Bureau was bearing down on the Coronado Connection of which the Lewis brothers were a part. Much later I happened to see a segment on *Sixty Minutes* about the machinations of the Coronado Connection.

From all appearances the Coronado Connection began in a very untainted way. A Coronado High School teacher recruited from his classes intelligent, clean-cut male students to paint houses in San Diego during the summer vacation. The teacher acted as a labor contractor, paid the students well, and many students as a result remained in the painting crews after graduation. The Lewis brothers, who were not brothers at all, had been this Coronado High School teacher's students some years before. An esprit de corps developed to the point where the teacher could envision exceedingly large profits by enticing his former students into drug smuggling. The carrot stick which the teacher held out to the young men was large earnings and expensive cars.

The youthful smugglers made contacts with ships from Mexico and South America, anchored off the San Diego shore. Then they became dealers distributing drugs throughout the United States. When we returned from Europe, neighbors told us that they were mystified because our tenants would have on the same car Mexican license plates one day and California plates the next. Furthermore, we learned that our house was exceptionally quiet during daylight hours but a beehive of activity at night. The Federal agent informed us that our home was a perfect drop for drugs because it was more than a usual distance from the road, and the home was shielded by giant eucalyptus trees. According to *Sixty Minutes*, the teacher avoided prison by turning state's witness, but some of his previous students went to jail.

During our thirty years in Rancho Santa Fe, Aileen, Chris, and I were living our dreams. True, there were some agonizing tears, but there was more joyous laughter. Our threads of life were woven together when Bishop Furey married us in the Catholic Church; when on the occasion of our twenty-fifth anniversary, Monsignor McEneaney from Sioux Falls celebrated our anniversary Mass; and when Chris and Susan at the same time announced their engagement. All in all, we think that we have enjoyed the best life that any human beings could hope for.

CHAPTER XIII

San Diego Faces a Challenge

Although *TIME* magazine in 1960 tagged San Diego as The Bust Town, such an epithet is not true today. San Diego, now the sixth largest city in the United States, has sky-rocketed in limitless phases of education, medicine, resorts, and computer-related industries. The city fathers not only resented the *TIME* cover article, but they did something about it. They picked up the gauntlet and faced the challenge.

Christopher King's *VOX POP*, the first talk show in the southern area of California, was able to keep its ear to the ground as San Diego took its baby steps toward phenomenal development. Five nights each week for eight years, *VOX POP* was like a two party telephone line, the caller and the entire listening public from the Mexican border to Los Angeles. Talk shows enabled people to communicate with others about serious civic matters whereas unfortunately, in many cases today, they have become a medium of hype and exploitation.

San Diego Faces a Challenge

After many years of intensive lobbying, the California Legislature voted to build a branch of the University system in San Diego. To the best of my recollection, the first local political tug-of-war concerned the proposed site for the University of California at San Diego. Many supported an imposing bluff overlooking the expansive Pacific Ocean while a large number of residents claimed that a valuable tax base was being donated to the State of California when raw, undeveloped land was available about four miles inland. Finally the bluff was selected and all opposing forces closed ranks. The University of California at San Diego presently is ranked tenth in the nation among Harvard, Stanford, Yale and the Massachusetts Institute of Technology. The medical school, equipped with the most modern research facilities, attracted Salk Institute and Scripps Clinic. Thereafter the meteoric rise in medical science had no limits.

San Diegans for decades had supported a first class minor league baseball team called the Padres. The doers and movers along with the city fathers decided that San Diego in its progressive march forward should construct a major league baseball stadium to entice a major league team. A political cloudburst drenched San Diego. This time the opposition was splintered among taxpayer associations, educational organizations and the general public. For three years on *VOX POP*, residents aired their support or opposition to a stadium. At last the City Council decided to call a referendum because the warring parties were equally split. For years educators could not get a fifty-one percent vote on ballot issues, but the stadium proposition passed with a seventy-two percent endorsement. The stadium was constructed at a cost of over forty million and was named the Jack Murphy Stadium in honor of a beloved sports editor of the San Diego Union. Affectionately it is called The Murph.

Live Your Dreams

There were times in my career when I went from one post to another. During the day I taught English classes at Mesa College. From there I drove to the *TIME-LIFE* TV station to do an interview or commentary on the *Six O'clock News* and after going home for dinner, I returned to the radio studio to host *VOX POP* from ten to eleven, five nights a week. For eight years it was a grueling schedule, exciting as well as enlightening, but the body can tolerate just so much. So I phased out the television and radio, and gave my full time to teaching. Furthermore, this gave me the freedom to lecture at New England resorts during the summer.

Mesa College was founded in the early 1960's as an offshoot of San Diego City College, which had been established during World War I. Mesa College was constructed on undeveloped land in its natural state and the only building on the street was an aged National Guard Armory; therefore, the street was named Artillery Drive. During my tenure as faculty president, there occurred two issues which were not earth shaking, but they demanded immediate attention. The three political entities that were involved were the State of California, the City of San Diego, and Mesa College. The solution struck me as quite simple, but very quickly I learned it to be otherwise. To me common sense dictated that the street should be renamed Mesa College Drive because the new college, which comprised five buildings, was actively serving five thousand students, whereas the Armory was seldom used. The State objected to the plan claiming that it was too expensive to change large overhead freeway signs which are posted at various intervals from three miles to the turnoff ramp. The City demurred because it would be necessary to change all auxiliary road signs relating to Artillery Drive.

The Mesa faculty proud of their newly established college harbored two reasons for the name change. The signs marked Mesa College Drive would immediately identify the College, but the faculty also realized that the signs would be extraordinary free advertising for three miles in each direction on the freeway. The meetings in Sacramento and San Diego consumed time, required patience, and demanded compromise. Finally, the State of California agreed on two conditions; the cost of ten thousand dollars would be divided three ways among the State, the City of San Diego, and Mesa College; then too, the City Council of San Diego must approve.

Governor Pete Wilson at that time was president of the San Diego City Council that was stretching and straining the budget. I knew Pete Wilson and all the Council members because they had appeared many times on VOX POP when they were running for office. Furthermore, I counted them among my friends. Although the City Council listened attentively to my presentation, I could not decipher from their facial expressions what the final outcome would be. Even to this day I remember my closing statement, "If the name of Artillery Drive cannot be changed, then I guess we will have to change the name of Mesa College to Artillery College." It was the custom of the Council to vote by pressing one of two buttons, green for passage, red for denial. All the lights flashed red. My crusade had failed. Then suddenly all the lights flashed green as the Council members broke into laughter.

At Mesa College a hornet's nest was building up in the Culinary Arts Department. Students were being taught to cook for employment in run-of-the-mill restaurants and fast food places, but they were not encouraged to use ingenuity in devising, developing, and supervising the preparation of gourmet menus. Two factions in the community were at loggerheads. One espoused courses in fast, fried food because that was where the action, the profits, and the employment had been while the other bloc supported in-depth education encompassing all the culinary arts, especially in the preparation of gourmet food. During my term as faculty senate president, not only the senate, but also influential business interests lobbied the Board of Trustees to appoint an experienced gourmet chef as head of the Culinary Arts Department. Four and five star resort hotels were surveying the San Diego area, and one of their principal concerns was a labor market of expert chefs who knew and concocted fine food. The Board acted quickly. They lured the head chef from the Belgian Embassy in Washington, D.C.

André, the Belgian chef, had been at the Embassy for many years. One day I asked André why he accepted the position in San Diego, especially since he was forsaking the glamour of the Ambassador's residence and the glitter of Washington. He was very frank in explaining that the atmosphere is atingle with excitement, yet the daily routine is filled with tension, uncertainty, and long, indefinite hours. "A fifty-year-old man can endure that atmosphere for just so long," he remarked.

As soon as André arrived at Mesa College, he started doing what he does best, teaching the students gourmet culinary arts. Under his supervision, the faculty lunch room was transformed into an upscale dining room. Table linens and a fresh flower on each table was the order of the day. No longer were there cafeteria lines because the members of André's classes were being taught to serve meticulously. He showed the young people how to prepare menus for posh restaurants with the chef's specials such as steak au poivre, gâteau de crêpes a la Normande, salade nicoise as well as ramequin forestière.

As André's success circulated around the community, a question surfaced. The expenses of the building, the equipment, and André's salary must be a part of the college budget as specified by California law. Moreover, the Culinary Arts Department cannot be a profit making enterprise. Therefore, only the cost of materials can predicate the cost of a meal. As a result, the price of baked Alaska would be 35 cents, tenderloin of veal with mushrooms would be priced at 65 cents, and coq au vin would cost 45 cents. Word circulated around San Diego that faculty members were dining like kings or at least like ambassadors. The furor, however, subsided when the Board of Trustees spelled out for the public that this was a concerted effort by the City Council, the Trustees, and the Chamber of Commerce to attract five star hotels to San Diego. It worked. Today tall, luxurious, five star hotels stand like sentinels against the skyline of San Diego.

A digression relating to André I find amusing. It is impolite, as Aileen tells me, to talk about money, but money is the core of this incident. One evening Chris and Susan, with Susan's parents, joined us for dinner at Sabrina's, a very chic restaurant in Rancho Bernardo. Dr. Skowron and I ordered Coquilles Saint Jacques which was $12.75 for just the entrée. About two weeks later André had Coquilles Saint Jacques listed as the chef's specialty in the faculty dining room at Mesa College. The price was 75 cents. The chef's specialty in every detail resembled the entrée at Sabrina's. On the way out, I spied André and mentioned to him the similarity of the two Coquilles. He motioned for a young man in the kitchen to join us whereupon André said, "This student learned how to prepare Coquilles Saint Jacques in my college kitchen. Evenings he works at Sabrina's specializing in Coquilles Saint Jacques."

When Aileen retired after teaching Latin and English for twenty-one years, I arranged with André to supervise a festive soirée highlighting an international motif. Since André, as a young man had apprenticed in Belgium, France, and Switzerland, he obviously was the ideal chef for the occasion. In our home, on the patio, and on the lawn he arranged tables featuring on each the exotic delicacies of the three respective countries. Aileen knew that a simple party was being planned, but she was overwhelmed when sixty of her colleagues and their spouses attended. To say that the party was a joyous occasion is the best way to describe it.

San Diego for the last thirty-five years has been a city building its dream. It is made up of individuals with private dreams and the totality of those individuals' aspirations comprises an all-embracing Metropolitan vision of the future.

No story is more typical than "Mama" Ghio's dream to open a seafood restaurant on San Diego's waterfront. The year was 1946. World War II had just ended and three of her sons were coming home. For generations, Mama's family had harvested the seas off Italy and California. In her little San Diego kitchen, she perfected Old World recipes and developed innovative ones. Friends encouraged her to live her dream, so in 1946 Mama Ghio, her sons Tod and Anthony, as well as her son-in-law Roy Weber, opened the doors of an eighteen seat diner, the first Anthony's Fish Grotto.

Fifty years later Mama's famous original recipes and her batters along with her sauces and dressings are still served in her six restaurants. Although Anthony's now waits on more than a million customers and sells five million pounds of fish a year, Mama's legacy of freshness, quality, and atmosphere still remains.

On one of our recent return visits to La Jolla, Aileen and I had lunch at Anthony's Fish Grotto in Rancho Bernardo. Our waiter was a good looking young Mexican about thirty, very well groomed, and exceptionally genteel. During lunch,

San Diego Faces a Challenge

Aileen and I were discussing some of the details in the second chapter of this book and the names John Adams and John Quincy Adams repeatedly kept coming into our conversation. Unobtrusively the waiter blended into our dialogue, "Pardon me. John Adams was the second President of the United States and his son John Quincy Adams was the sixth President." The waiter was so proud he continued to expound, "John Quincy Adams served as Secretary of State under President Monroe when Florida became a part of the United States." I presume our faces showed wonderment because he explained with an air of gladness, "I'm studying for my final naturalization exam. I've been a green card carrier for nine years, but now I'm going to be a real American citizen."

Since 1960 when *TIME* described San Diego as a bust town, the City not only has discarded the entrenched impediments to progress but also has retained the basic elements which have nurtured expansion. A typical example is the San Diego International Airport which is located on the same ground from which Lindbergh in 1927 took delivery of the Spirit of St. Louis from Ryan Aeronautical. The San Diego Airport today is situated in the middle of downtown San Diego and is one of the few airports in the United States where jumbo jets land in the center of a busy city.

Instinctively one will ask, "Isn't that a very dangerous area for an international airport?" Yes, it is; however, commercial pilots as well as private pilots are aware of the hazards and for that reason they take extra precautions on every landing. The City furthermore through its building code had made certain that the height of buildings in the landing pattern is restricted. Only one crash of a commercial plane has occurred in the history of the airport, and on that occasion a private pilot became lost with the result that his plane hit the underbelly of a commercial liner which was making a landing approach.

The upbeat attitude which permeates San Diego's success has engulfed Tijuana on the border of Mexico. Tijuana, only fifteen miles from the heart of San Diego, is a teeming city with over a million residents. It cannot be denied that Tijuana citizens over the years have been victimized not only by their own political leaders but also by some Americans.

During the Roaring Twenties the Volstead Act, popularly called Prohibition, was strictly enforced in the United States. A person could be arrested if a cop smelled liquor on one's breath because such would be proof of the consumption of alcohol. I can recall that as a very young boy, I had friends whose fathers made "bathtub gin" to circumvent prohibition. The Eighteenth Amendment opened up the infamous Tijuana Trail from Los Angeles to Aguas Calientes in Mexico. Many of the Hollywood celebrities would drive southward to Caliente to drink and cavort for a long week-end, and then bleary-eyed and unsteady, would make their way back to Tinsel Town. It has been reported that F. Scott Fitzgerald and his wife Zelda on their way back to Los Angeles would frequently stop at a cottage at The Cove in La Jolla—it is still standing—to sober up.

The continual traffic across the border supplied tidbits for the eventual stereotype of Mexicans as lazy, irresponsible, dishonest people. All stereotypes of any race or nationality are unreal, unfair, unjust, and are sprinkled with a seasoning of hostility; they are the device of the unthinking person.

Even a Mexican-American salsa company used an aspect of the Mexican stereotype for the labels on their products. The name of the national company I do not recall, but I remember their label, a graphic of a Mexican peon in a sitting position with a sombrero over his face and resting against a saguaro cactus. The stereotype is unreal. A Mexican would never lean against a saguaro cactus and if he did, he would bleed to death from the punctures of the needles.

As late as the 1960's, Tijuana was still a rough and tumble city. A fender bender, especially if one driver was from the States, would land him in jail for a few days until the authorities made up their minds about who was guilty. A group of San Diego attorneys and their wives drove fifteen miles southward from the border to the Rosarita Beach Hotel for a weekend of seminars and sunbathing. The Federal officials in Mexico City were at odds with the local politicians, so the Feds raided the hotel for gambling and incarcerated the lawyers with their wives for a few extra days. When it was discovered that the Americans had nothing to do with the gambling, the attorneys and their spouses were released after a time of uncertainty and discomfort.

In the late 1990's, the scene in Tijuana is radically different. Most of the streets are paved, motorists obey traffic signals, and even the police are now cooperating to make Americans feel safe with a sense of pleasurable ease. Hole-in-the-wall bazaars have been replaced by modern shops; continental dining is available in many parts of the city; and no longer do customers haggle with merchants about the price of an item.

During our thirty years in San Diego, we experienced many incidents involving Mexicans as well as Mexican-Americans and two are particularly memorable. Mrs. Enriquez was our Mexican-American housekeeper for thirteen years until she retired to become a nanny for her own grandchildren. She was a wonderful woman, clean and neat, and a devoted mother. Some of her children had graduated from college; one girl became a school teacher; and another daughter, equally conversant in English and Spanish, held a responsible position in a school district office. Some mornings when Mrs. Enriquez arrived, she would be carrying a covered dish which contained two tamales for Chris's breakfast. Even now Chris, who is forty-three and the father of three children, enjoys a tamale along with other Mexican food.

When Aileen was decorating our new Florida home at Panther Woods Country Club where we now reside, she decided that three stained glass panels, four feet by two feet, would blend beautifully with the decor of our morning room. She and I had often admired stained glass in churches, but we knew nothing about the complicated method used in assembling the small pieces of glass. The broad reputation of Mexican stained glass artists was quite generally known in San Diego, so we went south of the border to investigate. Before we departed, some of our friends warned us not to pay until the panels were delivered because they felt that Mexicans could not be trusted.

We came upon a small shop operated by a young man in his early thirties. Behind the office five artisans were working with lead and colored glass. When we made known our proposal of three stained glass panels, the owner reacted enthusiastically and seemed to comprehend our request as well as the challenge for him. After he precisely detailed the procedure and the date of delivery to Florida, he asked for a fifty percent down payment. Contrary to the advice of our friends, we gave him the advance money, and he in return handed us a receipt.

Three weeks later, the United Parcel delivery man handed Aileen a large package sent from Tijuana. Opening the box, we noticed three rolled paper panels along with a mass of small pieces of colored glass, each piece with a different number taped on it. As we unrolled the panel sheets, we observed that the surface on each was covered with numbers. In the bottom of the package was an instruction sheet. As Aileen and I were matching the numbers on the small pieces of colored glass to the numbers on the paper, we gradually became aware that a masterpiece of stained glass was unfolding. Extra glass chips were included so that we could lighten or darken the original colors.

Finding the corresponding numbers was like doing a jigsaw puzzle. At last we completed the process, returned the panels as well as the pieces of stained glass and then waited for the arrival of the three objects of art. On the designated day at nine in the morning, three magnificent panels arrived in perfect condition. When guests inquire if we purchased the stained glass in Europe, we do not hesitate to inform them about the master craftsmen in Tijuana.

By bits and pieces we learned about the origin and history of the Tijuana stained glass enterprise. The young man's grandfather had apprenticed in Spain, then moved to Mexico where he made stained glass windows for churches. The father of the gentleman with whom we did business not only continued the craft but also broadened the scope to include residential decorations. Furthermore, the suppression of the Catholic Church by the People's Revolutionary Party had almost depleted his list of ecclesiastical customers. The present owner, the young man with whom we transacted business, realized the potential for international expansion, so he enrolled at the University of San Diego where he earned a Bachelor of Arts and a Master's degree in Finance. His efforts have been rewarded because his custom stained glass lamps can be found in some of the best boutiques in the United States.

Live Your Dreams

The stained glass panels are a focal point in our morning room where frequently for informal dinner parties we entertain friends. Almost always someone will comment on the artistry of the panels and that observation usually will initiate conversation about our relationship with the Mexican people. After thirty years of living close to the border, we have found the Mexicans to be honest and hard working, devoted to their families, and proud of their heritage.

CHAPTER XIV

Outward Bound

A dream is not wishful thinking. It is not a frivolous fantasy granted by a mythical creature waving a star-studded wand. It is real. It is serious. It demands concentration and perseverance. Usually there is an element of compromise, especially when spouses are involved.

For years I had dreamed about us taking a freighter cruise. From research, the few passengers, the unexpected ports, and the complete relaxation at sea enticed me. Every time I mentioned the subject, Aileen would respond, "It's not my cup of tea, but if you really want it, I'm willing to give and take. We can't do anything until retirement. A freighter cruise, as you have read, requires absolute freedom of time."

"I know it, dear. I'm just dreaming."

In 1980, retirement was only a year away, so I began to investigate freighter cruises through brochures from various shipping companies. A freighter cruise is a time when cargo takes precedence over passengers. We made reservations eight months in advance. There were only two firm commitments: the *Jean Lykes* would leave from a Great Lakes port sometime between July and October, and the itinerary would be somewhere in the Mediterranean.

Characters weave in and out of a dream like actors entering and exiting in a drama. Little do they know the impact they make. Such was the situation at *La Chaumine* in Pacific Beach when our son Chris and his wife, as well as her parents, joined Aileen and me for dinner one summer evening. After surveying the atmosphere and overhearing the conversations of one waiter with another, I was convinced that it was a true French bistro.

Our waiter spoke fluent French, but he looked Arabic. When he learned that Aileen had been a French major in college, he conversed with her in French throughout the entire evening. Of course, when he recited the specials of the day or answered one of our questions, he spoke excellent English.

After dinner, as we were about to leave, he turned to me and inquired, "What do you do?"

Taken aback by the question I replied, "I teach at a local college." Two months later on the first day of the fall semester, there before me in a front seat was Mohammed, the French speaking waiter from *La Chaumine*.

That academic year of 1980-81 was my last year of teaching before retirement. In a college of more than twenty-five thousand students, there is not the relationship between professors and students as in a smaller college. Since Mohammed was not enrolled in my class during the spring semester, I never saw him again until one April day when I happened to see him on the college patio. After the exchange of pleasantries, he in his usual abrupt manner asked, "What's new?" When I told him that I was retiring in two months, he pressed on, "What are you planning? Are you going any-where?"

"Yes," I said, "We're taking a sixty-eight day freighter cruise from the Great Lakes to Casablanca, Port Sudan, Cairo, and Leghorn in Italy.

"I was born and grew up in Casablanca," he interjected. "My brother-in-law, Malhoud, is King Hussein's personal photographer. He goes everywhere with the King. Tell you what I'll do. Can we go to your office? I'll write two letters of introduction, one to Malhoud to be mailed and the other for you to present personally to Malhoud when you arrive in Casablanca."

Straightaway we went to my office. Mohammed wrote the two letters in French. We both went to the college mailroom where I bought the necessary postage. One letter went into the mail slot and the other into my inside coat pocket.

I believe that Aileen's diary best describes the events and the emotions of that sixty-eight day freighter cruise. To-gether we opened to the first page of the diary and there read, "September 15, 1981, aboard *S.S. Jean Lykes* in beautiful downtown Cleveland." The observations, the reactions, and the comments about people and places are not edited or para-phrased, but are copied as they were written in Aileen's diary more than fifteen years ago.

September 15, 1981: Today we met all our shipmates. We like them very much and look forward to many happy times with them. In the next cabin to us are two ladies—both retired—from Holland, Michigan. Another couple from Michigan are Mary and Don McDowell; he is a retired Ma-rine officer and has spent a lot of time in San Diego. Another couple, Jean and Harold Skinner, is from Vancouver, Canada. They have traveled extensively and have been on freighters before. Sandy and Ambrose Newland are from Chico, California. At dinner we realized that four of us are from California, four are from Michigan, and we have the couple from Vancouver to referee!

September 16, 1981: We are still in port but will be sailing at 2200; i.e. at 10 p.m. We walked downtown to do last minute shopping which included an electric coffee pot and two pounds of Maxwell House coffee. After walking around town my feet were sore so we took a cab back. At dinner there was an air of excitement. Despite the rain and cold wind, we all dressed in our warmest coats and sweaters and went up on the top deck as we pulled out of Cleveland. We were all exhausted—the Newlands and we went to the kitchen (I don't know what you call it on a ship) for coffee and more conversation before retiring.

Before retiring: Our cabin is C-1, and after seeing the others, we think we got the best one. My bed is very comfortable; B.'s is one that makes up into a couch by day. The cabin is quite spacious—we have a round table and two chairs between the beds. Over my bed is a wide shelf where we have a few things to make it seem like home. Two closets with six drawers each and a dressing table complete the room. The bathroom is adequate with shower, toilet, and a medicine chest over the wash bowl. Howard is our steward. He's affable and accommodating. We have a large picture window facing the bow. The accommodations compare favorably with those on Sitmar or Princess cruises to the Caribbean.

September 17, 1981: We arose early and after breakfast (so far I'm not impressed with the food or service in the dining room—B. seems to think it will improve) we dressed warmly again and went up to the top deck to view the ship going through the locks. We went through eight of them today, the last one about 7 p.m. It was quite a sight as we would descend 47 feet and were all walled in. Then we would wait for the gate to open and we would slowly sail away. The *Jean Lykes* was over 300 feet higher in the Great Lakes than she will be in the St. Lawrence Seaway. At each lock we dropped down between 45 and 55 feet. We watched and listened to the Pilot give orders—the ship was so close to the edge—yet never was there bumping or hitting the sides. Other ships passed us at various times, some barges, a tanker from Turkey, another from Norway, one from the Philippines, and various ships that ply the Great Lakes regularly. Tonight we are sailing out of the locks into Lake Ontario. We expect to see the Thousand Islands tomorrow and will probably pull into Montreal on Saturday.

September 18, 1981: When we woke up today, Friday, we were at the Thousand Islands. What a beautiful sight—islands everywhere, and at least one home on each. Some had more, but none was crowded. Some had homes that looked like English castles, magnificent structures. Most seemed to be closed up after the summer season.

B. and I decided to have a cocktail party in our cabin, so we invited all the passengers to come at four. They seemed to enjoy it and thought it was a fine idea. Someone had to get the social life rolling!

We are all complaining about the food. Someone suggested that Bernie be the spokesman and speak to the captain. I don't know whether he wants to do that or not. He keeps thinking it will improve, and B. is not a complainer. We will be arriving in Montreal about two o'clock in the morning.

September 19, 1981: We were up early today. Everyone was at breakfast and we decided to meet at the gangplank at nine to see Montreal. All ten of us took the bus and Metro to the city. Some split, but six of us took the bus tour of Montreal. We passed the *Basilica of Mary Queen of the World*, the Cathedral that is a replica, nearly one-third the size of St. Peter's in Rome. I really wanted to stop, but instead we had a stop at Notre Dame de Montreal, the most magnificent of French Canadian churches and among the largest in North America. The chapel behind the main altar had recently been destroyed by arson. It had been used primarily for weddings and must have been a spectacular setting. The church now has only 200 parishioners because it is in the heart of the financial district. There are many churches and hospitals in Montreal as well as convents and seminaries.

In one area we noticed the architecture of the homes with outside staircases, built this way to provide an extra room inside. Other houses were painted with garish colors—sometimes half a dozen different colors on one building.

After the tour, we all went our own ways—B. and I went to The Bay (La Baie), a department store. He settled in on the fourth floor in the TV department to watch the Notre Dame-Michigan game. N.D. was badly defeated. I went to the floor above for shampoo and set. We went to a little French restaurant, *Alexandre's*, for dinner—it was very pleasant and the food was excellent—a nice change from the food on the *Jean Lykes*. We found our way back to the ship without any trouble. It was a lovely day and we found the Montreal people very friendly and polite.

<u>September 20, 1981</u>: We forgot it was Sunday. It seemed like every other day. B. and I slept until ten and by the time we were ready to venture forth, it was lunch time. B. stayed up until after midnight when the ship weighed anchor. He visited with the Pilot on the top deck until quite late. B. finally unpacked the binoculars he had received as a retire-

ment present from his English Department and enjoyed all the sights along the way. I didn't go outside all day long.

The Newlands had a cocktail party in the ship's lounge this afternoon. Everyone seems to enjoy getting together—it's good conversation and we are speculating how long we will be in particular places and what there will be to see and do.

The cabin across from us was empty. Linda Van Natta moved out of the cabin she was sharing with Gloria Smith. The Captain had told Linda she could occupy the empty cabin if no one came aboard in Montreal. Gloria seems hurt. Linda feels bad, but she likes her privacy.

We had good steaks at dinner and pecan pie for dessert. Things are looking up. As we sat in the lounge after dinner, the captain joined us. He's such a nice guy. Bernie jokingly said to me, "What do you want to do tonight?" And I jokingly replied, "Oh, let's go to the movies!" Whereupon the Captain went and got the tape of *Nine to Five* and put it on TV.

Today was quiet and pleasant; tomorrow we'll be sailing between Newfoundland and Nova Scotia.

September 21, 1981: Monday before breakfast. B. was up at 6—we're really swaying. We need our sea legs today. We made coffee in the cabin and sat around sipping until 7:45, the time for breakfast. Linda and Gloria are seasick and the Newlands are not feeling too well.

We had our first fire drill today—we dressed as if we were going to abandon ship. We saw, for the first time, all the crew. Each seemed to know what his responsibility was. In the afternoon, we went to the ship's store which is open one day a week. I was looking for gloves (the North Atlantic is really cold), but none was to my liking. Maybe we'll get some lovely leather gloves in Italy.

Live Your Dreams

After dinner (still bad) all the ladies were doing their handiwork in the lounge. I'm knitting on my sweater and it's coming along very fast. Jean Skinner is a superb knitter, so I feel secure. It was too cold to go up on deck so I stayed in all day.

September 22, 1981: We set the clocks ahead one hour last night. It was rough sailing all night—there was a lot of noise, creaking, and the like. At daybreak the sun was shining and by noon it was very calm. It was starting to warm up and the Captain says either tomorrow or the next day we'll be wearing our California shorts.

We were all invited by the Captain for cocktails at 3:45. It was very nice with lots of good things to eat and a variety of drinks. I had Greek wine which was very tasty. Two other officers were with the Captain. One was Mr. Mangrum, the brother of Lloyd Mangrum, the famous golfer. We had met Lloyd when *Sounding Board* originated from California's Apple Valley Inn. The other was Mr. McDowell from El Paso—a very interesting conversationalist and an expert in navigation. He answered all kinds of questions.

We have been here only a week but it seems much longer. I have a feeling that these freighters are not what they used to be or what the brochures say they are. Even the officers complain about the food. They explained that they have to take the help sent by the Union. If the help is not good, they can get rid of them when they return to the U.S., but meanwhile there's nothing to do but put up with it. Our waiter Jake seems to be trying, but he gets things pretty fouled up. For example, he often serves dessert first and soup last. The Captain has tried to teach Jake, but Jake insists on doing it his way.

After dinner, a group played bridge while B. worked his crossword and I knitted. In conversation with Linda today, we learned she has a son Randy who is an anaesthesiologist in Redding, California, so we had an informative talk about Redding since we had just sold some acreage we owned there.

September 23, 1981: We slept late again today. It's a beautiful, sunny day and the ship sails along as smoothly as on a lake. After lunch we had a tour of the bridge which gave all the passengers much more confidence.

I am proud of the American Merchant Marine. I read about their courage during World War II, but after a visit to the bridge, I am convinced that these men know what they're doing and are professionals doing it.

B. and I did the laundry and found the facilities very adequate. Both washer and dryer are new. We were told the laundry would be locked when we are in port. Natives come aboard and steal everything. In port we must keep our cabins locked at all times. Money and jewelry go into the Captain's safe.

The Captain showed a movie tonight called *Changing Seasons* with Bo Derek—silly little plot, but it doesn't take much to amuse us at this point. B. is going to play golf with Tex Mangrum (Lloyd's brother) the first chance they have.

It's the same old grubby food. Bernie has written a letter to the Chairman of the Board of Lykes Lines to be mailed from Casablanca. Tex told us today that he has been an officer in the American Merchant Marine for twenty-one years and this is the worst service and food he has ever had on a trip.

I started reading *The Covenant* today. It's incredible how fast the days go with so little to do. We spent some time today in deck chairs and the weather was gorgeous. B. is starting a cold; I do hope he feels better tomorrow.

Live Your Dreams

September 24, 1981, Thursday: We were up in time for lunch again; we certainly sleep late here. Howard doesn't make up the cabin until afternoon, so there's no inconvenience. There is no wind today, but *Jean Lykes* is rocking. We sat up on deck with the Skinners who are fairly interesting. Everybody is nice but so dull—never have I been with eight other people who won't discuss something. Even B. can't get them going, and that's been his business for almost 30 years. Everything seems to fall flat. But they are nice people, really nice. Oh, well.

After dinner B. went to the crew's quarters and got a haircut. Howard is the official barber for everyone, including the passengers. It was a good haircut. Poor B. doesn't feel well, but the cold must take its course. He is taking aspirin every four hours; and we both are taking Gloria's remedy (honey, vinegar and hot water) every night after dinner. It's a home remedy designed by a Vermont doctor, concocted to help with colds and allergies.

Bernie heard that not only is Tex a good golfer, but also was a skater in the Sonja Henie company. Tex is second to the captain on this ship.

September 25, 1981: We didn't make breakfast again although we had planned to. For some reason the alarm didn't go off, but I'm sure I didn't miss anything. The meals are getting more atrocious, but at least we won't gain weight on this trip. When corned beef tastes tough as shoe leather, there's something wrong. Even a cook from a Union hall could boil corned beef until it's tender. The ship is nose-diving but it doesn't bother us. The other passengers can't understand how we stay so healthy—no seasickness genes, I guess.

We are all trying to decide what to do when we get to Casablanca. Of course, we are going to look up Mohammed's brother-in-law. We have a letter to his brother-in-law, Milhoud, who is the official photographer for the King of Morocco.

At this point, we have decided not to go on any more freighter trips. I, for one, miss the activities of the cruise ships—at least, a selection of things to do. I tire of the little games, crossword puzzles, etc. They're fine for a while, but . . . . . . ! The days get long sometimes. Really, the trip is too long—I'm just not ready to sit and rock on this ship day after day.

<u>September 26, 1981, Saturday</u>: The Skinners entertained in the lounge at 4 o'clock. I had a cold and very sore throat, so came upstairs to bed right after dinner—B. got some tetracycline from the Captain and I started taking the medication every four hours. Tex, the chief engineer, took us on a tour of the engine room, which was very clean.

<u>September 27, 1981, Sunday</u>: I stayed in bed all day and took medication but I got up for dinner. Later we saw *Escape from Alcatraz*, which we had seen before. I gave the Captain my rings and earrings to put in the safe while we are in port. We shall arrive in Casablanca tomorrow- as the ship has a berth reserved for 11 a.m. The Captain says the passengers will be able to disembark around 1 p.m.

<u>September 28, 1981, Monday</u>: B. is not going to mail the letter of complaint to the *Lykes Line* because he doesn't want to jeopardize the Captain's position. Perhaps when we get home he will advise the Company of our disappointment.

It was a little after three by the time we got clearance to leave the ship. We all walked down to the Seaman's Club to buy cards and stamps. I phoned Milhoud, Mohammed's brother-in-law, and spoke to him in French quite satisfactorily. Except for the occasion at *La Chaumine*, I haven't used conversational French for years. It came back quickly.

Milhoud, who sounded very cordial, is meeting us at the Club at 2 p.m. tomorrow.

The dock men started unloading as soon as we arrived and worked until 8:30 p.m. Never have I seen so many sacks of flour! Each sack has printed on it, "A Gift from the American People." I hope the African people see the flour.

September 29, 1981, Tuesday: Everybody arose for breakfast. All, except us, went to Marrakesh. We took a cab to town and went to the El Mansour Hotel where I had a shampoo and set. Then we poked around the shops, bought a pair of jade earrings in the hotel gift shop and had lunch at El Mansour. We went back to meet "our contact" at Seaman's Club at 2 p.m. Two young men showed up, Milhoud and Abdou, Mohammed's brother. They both were very personable, amiable, and very gracious to us. The man in the office at the Club knew Milhoud, so he came and sat with us as we all became acquainted. He spoke both English and French, so he was helpful to us. Milhoud had an appointment so he left us in Abdou's hands to take a walking tour of Casablanca. Abdou must have covered every square inch! After nearly four hours of walking, my feet were about to fall off, but it was extremely interesting. I was the interpreter and by the end of the day, I was thinking in French. It's amazing how it all comes back. We saw all the new part of the city; then the old, the Casbah, and the cheap little shops. Casablanca is a small area where the mixture is strange. Some parts are so beautiful, with modern buildings and up-to-date transportation. Smartly dressed and attractive young women mingle with old women wearing veils over their faces.

We really like Casablanca; somehow I didn't expect it to be so modern. We finished walking around about 6 p.m. and sat at a table at a sidewalk cafe when who should come walking toward us but our Captain. He sat down with us until it was time to return to the ship. B. and I were too tired to stay out any longer. We said goodbye to Abdou and he departed. He and Milhoud plan to meet us tomorrow at noon when they will take us to Milhoud's house to meet his wife and children and have lunch there. We certainly are looking forward to another lovely day tomorrow.

<u>September 30, 1981, Wednesday</u>: We met Milhoud at 12 and he took us in his car out to the beaches, which are very attractive with villas overlooking the ocean. Public salt-water swimming pools as well as clay tennis courts are built on the sandy beaches. There are many restaurants and hotels, so obviously this is a tourist area. We drove through a very wealthy section with large mansions surrounded with manicured gardens. We stopped at a luxurious country club, mostly frequented by Europeans and Americans.

Then we proceeded to Milhoud's house which is walled-in and has multi-colored gardens. It has a living room, dining room, kitchen and bath downstairs, with bedrooms upstairs. His wife Fatima is a charming, pretty girl—about 35. She had a smart coiffure, polished nails, and well-applied makeup. Fatima wore a caftan when we first arrived, but later changed into corduroy pants and a shirt and looked like the young suburbanite girls in the States. She used to work for Pan Am Airways directing French tours, but now stays home with her two sons—Aladdin, four years old and Yassin, seven months. She has her own car and Milhoud has his, as well as a motorcycle.

Fatima served mint tea when we first arrived. Then we had a typical Moroccan dish called cous-cous. Around the edge of a huge platter was a wide ring of fine wheat and piled in the middle was a mixture of vegetables (carrots, onions, peas, and yams) under which were chunks of young lamb. On soup plates in front of us she piled (and I mean "piled") so much food. I knew it would be polite to eat it all, so we did our best! It was very good. For dessert we had pomegranates along with a large bowl of fresh fruit. B. and I started eating with a large spoon, but Milhoud, Fatima, and Abdou ate with their hands, which is the way they do their eating. They rolled the food into a ball, then chewed on it. We had coffee in the living room after which Fatima, Abdou, Bernie and I went to the new Medina to shop. I bought two caftans, a brass bell, and some brass coasters as well as some sweets made of almonds and honey to take back to the ship for a treat tonight after dinner.

Fatima said that her father would like to meet us and would like us to come to his shop. As we entered the workplace, the father's eyes became moist. He was so happy that his son's professor had come to him—for him Bernie was a bond with the son whom he hadn't seen in nine years. In his shop he makes beach umbrellas, canvas chairs, and tents for the King. It is one big hole in the wall where he has several employees including a couple of sons. The father served lemonade and then invited us to his home on Friday for lunch. He spoke to Fatima in Arabic, she gave it to me in French, and I in turn gave it to Bernie in English. While this conversation was going on in different languages, B. just sat there with a smile on his face. At last the father said in broken English, "He looks like Jimmy Carter."

After conversing with her father in Arabic, Fatima asked me if we would be free for lunch on Saturday. I immediately accepted and explained that either day would be fine for us. Of course, I was assuming that she was changing our luncheon date from Friday to Saturday.

"Oh no, you don't understand. My father has two wives. It is a custom here for a man to have as many wives as he can afford—but he must treat them all the same."

As we were leaving the tent shop, I quietly asked Fatima if her husband, Milhoud, also had another wife.

"Absolutely not," said Fatima with definite emphasis. "I would never stand for that. Most of those in our generation don't follow that practice any more."

Fatima drove us back to the port where we ate dinner with the officers, since the others had not returned from Marrakesh. When they came in, we all exchanged stories about what had happened that day.

<u>October 1, 1981, Thursday</u>: At 8:30 a.m. we boarded the Volkswagen bus for ten passengers and together with the driver and tour director called Pee-Wee, we took off for Rabat, the capital. It was about a two hour trip. Pee-Wee didn't offer us much information en route and vaguely answered our questions. At one point when we asked the name of an impressive church, he said it had no name. There are many churches with crosses on them because Rabat is where the foreign diplomats live. Even so, Pee-Wee called them all Sacre Coeur. Pee-Wee didn't know very much about anything and obviously was trying to bluff his way. I did not care for him at all—just a little too cute!

We visited the Royal Palace, but we could only look at it from the outside. The King has a Royal Palace in every major city of Morocco and at most palaces he has an 18 hole golf course. The King often invites Billy Casper to be his guest at the Palace for a round of golf.

Next, we visited the mausoleum of King Mohammed V. We looked down from a balcony onto the marble tomb where a man recites prayers form the Koran constantly, day and night, and is relieved every two hours. We had lunch all together in a private dining room—some had cous-cous, others had Tige while B. and I had soup.

The ride back was tiring; we had not found Rabat terribly exciting, except for going through the Casbah in a little town across the river from Rabat. It was dirty and expensive. Linda Van Natta bought a caftan with hood for $50 American money, which most of us considered outrageous for what she got. They maintained it was wool, but I doubt it. But, "chaqu'un à son gout."

October 2, 1981, Friday: We met Abdou and his half brother Abdou Rahim at the Seaman's Club at noon. Before going to their father's condominium for lunch, we were given a tour of the coast where Milhoud had taken us on the way to his house. This time we alighted and walked along the boardwalk where we passed The Tropicana, The Miami Beach, and The Tahiti beach clubs with volleyball courts, swimming pools, and night clubs—a real resort area. From this section we drove to Papa's condominium. As we entered, we were ushered into a living room at the center of which was a round table with circular lounges. First, mint tea was served and we met members of the family including the wife, who is the *mater familias* in this house. She is the mother of Fatima and Abdou as well as Saida, whom we shall meet later. Another son, 21, Mustapha appeared. He speaks English quite well and plans to go to San Diego. He and Abdou smoke and love American cigarettes. B. kept them well supplied, but they don't smoke in front of their father as a matter of respect.

Soon Papa came from work in his brown caftan and promptly changed to a dressy white one before sitting down with us. We went into the next room for lunch which was really their dinner. It turned out to be a feast. The first course was the radishes, the beets, and salad greens; the family all eat from a large dish for each vegetable, but we were given individual plates. Next came a huge platter with roasted chickens anchored somehow to the platter. They went at the chickens, but only with the right hand. The left hand is never considered clean, but B. and I didn't know it at the time, so we dove in with two hands to try to break off chunks of the bird.

We ate as much as we could when lo and behold the next course was a platter of lamb. We tore into that with our hands trying to do as the Moroccans do, which, of course, pleased them. Little did we know there would be a second entrée. We were surprised that the mother did not sit at the table with us. Only the father and the sons and daughters who were around (Milhoud, Fatima, the two Abdous, and the young 21 year old, also a young daughter, El Arfaoui). I'll have to find out who all these people are when we get home and see Mohammed. Pears and grapes were served for dessert, after which Papa went back to work.

I mentioned to one of the sons that Papa was hardworking and he said, "Yes, it's true." I realize that he must work hard because he has two wives and two families to support. He works six days a week from 8 a.m. to 7 p.m. The custom of more than one wife seems to be dying out because none of the young people favor it. More than one wife seems to be a mark of prestige among the older generation because a man takes only as many wives as he can adequately support. Young people maintain there is no problem whatsoever with the two wives. Father goes home one day to one home; the next day to the other, and so it goes. All the children of both families call one another brother and sister and have two mothers. They all seem to love each other very much and of course, kiss one another every time they meet. They told us that Papa each year goes on a trip via Swiss Air to Switzerland and then on to Mecca for a month, staying in five-star hotels with both wives and the children say, "No problem."

I wanted to ask about sleeping arrangements at the 5 Star hotels, but I didn't want to appear uncouth! I did tell them in French that in my country there certainly would be "beaucoup de problemes" if a man had two wives. They translated this into Arabic for Papa, which was the first time we had seen him smile! Incidentally, Papa is 70 years old. After a while Abdou and Abdou Rahim took us back to our ship. We invited them to see our stateroom, the dining room, lounge, etc. and they were quite impressed.

October 3, 1981, Saturday: This is the day to go to the other wife's condo for lunch. So we meet at the Seaman's Club again and this time Abdou and Abdou Rahim came and we went directly to the father's house. This wife was older, quite stout, and very outgoing. She kissed me at the very outset. This one is Mohammed's mother and she misses him so much. Around the world, mothers are the same. She immediately identified with us because we were the link between her and her son.

Again, we were in a condominium—this one closer to Papa's shop and not in quite as good a neighborhood. I suppose it's because this is the first wife, who had 8 children, and I think they all grew up here. Many of them came to lunch because many live in the same apartment building.

Khadija was one whose husband was killed in a car accident and she was left with two young children. Another son, Hammed, and his wife whom we refer to as "the shy one" also have an apartment in the building. This son is a mechanic with seven men working for him in his body shop. From observing drivers in Casablanca, I judge he has a good business.

222

At this home the procedure was about the same as it had been in home number one. The entrée here was roast lamb, and it was really tasty. It looked like half a lamb, the biggest leg I've ever seen. Not only was it hot, but also very juicy and tender. The next entrée was beef, much like a pot roast.

Papa always makes the mint tea and it's quite a ritual; the beautiful silver tea service is brought in by a maid while another young maid brings in a kettle of steaming hot water and pours, according to Father's precise directions. He adds cubes of sugar, then the mint. He tries the tea for taste and decides how long it must steep before serving it.

Before the meal, a maid comes in with a kettle of warm water and a basin. You hold out your hands for washing, then someone hands you a towel which, after using, you hand on to the person next to you. Of course, when we have completed the meal, everyone is up to his elbows in grease, so the same procedure of hand washing is used.

We returned to the ship, but not without having promised Hammed and his wife that we would go to their home for a fish dinner the next day! The hospitality is incredible—they keep hoping our ship will stay a long time. Sometimes we live such circumscribed lives that we don't know how the rest of the world lives their dreams.

We stopped on the way back at Notre Dame Cathedral, a very imposing edifice. Since we are not allowed in Moslem mosques, the two young men were a little reluctant to go into the church with us. They did, however, but remained in a dark corner at the back of the cathedral while we walked around. We didn't delay because they seemed uncomfortable. Strangely enough, there is only one Mass on Sunday in this huge church.

Live Your Dreams

<u>October 4, 1981, Sunday</u>: We persuaded Howard to give our cabin a good cleaning and I made coffee in preparation for the visit of Milhoud, Fatima and their four-year-old Aladdin. They stayed on board for two hours and we had lively conversation. This playing interpreter is strenuous, but I must say that I am becoming more fluent in French and do enjoy speaking it.

It wouldn't surprise us if this couple would come to visit us some day—Milhoud had been in Washington and New York with the King and wants to take Fatima to the U.S.—it would be fun to entertain them. We introduced Milhoud and Fatima to the other passengers and Gloria had some shiny new American pennies for Aladdin. I thought that was so sweet of her.

The other passengers wait for us every night to hear about our experiences with Papa's family and I must say, they are quite envious.

We rested in the afternoon and met Abdou Rahim at 4 p.m. to go to Fatima's sister's house for tea. She is Saida and her husband is Zouheir—an attractive couple with a three month old son. Their apartment is very pretty. Saida was wearing a beautiful white caftan and pink and green pantaloons. There was exquisite embroidery, four or five inches, on the sleeve, the hem and on the pantaloons. Her husband was attired in a white caftan also with embroidery; he was handsome with a full, well trimmed beard and sang beautifully.

Tea was served consisting of a sweet concoction resembling crushed chocolate cookies with almonds; next a bowl of popcorn; then crepes with peach jam and of course, mint tea.

All the wives have at least two live-in maids, who do housework, serving, cleaning, and caring for the children, all for $5 a week.

Abdou and Abdou Rahim had disappeared, but rejoined us at 7 p.m. to take us to Hammed's home for dinner. This truly was a strange ride. The sun had just gone down. B. and I were in the back seat of a very small Fiat. Abdou was driving and Abdou Rahim was sitting beside him. On two or three occasions during the week Abdou Rahim had mentioned his interest in diamond rings. I had two, one B. had given me and the other was bequeathed when Bernie's mother died. The lights of the city disappeared in the background, and we were driving around in all kinds of dark alleys. Suddenly, Abdou stopped the car, rolled down the driver's window, yelled in Arabic to a shadowy figure leaning out a 6th story window, and abruptly turned to us in the backseat and said, "Here's where we get out."

The street lights were out and so were the lights in the building. Upon entering the foyer, Abdou flipped a cigarette lighter to guide us up the stairs. In absolute silence we four groped our way up six flights. In complete darkness Abdou knocked on a door and quickly it opened. There stood a lady holding a candle; the lady was Papa's outgoing, gracious first wife. The solution to the mystery was very simple. The principal transformer in that section of Casablanca had blown.

We arrived about 7:40 p.m., but Hammed's fish dinner was not served until 9:30 p.m. In the meantime, he showed movie shorts of Charlie Chaplin and of Donald Duck. I'm sure the family had seen them before, but they laughed and laughed all the same. Finally dinner came, again a feast. A soup was served as the appetizer plus all kinds of raw vegetables—lettuce, beets, cucumbers, radishes, etc. There were five courses of fish—the first was sole followed by sea trout, shrimp, and clams, and then superb haddock. The shells and skin were placed on the oilcloth table covering, and after each course two maids lifted up the table cloth, carried it to the kitchen and returned with a new one. Hammed had gone to the wharf that morning to assure that the fish would be fresh.

Hammed's wife, the one we call the shy one, was in the kitchen all the time and we didn't see her until after dinner. Mama #1 sat on the floor to pour mint tea and wanted her picture taken for Mohammed. As we departed, Mama gave us a bronze mortar and pestle as a souvenir of our visit.

On the drive back to the ship, the young men asked us if we would like to go to a night club. We were too exhausted for any more entertaining. We thanked them for the thoughtful suggestion, but explained that we had to be back to the ship by midnight.

Hammed, Abdou #1, and Abdou Rahim drove us back. Abdou Rahim had trouble with the guards and finally ended up leaving the other two as hostages while he drove us through the maze of shipyard berths.

Abdou wanted so much to see us again, but we told him we needed Monday to rest, do laundry, get hair done, etc. Believe me, we needed a day to rest. So this was "au revoir" to our wonderful, interesting, generous friends in Casablanca. Although we sincerely appreciate the hospitality of our Moroccan friends, we are just worn out and are enjoying a day with no commitments. The Captain informed us that we should think in terms of weighing anchor the next day for a direct sail from Casablanca through the Suez Canal to Port Sudan. Although we had enjoyed the wonderful hospitality of the Moroccans, we looked forward to continuing our voyage.

Outward Bound

<u>October 6, 1981</u>:   Bernie was supposed to play golf today with Chief, Mr. Mangrum—however, Tex was down with the flu and couldn't play. So I went to the Royal Golf Club with B. and walked around. We had a caddy about 28-years-old who bore watching every moment. Bernie was hooking his drives, so the caddy suggested if B. would remove his wallet from his hip pocket and let the caddy carry his wallet, the shots would be straighter. Bernie took out the wallet, gave it to me, and I put it in my purse. Ever after that, the caddy kept trying to get me to open my purse for one reason or another.

The caddy kept insisting that he be paid on the course, but I said, "No way." After being paid at the clubhouse, he wanted to ride back to the center of the city with us in our cab. When I said that we were having lunch, and I did not know at what time we would be leaving, he asked for lunch money. At last, I spoke to him bluntly and said, "Get lost."

We also had an incident with a cruising cab driver—B. hailed a cruising taxi outside the clubhouse who was charging double the amount we paid to ride out to the club. B. refused to pay, so through an instant grapevine of cabbies, not a single taxi would stop for us.   With golf clubs in one hand and golf shoes in the other, B. did a juggling act boarding a bus for the port—honestly, I wasn't much help, but I kept reassuring him about all the money we were saving.

When we reached the *S.S. Jean Lykes*, we learned that Sadat had been assassinated.

<u>October 7, 1981, Wednesday</u>: Today is Chris's birthday, his 28th. I am so lonesome—how I miss him and Susan. We went to the Seaman's Club to telephone him, but because of Sadat's assassination, we could not get through to the States. What a disappointment!

Live Your Dreams

We went on to town and had lunch at the Mansour Hotel and again I had a shampoo and set. When we returned to the *Jean Lykes*, a couple from the ship berthed next to ours, whom we had met that morning at the Seaman's Club, were waiting for us. We were showing them around our cabin when the Captain came in and invited them to stay for dinner. It was unusual and very gracious of him. Then they invited all our passengers over to their ship to view the accommodations. They took us all over, served drinks and introduced us to everyone, even their Captain. Our quarters are luxurious compared to theirs. Their ship is registered in Yugoslavia.

<u>October 8, 1991, Thursday</u>: In the afternoon we watched the final preparations to sail. Getting all the tractors back on the ship and dropping them in the hold is a very precise feat. It reminded me of youngsters in a penny arcade with toy derricks trying to put trucks in a slot. Moroccan longshoremen on the wharf were yelling in Arabic at our crew on deck, with our crew responding in English—it was Babel. Tonight we had our first good meal—tender and tasty London broil; cauliflower, well-cooked and hot for a change; roasted potatoes and peach pie a la mode. Everyone was delighted and surprised. We sailed away from Morocco at 6:30 p.m. on a calm sea.

CHAPTER XV

Deep in the Heart of Africa

October 9, 1981:   When we arose for breakfast, we had already sailed through the Straits of Gibraltar. The radio man came to our cabin with a radiogram for Mr. and Mrs. Bernard Kane—my heart stopped. What news did it bear? The best two words I've heard in a long time, "I PASSED" signed Chris. Needless to say, we are proud and very happy that Chris has passed the Illinois Bar. How I wish we could see him. Now he and his wife Susan will settle in Chicago for sure and he will have lots of opportunities there.

The fog horn started at dusk and continued through the rest of the night. Tonight's movie was *Urban Cowboy* with John Travolta—everybody left before it was over except B., me, and the Captain. Captain says that we will be home for Thanksgiving and that we will disembark at either Miami, New Orleans, or Houston.

October 10, 1981:   It is still smooth sailing; we passed Malta today but couldn't see the island because of haze. The McDowells had their party this afternoon and it was very enjoyable. Then, the officers had a cookout and they said we would have ours the following Sunday. We spent the evening on deck with the McDowells watching the moon.

October 12, 1981: This was a "down" day. B. still has an earache, so I got a syringe and peroxide from Mr. McDowell. The paramedic and I worked on B's ear, but he still doesn't hear. To make matters worse, I lost a contact lens. Fortunately, I had a backup, but it was for distance. Yes, it really was a "down" day.

October 13, 1981: We dropped anchor today waiting to go through the Suez Canal. The night was perfect, balmy, a calm sea, and a full moon. There must be about twenty ships lining up to go through the Canal. We remained on deck and enjoyed the beauty of the Mediterranean. The McDowells dropped by our cabin and brought hot oil for Bernie's ear. It doesn't seem to be getting any better. B. has suffered an ear ache in the past and I've lost more than one lens—but when you're thousands of miles away in a strange land, the problem becomes magnified.

October 14, 1981: Don McDowell woke us at 4 a.m. as we were about to enter the Canal. It truly was a beautiful sight with exquisite buildings along streets lined with palm trees. Small boats were bobbing in the water around our ship. Several Egyptians boarded the *Jean Lykes*. The Captain warned us to lock our doors—everything that isn't stationary has been locked up. This is Port Said, about two days away from Port Sudan. Our ship was fortunate to sail into the Canal right away. It's one-way traffic, open for south-bound traffic at 4 o'clock and 12 o'clock. It was a magnificent sunrise. Flies were swarming in droves so we could not stay on deck. We saw where the Six-Day War was fought—not much to fight over. Today we were told not to take pictures

Bernie & Aileen at top of the Jungfrau
in Switzerland

At the Pyramids, Cairo

Entering Singapore Harbor

St. Mark's Square, Venice

The Blue Lagoon at Amalfi

The Bridge of Sighs, Venice

or use binoculars. We passed Sadat's summer home, which was quite unpretentious. We expect to be in Port Sudan Friday morning.

October 15, 1981, Thursday: The Captain today informed the passengers that their mail may never leave Sudan— much of it will be trashed. Also if it *is* ever mailed, it could take a month to reach the U.S. The *Jean Lykes* is scheduled to dock in Port Sudan tomorrow sometime around noon. It's too hot to sit on deck today—Thank God, the ship is air-conditioned.

Passengers are getting edgy actually 10 or 12 passengers are too few. After a while the level of conversation is pedestrian and monotonous.

When Don McDowell took his seat, after the movie had started tonight, one lady said, "Well, you make a better door than a window." Such a clever, original remark! Some of the women are so self-righteous and narrow minded that they have become the moral guardians of the *Jean Lykes*.

We've been on board ship one month today—I hope we survive the next month. B. seems to think we'll be disembarking in Miami about the 20th of November. Please God!!!

October 16 & 17, 1981: We are still sitting here waiting to dock. Tempers are getting shorter.

October 18, 1981, Sunday: Steak dinner tonight was like shoe leather or perhaps it was. B. never got his meal until 40 minutes after we were seated and everyone had finished the entrée. Truthfully, his dinner was inedible. One of the ladies reprimanded Bernie for being ungentlemanly because he expressed a complaint about the food. We're still sitting outside the harbor. I wish we could get in there and out and on our way. B. says we could fly home from Sudan except he is afraid of bombs on their planes. I'm almost willing to take a chance!

Deep in the Heart of Africa

<u>October 19, 1981, Monday</u>:   The abject poverty of Port Sudan is unbelievable—it is a showcase of misery. If I didn't see it with my own eyes, I could never visualize it. The heat is unbearable; in July and August the temperature goes to 135 degrees and it has not rained for two years.

An agent for the steamship lines, an Englishman named William Brazier, came aboard this morning and seemed so happy to find people with whom he could converse. He talked for about an hour and a half in the lounge. Passengers are not allowed off the ship because of the unrest here. Yesterday 1600 people who were Khadafy sympathizers, were arrested in Khartoum, the capital. Mr. Brazier said that his manager was stopped six times driving from Khartoum to Port Sudan, a distance of 800 miles, and the rebels took all his possessions, ransacked his car, and practically tore it apart.

There is no telephone or tel-ex service between here and Khartoum and there hasn't been for six months. Germans built the telephone system and left two helicopters to keep it in good repair, but the government appropriated the helicopters; the (so called) government substituted camels to climb the mountain slopes with drums of oil on their backs to service the phone system. The camels are slow; everything here shuts down on Fridays; one of the microwave stations burned out so the whole network is disabled.

The people change their clothes every six months and then wash them in the dirty Red Sea. I must say I have never seen such filth.

On the wharf there are boxes piled on boxes, thousands of them almost two stories high; goods from all over the world. William Brazier said they've been in the same place for more than six months. Two separate piles caught my eye, one with cases marked Bristol Cream and the other with "wine glasses" printed on each case. What in the world are wine glasses and

Bristol Cream doing in a Moslem country which stringently enforces laws against the consumption of liquor? Could it be that Port Sudan is a dumping ground for excess products, so that prices remain stable in the home country? I just don't know; I'm only speculating.

From the ship we could see a rusting sugar refining operation. Some country came in, set it up, showed the Sudanese how to use it, but there it sits, never utilized. The people don't want outside help; they want no intrusion.

So it will be, I suppose, with the heavy machinery we are going to unload—two large G.E. locomotives; but I don't see any rail tracks. Maybe the locomotives will end up the same way the rusting sugar refinery did.

The Chevron people are here. They can and will pay any price for service and, as a result, the inflation rate runs thirty percent. For example, a $7,000 car has a $3,500 import tax on it. Most of their money comes from customs. I don't imagine there will be any automobile assembly plants in Port Sudan for some time.

There's not a consulate of any nation here, which leaves one pretty much at the mercy of these guys. The people have no bathrooms—they defecate and urinate wherever they happen to be. There are no restaurants, lounges, movies, or shops—yet Port Sudan has a population of more than 150,000 people and is the third largest city in the country of Sudan. The average income per year is $340. The dock workers, who are about the best paid, make $4 a day for seven hours.

October 20, 1981, Tuesday: The Agent came aboard today and said he is trying to get passes for us to leave the ship and eventually, he got them. The best and only hotel is the Red Sea Hotel which was built in the early 1900's when Sudan was controlled by an Anglo-Egyptian Alliance. I can't compare it to anything because I've never seen anything so bad. The rooms are not air-conditioned and are infested with insects. The price for a room is $70 per night!

We saw meat stalls with the meat hanging covered with flies. Imagine no refrigeration in this heat! Mr. Brazier told us that he boils all his fresh meat in detergent before cooking it. Many of the people have no homes, and that is why we see so many lying asleep on the docks and in the streets. Some of the natives have rings in their noses and scars on their faces. It's a sorry sight. Women are not treated like chattel; they are chattel.

October 21, 1981, Wednesday: Mary McDowell woke us up to tell us the Agent was here. Not only had he procured passes for all of us, but also he was taking us in his car. By the time we got to the lounge, the first group had already gone so we went next with the McDowells.

We got out of the car only once. We went into a little hole in the wall where they were selling trinkets. They said the trinkets were made of ivory although they looked like plastic to me. I asked the price of a small elephant, thinking it might be $5 at the most. It was $50. My, did they see us coming! Mary and Don stayed downtown to walk around, but B. and I returned with the Agent. B. and I took showers before lunch.

October 22, 1981, Thursday: They finally finished unloading the ship at Port Sudan, after moving the *Jean Lykes* twice so they could have space to drop the heavy equipment on the dock. Our American crew did the unloading—all the officers worked three days with about eight hours sleep during all that time. There were some 20 or 30 Sudanese around as paid help, but did nothing. Some of them even slept on the decks while all the work was going on. It is the responsibility of the Sudanese longshoremen to unload, but, as the Captain explained, we could be in Port Sudan for two years if we waited for them to do it. At last we sailed from Port Sudan. I was glad to leave the terrific heat, the dust, and the filth.

B. and I are going to try to leave the ship at Alexandria, fly to Rome, spend about ten days in Italy, and pick up the ship at Leghorn.

October 23, 1981, Friday: We stopped at the Captain's office to discuss our leaving the *Jean Lykes* at Alexandria, flying out of Cairo to Rome, then running around Italy and meeting the ship at Leghorn. The captain thought there might be a possibility of trouble with the immigration people as far as getting a visa to leave Egypt since ours had expired. The visas were of three month's duration and since we were delayed in leaving the States, all passengers' visas had expired.

Then B. talked with Jack, the radio man, who suggested that we call the American Embassy in Cairo and ask them for a solution. We radioed at 12 and again at 3 to no avail—all contact was jammed up because of Sadat's death.

There's a rumor the Captain has ordered that no passengers would be allowed ashore for the rest of the trip. Everyone is now wondering whether there is unrest in Egypt, which could develop into something. Surely the Captain would not keep us on board in port for any other reason.

We didn't mention our conversation with the Captain to anyone. Yet at lunch Gloria Smith asked me if the Captain "saw eye to eye" with us about our plans—I was so stunned I couldn't answer. Gloria said, "I mean about your plans to leave the ship. I was in the hall and heard you talking with him."

The excitement around here today is that we have two stowaways from Ethiopia. They are being kept in the ship's hospital and we have been warned not to talk to them. The stowaways will be put ashore in Alexandria and handed over to the immigration officials.

October 24, 1981, Saturday: When we awoke today, there was much ado—another stow-away was found this morning—now the officers are wondering whether there could be more.

The Italy trip for us is off as the rumor is that we might not even go to Leghorn. Passengers were notified they could go ashore at Suez. The launch would come at 6:30 p.m. and return at 11 p.m. The Skinners and Gloria chose to go ashore, but we decided against it. Some of the officers, who have been to Suez on a previous trip, said that there was nothing to see.

Dinner, incidentally, was a fiasco. We had short ribs that were long on fat. Of course, Gloria said, "They were absolutely delicious!" One of the ladies had the nerve to tell Jake, the waiter, to pass the word on to the cook that the ribs were just perfect. Mary McDowell turned on her and chastised her, "Why do you do that when you can see the ribs are inedible?" Only Mary didn't say it so delicately!

October 25, 1981, Sunday: We were up for breakfast which surprised everyone. We told the Captain we had given up the idea of trying to do Italy because of all the complications. Chicken at lunch was not cooked long enough—now we know how a rubber chicken tastes. Even the officers were making remarks about the food.

We are sailing—left at 9 this morning and should reach Alexandria tomorrow. The McDowells came to our room in the evening and Jack, the radio man, came by also. At 9:30 Gloria knocked on the door and told us to be quiet. We then went to the dining room and sat around for awhile.

Live Your Dreams

<u>October 26, 1981, Monday</u>:   I told the Captain about Gloria getting upset last night. He said that he hadn't heard us and his quarters are adjacent to ours; furthermore, he said that there is no law of the sea against having a get-together in a cabin. That afternoon the Captain invited all the passengers to a Bloody Mary party in his cabin where he served delicious hors d'oeuvres, especially wonderful Greek olives.

<u>October 27, 1981, Tuesday</u>:   We arrived at Alexandria this morning and are anchored outside the harbor. The Captain says we will dock on Wednesday. We are in quarantine now because of the stowaways. The officials will come aboard to get them on Wednesday.

<u>October 28, 1981, Wednesday</u>:   We sailed into port at Alexandria where Blue Sky Travel came with its representative, Mohammed. He sold us a tour to Cairo.

<u>October 29, 1981, Thursday</u>:   We left at 9 a.m. for Cairo with Mary and Don, our driver, and Mohammed, our guide. After three and a half hours along the Delta, we arrived at the Egyptian Museum. Artifacts and monuments on display date back 50 centuries. We drove to our hotel, the Mena House Oberai, where Presidents Nixon, Ford, and Carter had stayed when they attended Sadat's funeral only a few weeks before. It's a lovely, first class, luxury hotel. We had a delicious luncheon before going on to Giza to see the Pyramids and the Sphinx—had a camel ride—what an experience! If our shipmates turned green when the sea was rough, they certainly would have the same feeling on the back of a camel. The camel drivers work an effective gimmick. They charge for a Pyramid camel ride, which I thought was round trip. At the Pyramid, however, the driver informs the rider that the return will be double the price. Of course, one can walk back, but trudging in soft desert sand can be laborious exercise.

Deep in the Heart of Africa

October 30, 1981, Friday: We met Mohammed at 9 a.m., and after mailing ten cards and letters, we went back to the Pyramids and the Sphinx. It is surely a magnificent sight; there is something magnetic about the Pyramids. Then we went into the city of Cairo. Cairo has 10 million people; it is noisy and congested. We stopped at Sultan Hassan Mosque and School and had to wear cloth coverings over our shoes— B. bought an ivory tusk shoehorn, a foot long, for $2. It was interesting that we were allowed to enter mosques in Cairo, but not in Morocco. A mosque is not like a church where the faithful are seated and led by a clergyman; on the contrary, the people roam about, some sit on the marble floor, and others lean against pillars. They individually pray and read aloud from the Koran. It seemed more like the public forums of the Romans. We were fortunate to have an excellent guide.

We stopped for lunch at Hotel Shepherd. This hotel goes back in age to the days of English colonialism in Africa. I could just picture a Rudyard Kipling character sipping his cognac in the ornate lobby.

We left Cairo and took the road through the Sahara Desert to Alexandria. It was quite a lonely road—I'd hate to have a flat tire. The driver wearing his little, white embroidered skullcap evidently thought he was driving in the Indy 500—he was weaving in and out of camels, broken down trucks, and people walking in groups, never taking his foot off the accelerator. Very tired, at 5 p.m. we arrived back in Alexandria.

October 31, 1981, Saturday: We were up for breakfast and met our guide and driver for a tour of Alexandria. Our first stop was the catacombs where there was an electricity outage, so we made the tour with each one holding a candle, much like the early catacomb visitors centuries ago. Next was Pompey's Pillar dating back to 297 A.D. built in honor of the Emperor Diocletian.

We proceeded to the Roman Amphitheater which has twelve marble galleries forming a semicircle. The Amphitheater was recently unearthed. In the Graeco-Roman Museum we saw antiques of great historical value going back to the B.C. era.

Lunch was at the new Sheraton Hotel. I remember well, when I was at Harvard Graduate School, that a man by the name of Henderson owned three very small hotels in the Boston area called The Sheraton. Little did I think that one day I would be lunching at a Sheraton Hotel in Cairo. Anyway, we drove across the street to see the Montazah Gardens, the Palestine Hotel, and the Palace of King Farouk. Our group stopped and entered (sans shoes) the Mosque of Abul Abbas with its high minaret and four domes.

November 1, 1981, Sunday: We arranged to hire Mohammed, the driver at Blue Sky Travel, for several hours and met him outside the gate at 10 a.m. to go shopping. We told him emphatically that we did not want the bazaars or souvenir shops, but one good store. He found it for us and we did all our shopping there in one spot.

Then we went for Egyptian coffee and subsequently to St. Catherine's Cathedral in Alexandria run by Italian Franciscans. Masses are in Arabic, Italian, and French; the noon Mass we attended was in French. It didn't look much like our cathedrals or churches since it was pretty run down.

We returned to the ship which weighed anchor at 5:30 while we were at dinner. What a thrill to be going home! People speak so highly about freighter travel— maybe it is for some people, but definitely not for me. B. I think, enjoyed the freighter cruise more than I. He likes adventure—I guess

Deep in the Heart of Africa

I like to be pampered. Two ports in two months is the gamble one takes. I don't consider Montreal or Port Sudan ports of call because Montreal is a suburb of New England, and we were only one hour on the terra firma of Port Sudan. After all, we knew that uncertainty would be the only certainty before we sailed. I still say, "Ten people confined to such close quarters for such a long time can be a problem."

<u>November 2, 1981 to November 7, 1981</u>: Here it is almost a week later. I must admit I don't know where the days went, but the time passed very quickly. Days are much the same—B. and I are playing Scrabble every day and we spend considerable time on the bridge. The weather so far has been just about perfect, no rough sea and the air is clear and invigorating. We definitely are not going to make a stop in Italy. The itinerary is straight home and we will disembark at New Orleans.

The Captain invited us all to the lounge on Wednesday afternoon for boiled shrimp which he cooked himself; he cooks them in beer. Were they delicious! Gloria didn't attend; she sent word she wasn't feeling well. Strange that she gets sick whenever the Captain has a get-together. I mentioned the fact to Sandy and she remarked, "Gloria doesn't like parties where there's liquor. After all, the Captain is cooking the shrimp in beer."

Packing has started and I have already made out our customs declaration. Jack Littman, the radio man, is betting we'll dock in New Orleans November 16th. I can't wait to see Chris and Susan and then to get home and settled.

<u>November 8, 1981 to November 15, 1981</u>: The Captain fired George and Jake, the cook and waiter, because "they weren't doing their jobs." The Captain was obviously boxed into a dilemma. He couldn't very well fire the two men in Port Sudan because that would be cruel and abusive treatment.

Live Your Dreams

The Captain was a good diplomat in the manner he retained the worthless cook and waiter and at the same time appeased the passengers.

The weather is gorgeous, and the sea is so beautiful. There's something fascinating about looking down at the sea. Tonight there's a full moon—the kooks will be out tonight!

Every day is so beautiful. It's hard to believe that we have had no rain on this trip since we sailed from Cleveland on September 15th. Tomorrow, November 16, a pilot boat directs us into the dock at New Orleans. That's it, Dear Diary.

* * * * * *

I would never have remembered all the details of the freighter cruise without Aileen's diary. This cruise has now become a part of our life's dream. The unexpected and the uncertain have been integral parts of the experience, but we anticipated them. There's no such thing as heaven on earth, so why should we expect it on the *Jean Lykes*? It has been an adventure and I wouldn't have missed it for the world.

The saga of the *Jean Lykes* reached even another climax as we docked at New Orleans. The customs inspectors, of course, were there; however, five other official looking men boarded the ship. With formality and very serious demeanor the gentlemen introduced themselves, and then the spokesman inquired, "Where is Mr. Kane?"

I had written a letter of complaint to the Chairman of the Board of *Lykes Lines*, and had mailed it from Alexandria. The five men were executives from the *Lykes Lines*; they interrogated each of the passengers and each of the officers and then they departed.

242

Deep in the Heart of Africa

Five weeks later Aileen and I received a letter containing two checks; each check was a thirty percent refund of the price we had paid for the freighter cruise. Not only did the *Lykes Lines* make restitution to us, but they also gave back thirty percent to the other eight shipmates as well.

In fairness to the *Lykes Lines*, which is one of the largest cargo shippers in the world, I must state that they followed precisely the letter of their Union contract. Their problem, I later learned, revolved around the employees associated with the culinary services on the *Jean Lykes*.

The following are suggestions we have jotted down from our own observations and from the comments of other passengers on freighter cruises. Choose a bulk ship in preference to a container ship because, at the assigned dock space, bags, boxes, and cartons are unloaded individually. In contrast, on a container freighter, all bags, boxes, and cartons have been packed into huge containers at the point of origin, and are unloaded from the ship by derricks in a matter of hours. This means that a container ship can enter a port, unload, and be gone within eight hours whereas a bulk ship can be in port for as long as two weeks. If one wants to see plenty of water and very little terra firma, then a container ship should be the choice.

Freedom of time is absolutely essential because you are never certain when you will sail, where you are sailing, and how long it will take. The passenger has a general idea of the ports of call, but there is no guarantee.

Don't expect planned entertainment. Bring plenty of books you had hoped to read, but never have had the time. Prepare to unwind completely.

On American freighters, no liquor is served. Crew members are not allowed to bring liquor on board, nor are they allowed to consume liquor on board with the passengers. Passengers may bring liquor on board, but they must purchase it on shore.

From personal experience, I would choose an American ship with an American registry. Too many foreign ships are registered in Liberia where the owners pay a one time exorbitant fee, and the ship is never inspected again. On the other hand, the United States Coast Guard is very strict with ships of American registry. The Coast Guard insists on partial and complete inspections every few years with periodic reexaminations of the officers and the crew.

The officers and many of the crew on American freighters make the Merchant Marine a lifetime career whereas in many foreign countries the officers of a freighter are rewarded for their worthy service in the army. Many of the crew are military draftees. They undoubtedly are good people, but they definitely are not qualified for sea duty. We saw many examples of this circumstance in Casablanca and Alexandria on ships that were berthed next to the *Jean Lykes*.

CHAPTER XVI

Join the Navy—See the World

Retirement means different things to different people. Some individuals look forward to playing golf whenever they feel like it. Others enjoy volunteer work. Some like to travel, and a few plan to embark on a second career. It seems incredible to me that there are those who would be content to just sit and rock.

A physician, a friend of mine who treats senior citizens, said to me one day, "Many of my retired patients who had been tycoons of industry, fighting daily for millions of dollars, now on the golf course are just as competitive for twenty-five cents a hole." In retirement, our personality doesn't change; the pace and the place do.

We all dream, whether it be in the teens or in later years. In the teens the world is our pearl; we can accomplish anything. In later years, we have matured. We acknowledge our limitations and endeavor to live within them. There is, however, one irrefutable fact which a national insurance company has been telling us for decades, "The future belongs to those who prepare for it."

Retirement is merely another phase of life. It can be fully as exciting and rewarding as all the other stages we go through. Furthermore, retirement can be a combination of many interests because we have more time and less pressure.

Somewhere I had seen a United States Navy pamphlet seeking retired college professors to conduct classes on board ships in the Pacific. So I wrote a letter of inquiry to the Navy headquarters in San Diego. To my surprise, the officer in charge of the educational program telephoned requesting that I come in for an interview the next day.

When I informed Aileen about the telephone call, she expressed her sentiments firmly yet kindly. "You have been dreaming about a trip to Australia for a long time—now here's your chance. For me, it's just too far, and I can see kangaroos in the San Diego Zoo. I think you should go, if you want to."

The next day I went for the interview. At the Naval installation in San Diego, the procurement officer explained the reason for the P.A.C.E. program as well as the results it was designed to accomplish. The initials P.A.C.E. mean Pacific Area College Education.

He narrated first how the educational plan came into existence. Congress realized that it was unfair that seamen stationed on shore could attend classes at local community colleges while others assigned to a ship for six to eight months sea duty had no opportunity to gain college credits. As a result, Congress launched and financed a project to make college courses available to sailors on long tours of duty. The major emphasis was on freshman college courses such as English, math, psychology, and economics. The credits were good for seven years. In this way, a young seaman who had

246

dropped out of school could complete his high school requirements on his return to shore-duty and be credits ahead as he began his college career.

While the interviewer and I were talking, the telephone rang. There was a brief pause in the telephone conversation, and then the officer placing his hand over the receiver said, "The *U.S.S. Cleveland* is sailing in three days. They need an English professor. Do you want to go?"

This was fast action especially since I had gone to the Naval headquarters only for information. I had expected to be put on a list and perhaps be contacted sometime in the distant future. My commitment to Aileen was foremost, so I informed the officer that my wife and I would discuss the proposal and let him know our decision at ten o'clock the next morning.

The next twenty-four hours were a span of decision and indecision. Apart from my admiration of the United States Navy, the basic principle of P.A.C.E. impressed me, and if I could make any small contribution, I desired to do it. The minimum tour for college teachers was five weeks, and I had advised the interviewer that I would not consider a longer time.

There was the question of whether Aileen would remain in Rancho Santa Fe or spend a couple of weeks with our son and his family in Chicago. Could I get packed in three days was another concern. Then too, my birthday was the next week, and in retirement, birthdays have a very special significance. We were not reaching any conclusion because there were too many details to settle. Throughout this day and night of tentativeness, Aileen in her quiet way knew that the forces of uncertainty were battling within me, and yet in no way did she try to influence me. At last she suggested, "Let's call Chris to get his opinion."

Live Your Dreams

When our son heard the facts, he quizzically asked, "And you're going to leave my mother for five weeks?" He went on to state that the final decision, of course, was ours, but he did not think a tour of duty with the Navy at my age was a good idea. He further suggested that if I decided to accept the offer, Aileen could spend the five weeks or any part of them with him and his family. Aileen and I dearly love our son's family, and that invitation truly softened the blow of separation. As I put down the receiver, Aileen sidled up to me and calmly said, "After being married to you for forty-two years, I know you pretty well. You should go. I want you to go."

In the morning I phoned the procurement officer to tell him that there was only one obstacle to the acceptance of the Navy's offer. The next week was my birthday and I really wanted to be home on that day. He said that he would call back in half an hour. Within thirty minutes the officer returned the call and stated that the obstacle had been overcome. The Navy would fly me on United Airlines to Hawaii where I would join the *Cleveland*.

On Navy ships chaplains are responsible for the educational programs and for the ship's library. The chaplain of the *Cleveland* met me at the Honolulu Airport and we drove directly to the ship. We went straightaway to the Skipper's quarters where the chaplain introduced me to Captain Roger MacPherson, a tall, trim, athletic man. The Captain's warm, pleasant greeting indicated that he was a kind, friendly person and within the first week that judgment proved to be true.

After a cursory tour of the *Cleveland*, Captain MacPherson led the way to the officers' mess. The men were gathering for the evening meal when suddenly a voice behind me called out, "Welcome, Mr. Kane, to the *Cleveland*.

Perhaps you don't remember me, Mr. Kane, but you flunked me in English at Mesa College." With a genial smile the Commander—I had noticed his stripes— recounted some of the episodes in his life since freshman college days in San Diego. Back then, when the tide was up, surfing for him was the only thing that mattered. Before it was too late, he realized that not only was he wasting time, but also he was not preparing for the future.

He told me about the Rhode Island preparatory school where he took crash courses to ready himself for the Naval Academy entrance exam. He proudly explained that Annapolis had changed his life. Now he was happy and proud to have a wife, two teenage daughters, and the rank of Commander. As we were talking, a Lieutenant, Steve Ethridge, joined us and said that he would sit with us at supper and acquaint me with the living arrangements aboard the *U.S.S. Cleveland*. Steve was comparable to the manager of a hotel; he was responsible for accommodations, all food services, and recreation. With the passage of time he and I became very good friends.

The private room, which Steve assigned me, was small but adequate. After all, I was in the Navy, not in a resort hotel. It was furnished with a steel bunk bed, a small desk with a chair, and a wardrobe. There was no private bath. The officers' common toilet facilities were at the end of a long corridor.

Since the *Cleveland* was scheduled to sail in three days, Captain MacPherson suggested that he, Doctor Rocco, Steve, and I have dinner at his favorite restaurant in Hawaii. Later I learned that the other senior officers could not join us because they were working long hours to weigh anchor in a couple of days.

Live Your Dreams

At one point during the dinner, Captain MacPherson abruptly changed the conversation, "Professor, is your cabin satisfactory?"

"Indeed it is, Captain," I responded. "Living arrangements are my least concern on this voyage."

The next morning in the Captain's quarters, he stated that my answer to his question about the cabin being satisfactory subtly revealed my true reason for joining the *Cleveland's* crew. Then he proposed that I occupy the Commodore's suite. He went on to explain that in our flotilla of five ships, the Commodore always lives on the flagship, and therefore, it was unlikely that he would join a landing craft vessel like the *Cleveland*. This opportunity could not be offered to an officer because protocol prevails. It was good fortune to be a layman on a military ship.

The Commodore's suite consisted of a good-sized living room, a standard bedroom, and a private bath. The appointments were attractive. In the living room the decor was blue and white with wall to wall carpeting, a comfortable sofa, casual chairs, various lamps, and a very large desk. Only a few places on the ship had air-conditioning and the Commodore's suite was one of them. I smile when I think of a remark Captain MacPherson made as we were dining one evening at the Subic Bay Officers' Club in the Philippines. He commented that I must have an unusual rapport with the students because he observed so many coming to my quarters with books under their arms. Frankly, I was flattered by the Captain's awareness, but I must confess that in 100 degree heat, my air-conditioned cabin was very likely a motivating factor for the students.

Join the Navy—See the World

Teaching on board a ship is a much different experience from teaching at a land-based college. The classroom is wherever space is available. The students are available only when they are free from their Navy commitments. Blending these two aspects with the number of hours required for college credit is a balancing act, but it can be done with success. The two courses, which I taught, were basic *English Composition* and *American Literature.*

The mix of students was extraordinary. There were senior Navy officers, young sailors who were financially qualifying for a college education by service in the Navy, and also a substantial number of high school drop-outs. The entire crew were males because females at that time did not serve on ships at sea.

Although attendance at the courses was voluntary, Captain MacPherson was a quiet persuader as he effectively recruited for my classes. He passed the word among younger officers on the Cleveland—many of them Annapolis graduates—that the ability to write brief, substantive communiques was an essential requisite to reach the rank of captain. From his own experience Captain MacPherson cited instances in which officers perfectly skilled in naval sciences did not write what they meant and did not mean what they had written. As a result, five officers enrolled in my *Freshman Composition* class.

Frankly, *Freshman Composition* is repetitive and mechanical whereas American Literature can be a literary adventure. The literature class turned out to be an experience both exhilarating and rewarding. Many of the seamen were taking the course for college credit whereas some of the officers considered the literature class a source of personal enrichment. At the termination of the five week course, I asked each member to write a three-page critique about his favorite author's style and content.

Since at least fifty percent of the class had been high school dropouts, and some of these dropouts were tough young men from the streets of New York, Chicago, and Los Angeles, the cumulative result of the critiques stunned me. I had expected Hemingway, Steinbeck, F. Scott Fitzgerald, or Thomas Crane to be the favorites. Contrary to my anticipation, Emily Dickinson was the outstanding fair-haired writer. Her mysticism, her subtleties, and brevity appealed to the young men. Thereby I learned that you can't judge a book by its cover.

Throughout the years I had read stories about the courageous escapades of Navy Seals; however, the concept of their precise, daring deeds was vague until I observed first hand the assault of Navy Seals on a beachhead at Iwo Jima. Not only must a Seal be physically strong, but also he must possess superior mental alertness. On a dark, cloudy night about fifty Seals participate in a silent attack on an enemy's shore. The quiet onslaught occurs close to midnight. During the twelve hours prior to midnight, lengthy briefing sessions are held so that every man knows exactly what his role will be.

Eleven at night is the hour when Seals blacken their faces and bodies with a paste so that, if the moon should appear from behind a cloud, they will not be exposed. Then each of these brave men dons only a pair of black bathing trunks. His only weapon is an ebony stiletto attached to an ebony, leather belt containing a black sheath. At the designated minute, fifty gallant men slither off the *Cleveland* into the night's darkness and on shore slash away to prepare for the beach landing of tanks and the hovering of overhead helicopters. Then the amphibious tanks roll into the water from the hold of the *Cleveland*, and simultaneously in formation, the helicopters fly off the flight deck.

The military exercise was a mock assault on Iwo Jima; it was executed, however, with the same preparation, preciseness, and courage as if it were a real invasion. Miles away and years later in the middle drawer of my desk is a vial of black sand from the beach at Iwo Jima. That vial reminds me of a Navy Seal on the *U.S.S. Cleveland* who, as he handed it to me, said, "This is a small token of appreciation for opening up to me a wonderful world of literature I never knew existed."

The first port of call after Hawaii was Subic Bay in the Philippines. There the ship took on provisions, added to its water supply, and underwent minor repairs. A skeleton crew remained on duty while most of the men enjoyed shore leave. Shopping, sight-seeing, international dining, and especially golf were the main attractions on shore leave.

A golfer, whether a par-shooter or a hacker, has never really tested his ability until he has played the Navy course at Subic Bay. The eighteen-hole course beautifully edged with tropical flowers and colorful trees is, in no sense of the word, ordinary. Always the unexpected and the unusual happen. A straight drive down the middle of a manicured fairway frequently can result in a lost ball because a monkey will swing from a tree, grab the ball and retreat into the wilderness. The monkeys in the trees, furthermore, help to find a ball hooked or sliced into the rough. The question, however, is: does the golfer or the monkey find the ball first?

In 1983, the caddies at Subic Bay were paid seventy-five cents per round. Their standard attire was bathing trunks. Whenever a golfer hit his ball into the water, the caddy would 7trieve the ball. At some holes the golfer must assume the role of an Alpine mountain climber as he ascends on a rope ladder from a green to the next tee. The Subic Bay Navy golf course definitely is an unusual challenge designed by a masochist.

One day as I was set to drive off at the tenth tee, a voice on the nearby putting green called out, "Hey, Mr. Kane." I turned and there was Mario who had been a student of mine ten years before. I remembered him well because his background was extraordinary. Before he joined my English class at San Diego Mesa College, Mario already had earned a Bachelor's Degree in Manila and had joined the Navy as a steward so that American citizenship would be easier for him to obtain. After the completion of his enlistment, Mario with his wife migrated to San Diego. Soon after their arrival, Mario enrolled at Mesa College to begin studies toward a second Bachelor's Degree, this time in hotel management. After two years, he went on to San Diego State University, earned his degree, and in 1983 was the executive manager of all officers clubs at Subic Bay.

We stepped off the tee for a brief téte-a-téte and as we were concluding, Mario suggested that I invite the Captain as well as the available officers to be his guests for dinner at the officers' club. We accepted, of course, and at least for one evening the officers of the *U.S.S. Cleveland* were treated like admirals.

Steaming out of Subic Bay the *U.S.S. Cleveland* headed south for Perth, Australia, our next port of call. Australia for many years, had tweaked my imagination because I had heard that Australia today is very similar to the United States of fifty years ago. Now and then throughout the years gentle hints to Aileen about a trip to the continent down under fell on deaf ears, but now the United States Navy was about to fulfill a secret desire. Since my tour of duty was scheduled to end in

Perth, the most western city in Australia, I could visualize that highly publicized train trip eastward across the continent on tracks so straight that they vary less than a foot for hundreds of miles. In my mind, I could picture the train chugging toward Sidney offering a kaleidoscopic panorama of vast desert with its kangaroos, its aborigines, and its outback with sheep stations scattered far and wide. There also would be an opportunity to view Old Australia in Adelaide and New Australia in Sydney. But alas, as the Greek poet Homer wrote, "Zeus does not bring all men's plans to fulfillment."

I did not see Australia. The *U.S.S. Cleveland* hit a tree in the Pacific Ocean. In truth, trees do not grow in the Pacific Ocean; large fallen trees, however, drift throughout the Pacific Ocean and occasionally knock out a screw propeller. That happened to the Cleveland with the result that she limped into Singapore, the nearest port, at five knots an hour. Two weeks of dry dock for repairs was necessary. During that time I held daily classes, gave the final exams, and was able to play a few rounds of golf.

Before leaving Rancho Santa Fe for the Pacific tour, I had promised Aileen that on my return trip we would meet in Maui and spend two weeks together at the new Intercontinental Hotel. A problem, however, developed; M.A.T.S., which stands for Military Air Transportation Service, did not have landing rights in Singapore. After negotiations between the United States Consulate and the Navy, it was decided that I would fly Singapore Airlines to Hong Kong, Japanese Airlines to Tokyo, and Pan Am from Tokyo to Hawaii. Aileen's plane from San Diego touched down one hour after my Pan Am from Tokyo. We enjoyed a wonderful reunion in Maui. Samuel Johnson best describes those two weeks. "The joy of life is variety; the tenderest love requires to be rekindled by intervals of absence."

Live Your Dreams

Another quotation from Samuel Johnson brings to mind a different episode in our retirement years. Johnson wrote, "Exert your talents and distinguish yourself, and don't think of retiring from the world." It was seven years after my final broadcast on radio and television and the same amount of time after our mutual retirement from academia that Aileen and I sold our home in Rancho Santa Fe, California, and built a new residence at Panther Woods Country Club on the Treasure Coast of Florida. Each successive flight from San Diego to O'Harc to visit our son's family was becoming more strenuous, and we were aware that the situation, in view of our age, would worsen. Aileen and I had been in Florida only once, thirty years earlier when a series of *Sounding Board* programs had originated from Sarasota.

Resettling from the West Coast of the United States to the East Coast involved adventure as well as a certain amount of apprehension. The transition, however, was made easier through the kindness of Clarise Schuenaman, a neighbor at Panther Woods and the first friend that Aileen made here in Florida. Clarise's seventieth birthday was approaching, so Aileen suggested that we host a formal dinner party to celebrate the occasion and to thank her in some small way for making us feel welcome. The plan was that Clarise would invite eight couples, who were her friends, to our home for the festivities. It turned out that we did not know any of the guests.

The conversation at the dinner party ran the gamut from golf through politics to the decadence of television. Eventually the chit-chat involved the sloppy attire of personalities appearing on TV. I interjected the fact that, *TIME-LIFE* Broadcast, for whom I had worked many years, insisted on meticulous dress at all times. *TIME-LIFE* Broadcast, like their two original magazines, always demanded quality. I mentioned furthermore that usually on television I wore a suit and tie, but occasionally when the interviewee happened to be a sports or theatrical celebrity, I would wear a sport coat with an ascot.

An ascot is a silk scarf that ties around the neck and goes under an open shirt, made popular by David Niven, Cary Grant, and their counterparts. The ascot is total casual elegance. After gaining a few retirement pounds, I realized my collars were too tight, so I sought out the former stylish accessory only to learn that men's haberdasheries and popular department stores had quit carrying them ten years before. In New York, Chicago, and San Francisco, when Aileen and I would inquire whether a store sold ascots, we received a variety of answers: "Haven't carried them for years." "Is it some kind of a dog?" "What do you do with an ascot?" "I'll ask the manager."

The lamentation caused a response from Pauline Cossey, the dinner guest on my right. Pauline offered to make one for me, but at that time, I did not know that she owned *The Dance Wearhouse* and designed many of the shop's dance costumes. She came up with what could be called the clip-on cravat. Instead of a scarf, she sewed two separate pieces from her own pattern to make it look like a tied scarf, but actually it fastens around the back of the neck with a material called Velcro.

As an aside, I should like to relate how Velcro became a reality by accident. A retired university professor, with whom I play golf at Panther Woods, related the story. One of his academic colleagues was working toward a Doctorate in Agriculture. While doing research in the fields, this doctoral candidate at the end of each day spent much time pulling stubborn briars off his pant legs. This nuisance resulted in the creation of Velcro. The doctoral candidate switched from agriculture to economics.

Every time I donned the unusual accessory, golfing friends as well as party patrons would ask me where I bought it. So Pauline made more, adding fabrics and colors for variety. She had special requests for red, white, and blue as well as St. Patrick's Day green, college logos, athletic symbols, and holiday emblems among others. Ten guests at a wedding in New York ordered ascots. And that is how *Bernárd of Palm Beach* entered the ascot business.

The formation of the company was not only different, but also very unique. I was listed as president, Pauline as vice-president, Aileen as treasurer and Bob Cossey, Pauline's husband, was secretary. We kept accurate records, but there were no established policies. A legal contract did not exist among us four because every commercial action was expedited by consensus. Our son, the attorney, many times recommended a contract, but we four preferred to conduct the business amicably by mutual trust. It worked very successfully.

Our bimonthly executive meetings were held late in the afternoon on Sundays after golf and never lasted more than forty-five minutes. They were held at our home. After the session, cocktails and Sunday supper were served. Aileen does not like to cook, but she loves to cook. By that, I mean Aileen is not thrilled to prepare a routine repast; she, however, enjoys experimenting and developing new and unusual menus. Entertaining is one of her favorite pastimes.

We targeted our advertising at upscale markets where the ascot is respected: Long Island; Southern California; Charleston, South Carolina; and Lake Forest, Illinois. The ascots were particularly well received at horse shows and racetracks because Pauline had designed an exceptional horse's head logo for special ascots.

Ascots had fallen out of favor sometime in the 1970's because the knots slipped and needed pins and because they were a symbol of the upper class. You don't have to play polo to wear an ascot. There are many practical features. If the shirt is too tight around the collar, unbutton it and wear an ascot. If it's sweltering on the golf course, wear an ascot made of washable fabric to soak up the perspiration. In our advertising, we never suggested that ascots should become a substitute for neckties, but rather, there should be at least one ascot in every closet for variety.

One day as I drove up to the barricade of Panther Woods, the guard wearing a white cloth around his neck approached my car. Without my asking, he explained about the large white handkerchief. He told me that recently he had undergone a tracheotomy and the white cloth was hiding the scar. I drove home, picked out two pastel ascots, returned to the guardhouse and gave them to him. Two purposes were served. The ugly scar was brightly covered and the guard, happy as he could be, was a walking mannequin eight hours a day, five days a week.

There were problems, of course, in the ascot business, but nothing serious. One incident was amusing because our stuffy ascots stirred up a hornet's nest in a stuffy country club. It seems that a local haberdasher had sold an unusually large number of ascots to the male members of this particular country club with the result that at dinner men were wearing more ascots than neckties. Some of the ladies became agitated and complained to the manager. When I heard about the uprising, I immediately phoned *The Ritz-Carlton* in New York, told them I planned to have dinner in their main dining room and inquired about the dress code for gentlemen. The crisp, autocratic voice informed me that gentlemen must always wear a jacket and that a necktie or an ascot is acceptable. Thus a social brouhaha was quelled.

Obviously, *Bernárd of Palm Beach* was a loosely knit company. Pauline Cossey designed and supervised the production of the neckwear and I filled the role of salesman. During retirement years, more time and less pressure unquestionably influence any venture, and as a result, fun prevails and coercion really is non-existent. This exuberant atmosphere prevails even on sales trips to different areas of the country. Charleston, South Carolina, was a city Aileen and I had always desired to see, but we had never visited. So we casually drove northward from Florida to Charleston as I peddled ascots at haberdasheries along the way in St. Augustine, Savannah, Sea Island, and Hilton Head. Financial survival in no way was the reason for these sales expeditions, and as a result, the trips were fun.

Occasionally, the Cosseys and the Kanes together would drive across the country on a junket making contacts to merchandise ascots at upscale men's shops. As we were returning from California to Florida on one of these jaunts, my handwriting on the gasoline credit card slips became less and less legible. The more I endeavored to make my signature readable, the more it became a mere scribble. I knew something was wrong. As we entered our driveway at Panther Woods, I mumbled to Aileen, "Take me to the hospital. I'm having a stroke." After two weeks of recuperation in the hospital and three months of physical therapy, I am playing golf twice a week and enjoying life as I always have. You laugh and cry until you die. That's life. By the weirdest coincidence Pauline Cossey suffered a slight stroke four months after mine, and that forced the liquidation of *Bernárd of Palm Beach*.

CHAPTER XVII

A Potpourri of Memories

It was almost two years ago when my husband, the author of *Live Your Dreams*, asked me to write a few thoughts on living my dreams. I casually agreed, thinking that he might forget about it or perhaps decide against it. Such, however, has not been the case, and since a promise is a promise, I realize my obligation. I am, by nature, a private person; therefore, my opinions will be neither explosive, nor shocking. They will, however, be sincere and genuine.

My greatest pleasures in life are my family and friends. One of the advantages of writing these comments is that I can comfortably brag about our grandchildren. Even though parents want to and often do brag about their own children, they aren't really comfortable doing so; but with grandchildren, I have found that I can boast about them with reckless abandon. I figure if people don't want to hear about the wonderful grandchildren we have, it's best not to ask, "How are the Chicago Kanes?"

Live Your Dreams

At Grand Hotel in the summer of 1953, I was expecting my first child. During those months of pregnancy, I quietly and in my privacy would dream about the child about to be born. My private dreams overflowed with speculation. What would this son or daughter be like and what would this child be doing in later years. During that same summer of 1953, there was another pregnant lady, a guest at Grand Hotel. Strangely enough, she and I never met at the hotel that summer. Actually we didn't meet until twenty years later when her daughter Susan and our son Chris met at Notre Dame and began dating. They married in June of 1975. Now as Bernie and I look forward to celebrating our 50th wedding anniversary in the year 2,000, Chris and Susan will be celebrating their 25th. What a joyous occasion that will be!

Susan's mother, Helen Skowron, was one of my best and certainly is one of my most-missed friends. She and John became a part of our family as soon as we met them, when Susan and Chris first started dating as college sophomores, she at St. Mary's and he, at Notre Dame. The Skowrons spent winters at their condo in La Jolla, just ten miles from our home. We would spend every other day or evening together for various activities—dining, theater, museums, sight-seeing, or just plain chit-chat. I remember once, before our children were married, Helen seriously said to me, "No matter what—even if our children should end their friendship—God forbid—let's the four of us remain friends forever."

Helen's passing left a terrible void not only in the lives of her immediate family, but also in the lives of her many friends, and especially in my life. When Chris graduated from the University of San Diego Law School, he and Susan moved to Chicago where he started his law practice. They set up housekeeping in an apartment in Park Ridge, not too far from the Skowrons in Lincolnwood. The always-thoughtful and sensitive Helen kept us posted on the activities of the Kanes because she realized that young people get so busy with their day-to-day activities that there isn't always time for current reports. She also sensed that we were quite lonely without our son. That's the way Helen was, always aware of the feelings of others.

As the grandchildren came along, Helen would write us frequent notes to report the "cute things" the grand-girls were doing and saying. Once she wrote about walking along the avenue in Park Ridge with Melissa, looking in the shop windows. As they passed *Fannie May*, Melissa, holding her Nana's hand, stopped to peer at the goodies in the window and promptly asked, "Do we need anything in here?" Nana allowed that of course they did. After their purchase, they continued on because Nana had promised one toy to take home. It was getting late, so Nana urged Melissa to make a selection. Since Melissa was slow to make up her mind, her grandmother suggested a very colorful broom and dustpan that was on display near the entrance, but Melissa quickly dismissed that toy—saying, "Oh, no, that's not a toy—that's work!"

Emily was only five years old when Nana passed away. Being an unusually sensitive child, Emily has found it especially difficult to accept the death of her grandmother. We were riding with Susan to the funeral home when Emily asked her mother how she knew that Nana was dead. "How can you be sure?" quizzed Emily. Her mother explained in a beautiful way that there are two ways you can tell. If you put your ear next to Nana's face, you won't hear or feel her breathing. The other way is if you touch her hands and face, they will be cold.

The Kane family: Susan, Christopher, Melissa,
Chris, Jr., Grandpa, Grandma, Emily   (left to right)

The Chris and Susan
Wedding, 1975:
Mr. and Mrs. Bernard Kane,
Dr. and Mrs. John Skowron

(left to right)

Emily,
Chris, Jr.,
Melissa
(left to right)

A Potpourri of Memories

Obviously, Emily stored this information in her mind. At the funeral home, Bernie and I were standing with members of the family, not too far from the casket. We were greeting the friends we knew as they came to pay their last respects. Suddenly Emily let go of my hand and without a word, she walked up to the casket, stepped up on the platform, leaned over and put her ear next to Nana's face; almost at the same time, she reached over and placed her little hand on Nana's face. She returned, took my hand, and held it as tight as she could, looked up at me and said, "Yes, she's gone." I'm not sure how much of this Emily remembers, but it's a moment I'll never forget.

What a pity that Helen never had a chance to know Chris, Jr., but perhaps it's even more of a misfortune for young Chris that he is growing up without the loving attention of a very beautiful lady, his other grandmother.

There are no words to accurately describe the pleasure that little Chris has brought to his family and grandparents. Now when we talk on the phone with "Papa" Skowron, he proudly relates the remarkable accomplishments of our mutual grandson. We all smugly agree that his unusual talents must be due in some measure to his grandparental genes!

Right from the beginning, Melissa was like a little mother to Christopher. Often when Susan would start to tend to the baby's needs, Melissa would take over. She would change him, give him a bottle, put him to bed with lots of hugs—all without much ado, as if it were second nature.

Emily, because she was closer in age, has been like a playmate to her brother. I have seen her come home from school, and after a light snack, she would be on the floor playing cars with him, or on the sofa watching a video of *Barney* or *Winnie the Pooh*.

265

Live Your Dreams

John has remained among our closest friends—he *is* family. When we visit the Kanes in Chicago, we are often John's guests at the Evanston Golf Club, and we also frequently meet him for lunch at the Barrington Barn or at Chessie's. Of course, John and we are always together for the girls' dance recitals, tennis tournaments, First Communions, and birthdays. John and Bernie also play a few rounds of golf, weather permitting. Bernie maintains that it is usually either too cold or too rainy in Chicago. The men, however, do make up for it when John visits us in Florida every winter and the men play golf almost daily.

The last few winters, Bernie and I have spent some time in John's condo in La Jolla, California, overlooking the beautiful blue Pacific. What a glorious sight! We usually go ahead in early April and John meets us there for a couple of weeks of relaxation. We never seem to tire of trips to the Wild Animal Park, the San Diego Zoo, or the Mexican restaurants in Old Town. Recently we attended a Globe Theater performance of *Macbeth* in a natural forest setting in Balboa Park. San Diego is, without a doubt, one of the most beautiful cities in the world. When we lived there, we found it a superb place to entertain guests because of the temperate climate as well as the many historical and cultural attractions.

Bernie, Chris, and I are all only children, which perhaps accounts for our being so fiercely protective of one another. The family is a precious entity; it is especially appreciated by those of us who have but a few individuals to share our joys and sorrows.

As an only child, I have gathered many friends along the way. Some are like sisters to me and perhaps are even closer than many filial sisters. I think of Nancy in New Hampshire and her sister Joan and their dear parents. When I was a young, unmarried teacher in the small town of Sherborn, Massachusetts, I lived with the Parks family. They treated me like another daughter, seeing that my car started in the morning, making certain that I was bundled up on cold, winter days, and serving hot chicken soup at the onset of a cold. I still stay in touch with Nancy and Joan and consider them among the oldest and best of my friends.

Another long-time friend, Margery, roomed with me in Cambridge. She had graduated from Smith as well as the Yale School of Nursing and was employed at M.I.T. when I first met her. We have stayed in touch these many years and Bernie and I meet her and her husband for lunch whenever we go to visit our family in Chicago. At Bernie's 80th birthday party, when we had guests from New York, San Diego, and Florida, Margery made it known that she had been our friend longer than anybody else there.

Rose is my Jewish friend. She traveled from California to Chicago for Chris's wedding and we, in turn, recently flew from Florida to California to attend her granddaughter's Bat Mitzvah. Rose is such a good friend; obviously we would go the extra mile for each other.

My good friend Carolyn was always like a sister to me. Since her son Jim and our son Chris went to Rancho Santa Fe Elementary and University High School together, Carolyn was always there at the bus to meet "her other child" as well as Jim. On days when school was only a half day, she would take Chris home with her, feed him lunch, and keep a watchful eye on him until I was available after my teaching day was over. What would I have ever done without Carolyn?

Then there was Mrs. Enriquez, one of my dear friends who kept house for me for 13 years. Even after she left to care for her own grandchildren, I would stop by her house with a couple of Danish treats and she would put on the coffee. We always had a lot to talk about.

If I could choose someone to be my sister, my cousin Joan would be number one on the list. We practically grew up together, sharing our deepest secrets and planning our lives together. I am "Aunt Aileen" to all of her children, and I follow all of their activities as if each child were my own. I have rejoiced when Dan recently ran the Alaska Marathon, when Edwin passed the bar, when Ginny was promoted to Art Editor of *Soap Opera Digest,* when Meg announced that her third child is on the way, and when Tom graduated from Law School and is now preparing for the bar exam.

I am proud of my friends from the priesthood. They have been kind and charitable from the beginning, and over the years, our friendship has strengthened. I know now that Father Jim Sullivan, Msgr. John McEneaney, and Msgr. Bill Granville are among my strongest supporters and I, in turn, am among their most ardent admirers. I can't help wishing, however, that the Church would relax its stringent rules and permit a married clergy for those who would so choose. In my humble and honest opinion, most of the priests I have known would have been remarkable husbands and fathers.

Throughout my life, everything seems to have fallen into place without a great deal of effort on my part. Sometimes I stop and wonder—what did I ever do to deserve all this? Call it what you will—the luck of the Irish, being born under a lucky star, or perhaps the gods have been smiling on me all these years.

I believe that a good education is a solid foundation for success in life. I entered the teaching profession well qualified, with a B.A. from Trinity and a Master's Degree from Harvard. I am truly grateful for the educational advantages

A Potpourri of Memories

that I have had. A good education led to wonderful teaching days.

Teaching for me has been very rewarding, especially the twenty-one years in the San Diego city schools. Clairemont High School opened in 1960, the year I started teaching there. Many of the same teachers who started with me were still there when I retired and are still among my close friends. There was a camaraderie among us teachers that held us close together. We respected one another and demanded the same high standards of our students. It is known as professionalism. The parents were unusually cooperative; many of them became my good friends, especially after I had taught three or four of their children, and they had attended parent-teacher conferences for three or four years.

My subjects were English and Latin. One of my educational theories is that learning can be enjoyable. Often in the spring when my Advanced Tenth class was doing a poetry unit, the culminating experience was a trip to Balboa Park where we would sit on the grass among the towering eucalyptus trees, and each student would read his own original poem. The other students would offer a critical analysis, based on the rules of poetry that they had studied. The criticism was of a constructive nature and students accepted it as a helpful gesture and sincere interest in one another's efforts.

The Latin classes, besides learning declensions and conjugations, studied Roman history and customs. At the end of each year, the students had a Roman Banquet which was held at my home. Students were responsible for the entire affair. Everything had to be authentic and hence demanded a great deal of research. They planned and prepared the menu; I turned the kitchen over to them. They wrote a play in Latin, staged it, and a second cast acted it in English. They made their own togas and wore them throughout the day. They played games that they learned about through their research. One year a student made a crossword puzzle in Latin, a remarkable feat.

I never expected students in the 20th century to emulate the lives of the Romans. The discipline of learning another language, however, and the benefits of researching unfamiliar areas of knowledge were most rewarding to these students. Above all, they experienced the pleasure of learning.

The Latin classes, because they were small in number compared to the English classes, enjoyed a social activity that was somewhat unusual. Occasionally we would all go out to dinner together. This was always a dress-up affair; the boys wore coat and tie and the girls wore a dress as well as hose and heels. The parents again cooperated by dropping their offspring off at the restaurant and picking them up at the designated time.

One evening we were preparing to leave the restaurant when a couple who had been dining at a table near us, stopped by, asked what school we were from, then complimented the students on their excellent behavior. It's hard to say who was most proud—the students or their teacher.

Words hold a fascination for me. I like to know the derivation of a word, the various usages, and different interpretations of words. The word "prejudice" comes to mind. If I were to say, "Yes, I am prejudiced," most people would be horrified, but truly I am. My research of the word does not indicate that it necessarily refers to color, race, or religion, as many people believe. Activists have taken this word "prejudice" and "hyped" it to the extent that it refers primarily to color or race. My trusty Webster's refers to prejudice as an unfavorable opinion. Therefore, I must state unequivocally that I am indeed prejudiced—especially against hypocrisy, prevarication, irresponsibility, and laziness. I might further add that I am prejudiced against people who use bad language and tell embarrassing jokes. My prejudice is not based on any moral code. To me it is just offensive, undignified, and uncouth to engage in such unbecoming social behavior.

I am not an activist, but I am fiercely proud of the many achievements of members of my sex. Of course they don't know about it, but some of my role models are Sandra Day O'Conner, the first woman on the Supreme Court; Jeane J. Kirkpatrick, former United States Ambassador to the United Nations; former First Lady Barbara Bush, a real lady with class; Mother Teresa, an international example of courage and compassion; and Helen Hayes, whose whole life was good theater.

It is really almost miraculous that Bernie's mother and I did eventually become very good friends. It has been a source of great satisfaction to me. Of course there were many strained moments in our relationship—and this was always very understandable to me. As I grew older, I realized that I would have reacted in the same manner, perhaps even with less understanding than Bernice showed me. At any rate, we had many good times together and lots of "girl talks." I'm sure we understood each other, and each of us wanted to make up to the other for any unpleasantness we might have caused. I am so grateful for her forgiveness.

Among the many adages posted on my refrigerator, is one that I often read and enjoy. Since I do not know where the quote came from, I cannot give credit. I can only say this is the way it goes.

"Butterflies, children, happiness, and running water are just four of the many things we should never try to hold on to. It is only in the letting go that we have them to enjoy."

Live Your Dreams

I apply this bit of wisdom especially to children. There is a fine line between giving children a sense of stability and security and, at the proper time, allowing them to try their own wings. We have watched the purple martins who come from Brazil to Florida every January. They move into our twelve-apartment bird house where they nest, and very soon they have a flock of babies. We bird watchers are fascinated to watch the parents fetch food, bring it back to the babies, teach them to open their mouths and stretch for the food. Soon they bring their babies out on the balconies and introduce them to the big, wide world. Almost immediately they start the flying lessons. The birds swoop from one bough to another, take a little rest, and then fly back to the nest.

Each day they fly a little farther away from home base as they develop their wings and gain more confidence. Soon they glide out of sight and by the end of the season, they are ready to proceed with ease to their other home in Brazil.

When Chris graduated from the University of San Diego Law School, he and Susan moved to Chicago where he started his law practice on their dining room table. Little by little the firm grew as colleagues were added, and the J. Christopher Kane law practice became a reality. He had learned to spread his wings and to fly on his own.

I have not dwelt on the Bernie and Aileen romance because our relationship was most unusual. Obviously we were not in a position to date as young couples do before marriage. Soon after we met, we became best friends and each of us believed it would always be that way. Almost before we realized what was happening, however, we found ourselves hopelessly in love. There were hours and days of agonizing and indecision, of planned separations, but the farther away I went from Bernie, the closer I felt to him.

Chris, Jr., Susan, Melissa

Emily dancing

Chris, Jr.

Melissa, Emily

Father Jim Sullivan, Bernard Kane,
Monsignor John McEneaney (left to right)

Live Your Dreams

In the words of Tennyson, "Ask me no more: thy fate and mine are seal'd. I strove against the stream and all in vain."

During all these forty-eight years, Bernie has been my stalwart support. He has been totally involved in all my major and minor incidents. When I was diagnosed with breast cancer, he walked with me every step of the way. I have been free from cancer for fourteen years now. Early detection is the reason I am alive today.

Chris has been a faithful son, ever vigilant about our well-being. Whenever a crisis occurs in our lives, he is immediately on the scene and stays until the problem is resolved. This has been true in sickness and in health. Having an attorney in the family is most helpful and comforting, and I have often said to my friends, "Every family should have one." Equally compassionate is his dear wife Susan.

From the first time I met Susan, I felt a common bond. True, I had been conditioned by Chris's letters from Notre Dame which unfailingly mentioned, "You will really like her, Mom." Susan is not the kind of girl that grows on you; you like her immediately because she is just naturally thoughtful, gentle, and pleasant. There is no pretense about Susan; she *is* a natural.

Susan is the epitome of the perfect daughter-in-law. When Chris first brought her to our home in Rancho Santa Fe for a visit, I realized that I liked her very much. Now, twenty-four years later, I know that I love her as if she were my own daughter.

Susan is an artist. I first admired her oils in her parents' home and now I am proud to have her art work scattered throughout our home. One of Susan's special traits is that she always has time to help others. She often types legal documents for Chris when he has a deadline, and in an emergency,

Susan, Chris, Sr.

Chris, Jr., Chris, Sr.

Susan, Chris, Jr.

Emiley, Chris, Sr., Melissa

she will do the same for the girls. You can always depend on Susan.She frequently does art work for the school, such as making posters or decorating the gym, and always with the greatest of ease.

Chris was right when he wrote, "You really will like her, Mom." Yes, I really do.

When I depart, "Sing no sad songs for me" because I have been blessed with a charmed life. I sometimes muse on what changes I would make in my life, if it were possible for anyone to do such a thing. I can't think of any, not even those first days in Phoenix, when we were almost destitute. I don't know why, but I have never thought we were poor. I suppose I was in a dream world, but I knew with our good educational backgrounds and with our appreciation for the good life, those days were just stepping stones and wouldn't last forever. Actually they were kind of fun, and fortunately they didn't last too long! We did what we had to do, and with lots of luck, every day got better. It really was not a bad way to start a marriage.

Aileen Kane

AFTERWORD

More than fifty years ago when I casually remarked to Aileen, "My, what beautiful blue eyes you have!" little did I know then that life would never be the same. For half a century I have been blessed with a loyal, loving wife; a son and his charming wife Susan; and three wonderful grandchildren, fifteen, twelve, and the only grandson, four-year-old Chris, Jr.

Melissa, the oldest, is tall and willowy, a solid scholar, and the clone of her father in competitiveness and attitude. Emily, a Dresden china doll, sways to and fro with the rhythm of life and she loves every minute of it. Chris, Jr. has added a new dimension to the family. Until his arrival, the household revolved around dolls, dance recitals, and cheerleading, but now the toy box is filled with cars, trucks, and baseballs.

If you should ask me to describe the two girls, I would say, "Melissa is going to climb the corporate ladder to the top and Emily is going to marry the guy at the top."

Fifty years is a long time to look back. It's half a century of adamant decisions, fifty years of positive action, a time of personal accomplishment. Little did I know, when I told Aileen on that desolate Cape Cod beach that I loved her, what destiny had in store. She, our son Chris, and our three marvelous grandchildren have fulfilled a dream—a dream I may not have deserved but profoundly treasure.